D0604428

Advance Praise for *Lockdown*

Our personal liberties are so easy to take for granted, but if the growing gang of Socialists have their way, we will regret not having paid attention and assuming such a stupid thing would never happen in America. Cheryl Chumley is a gifted writer and courageously explains what's at stake. Don't put off reading this book and regret that you failed to realize the threat we face.

—Gov. Mike Huckabee, *New York Times*
Bestselling Author and Host of *Huckabee*

Lockdown is a deep dive into the radical Left's aggressive manipulation and politicization of the COVID-19 pandemic to advance their own toxic agenda and silence the American people. Cheryl Chumley has done it again!

—Rep. Jody Hice, R-GA and Host of *The Jody Hice Show*

When a plague originated in a Chinese Communist Party lab in Wuhan began spreading like a prairie fire across America, President Trump faced a no-win situation—how best to stop it. In *Lockdown*, Cheryl Chumley gets to the heart of the dilemma that POTUS warned us about on that March day—don't let the cure be worse than the disease. Cheryl Chumley is one of the most important voices in the Trump Movement and *Lockdown* is a must-read for those "Deplorables" who want to understand the real threat America faces.

—Steve Bannon, host of *War Room* and
Former Chief Strategist for Donald J. Trump

The pandemic reminded us of how fragile our liberties are. Cheryl Chumley shows us how close we came to losing them for good and what we can do to secure them in time for the next challenge.

—Cal Thomas, Syndicated Columnist and Bestselling Author

Despite different views Americans will hold about the pandemic and the vaccine, we can all be united about the value of liberty, and the need to be vigilant in defending it. The left looks for any and every opportunity to destroy it. Cheryl Chumley's book *Lockdown* will help you to be even more alert to this danger!

—Fr. Frank Pavone, National Director, Priests for Life

Cheryl has emerged as one of the most important writers in America today for one of the most important newspapers today. She made tremendous impact with her landmark book *Socialists Don't Sleep*. Now she extends her work in the brilliant Lockdown detailing how precisely collectivists like Joe Biden are, at this moment, doing their utmost to destroy freedom in America. Must read. Essential.

—Craig Shirley, Reagan Biographer and Presidential Historian

Cheryl Chumley, in *Lockdown*, provides a crucial warning for Americans about the left's never-ending lust to steal individual liberties—and then reminds of the power of God to stop it.

—Everett Piper, Bestselling Author of *Not a Daycare* and *Grow Up!*

Find out what is behind the tyranny of government stay-at-home orders, curfews, bans on attending weddings, funerals and backyard barbeques. Chumley reveals how global institutions are poised to make the "two-week" flattening of your freedom into a permanent Great Reset using climate change to bring George Orwell's 1984 dystopian vision into reality.

—Marc Morano, Bestselling Author of *Green Fraud*

The political divide in America became the mask divide. Those who believe in big government and phony science clung to masks, lockdowns, and Fauci far after the facts were against them. Chumley outlines how it happened.

—Jack Kingston, Conservative Activist

LOCKDOWN

The Socialist
Plan to Take Away
Your Freedom

CHERYL K. CHUMLEY

Humanix Books

www.humanixbooks.com

Humanix Books

LOCKDOWN
Copyright © 2022 by Humanix Books

Humanix Books, P.O. Box 20989, West Palm Beach, FL 33416, USA
www.humanixbooks.com | info@humanixbooks.com

Humanix Books is a division of Humanix Publishing, LLC. Its trademark, consisting of the words "Humanix Books," is registered in the Patent and Trademark Office and in other countries.

ISBN: 9-781-63006-209-5 (Hardcover)
ISBN: 9-781-63006-210-1 (E-book)

Printed in the United States of America
10 9 8 7 6 5 4 3 2

For Jesus, always.

For America the free.

And for those who would fight to the end for both.

Contents

Foreword

Any conservative who is familiar with Cheryl Chumley's work, knows she's a champion of human liberty. *Lockdown* reveals how anti-freedom, left-wing forces use events and tragedies like a pandemic to advance their barbarous assault on the human spirt. It's hardly a new tactic. They've done this throughout history.

Whatever issue left-wing extremists claim they care about, you can bet their goal is the acquisition of power to advance communist and socialist policies. They claimed they cared about public health, but instead used the pandemic as an excuse to commit a direct attack on the Constitution and the rights of the people it was instituted to protect.

Simultaneously, left-wing extremists deployed the use of race to divide our nation. Leftists claimed, with no facts, that the United States was founded on racism. Because of this canard, socialists in the American Democratic Party proclaim their desire to shred the U.S. Constitution and its protections for every citizen. The problem is, America's history is replete with racism coming from the Democratic Party. History shows that the KKK was the militant arm of Democrats in the past. In the present, terrorists in Antifa and BLM have assumed duties of threats, violence, and intimidation.

Socialists have instituted a curriculum in the government-run schools. This curriculum, called critical race theory, teaches white children to hate their skin color and heritage, and teaches brown and black kids to hate whites. The curriculum takes aim at America's foundations, bastardizes and rewrites history, and silences any dissent. Glenn Bracey, an assistant professor of sociology and criminology at Villanova, loves critical race theory because it is Marxism wrapped up in a false racism cloak. Bracey made the admission during a remote discussion about critical race theory on Zoom. The seminar was posted on Villanova's official YouTube channel, entitled "What is Critical Race Theory?"[1]

In his "Evil Empire" speech, President Ronald Reagan alluded to a destructive leftist ideology that destroyed Russia and threatened the world. In outing the Soviets guiding spirit, Vladimir Lenin, Reagan said that Soviet Russia repudiates "all morality that proceeds from supernatural ideas—that's their name for religion—or ideas that are outside class conceptions. Morality is entirely subordinate to the interests of class war. And everything is moral that is necessary for the annihilation of the old, exploiting social order and for uniting the proletariat." That's what socialists and Democrats are doing to America today. They falsely claim our Constitution was founded on racism, and that it exploits people of color. Thus, they claim Americans must get rid of it to unite America under their tyrannical rule. The entire left wing, in and out of the media, is in on the big con.

Whether its race, gender issues, sexual orientation, illegal immigration, or even a pandemic . . . no issue is beyond the reach of democratic socialists to politicize and divide. Everyone who loves this country needs to pay attention to this important book as it dismantles the tricks and tactics used by the radical left to advance their dark agenda. More importantly, Cheryl tells us what we can do to stop it.

Chris Salcedo

Chris Salcedo is host of the *Chris Salcedo Show* on NewsmaxTV & Radio. He's the Executive Director of the Conservative Hispanic Society.

Prologue

I ask you: Where has critical thinking gone?

On April 30, 2008, my husband, Doug, suffered a serious heart attack that left him in a medically induced coma for almost two weeks while doctors and nurses worked desperately to save first, his life, and second, his quality of life. Doug and I have four children—two boys, two girls—and their ages at the time were 13, 12, 6, and 1½. As you can imagine, the ordeal was difficult.

Doctors were clear: Doug was going to die. In fact, they were more than clear. They were unequivocal in their certainty. "Oh, he's going to die," one told me, with a strangely chipper tone. "He's definitely going to die." Others were more optimistic: meaning, they left a window of hope by saying he was going to die, but if by some small chance he lived, he would be brain dead. A vegetable. Totally unable to live and function as before the heart attack. Good news all around.

But the hits kept on coming. A balloon pump inserted at the top of Doug's left leg as a means of keeping blood flowing to his heart had the unfortunate consequence of cutting off circulation to his lower half. Around day two of his hospitalization came the news that doctors would have to amputate. The line went like this: Doug was going to die, and on that, it was certain. But in the zero-to-slim chance that he could live, the only way to save him was to amputate his left leg. Why? The toxins a dead leg would release into the bloodstream would prove fatal. On that, again, doctors were certain. I had the lucky job of signing the paperwork that gave doctors permission to amputate.

It was an agonizing decision. Can you imagine going to sleep with two legs and waking up with only one? But I signed. After dragging out the decision as long as possible, I signed. And shortly after, doctors amputated—performing an archaic "guillotine cut" because, after all, Doug was going to die. No need to worry about pain blockers or precision cuts. He was going to die. On that, they were certain.

And in May, when they removed all the tubes and wires and medical hookups that had been used to keep him alive, to keep him breathing, to keep his heart pumping, to keep him in some sort of state of consciousness, he opened his eyes. They spoke with him and they tested him to make sure his mental facilities were, in fact, intact. These same doctors, these same experts, these same certain doctors and certain experts, expressed shock and awe with their discovery: Not only was Doug alive, but he was well. He was cognizant. He was mentally competent. Minus a leg, he was basically the same as before his heart attack.

The same doctors who had been so certain of his death were suddenly amazed at his life. The same doctors who had been so certain of his vegetable state were suddenly amazed at his mental acuity.

Fast-forward a few years. Different hospital, different patient. I was roused from anesthesia-induced sleep to my knee doctor's pronouncement: "You'll never run again."

In fact, the prognosis was worse: I'd never jump again, never play sports again, never perform anything of high-impact aerobic activity again—never even go on long walks again. "You'll have to find a different activity," my doctor told me. "Bike riding. Or swimming." He was certain. No matter how many times I asked, no matter how many times I rephrased the question, my doctor was certain. "No," he said. "You can never run again."

I think of that often—usually while wrapping up my four-mile runs, my seven-mile runs, my thirty-minute high-intensity interval training workouts, my long walks, with and without weights. His certainty always brings a smile to my face.

Fast-forward a few more years. Different hospital, Doug again as the patient. Liver failure. Kidney failure. Total bodily distress—and doctors who once again offered the bleak outlook of death. At least this time, they couched their near-certain expectation of Doug's death on the fact they couldn't be certain how to cure him, because they weren't certain what was causing him to come to the point of death. They were certain in their uncertainty, and as such, were confident in predicting death. A few days later, a recovered Doug was released and sent home.

The common theme here? The takeaway point?

Doctors don't know. They don't—they just don't know. Their particular brand of science isn't always as settled as they say. They're educated, possess degrees, and are filled with all the knowledge the world has to offer, but in the end, no matter how high their IQ, no matter how esteemed their pedigrees—they just don't know.

If they did, Doug would be dead. Twice. I'd be inactive. And here's the thing: the world is filled with people who have been just as erroneously diagnosed—just as miraculously cured. Doctors may say this, scientists may say that, but in the end, it's God who has the final say.

So why is Anthony Fauci to be unquestionably believed? Why believe the experts at the Centers for Disease Control and Prevention (CDC) or the bureaucrats with the World Health Organization? Why, for goodness sake—why?—pay mind to the Microsoft-building billionaire Bill Gates?

Science is not sacrosanct. Doctors are not gods. But believing so has placed America's freedoms in chains. This is our national misstep; this is our nation's big mistake. With the pandemic, first fear replaced the ability to think and reason, then overreaching government exploited the situation to instill more fear and grab more powers. Then Democrats, progressives, globalists, collectivists, socialists, and Marxists saw opportunity to reshape an entire world, if only they could keep the fear going, press for even more powers, move goal posts farther down the field.

They're evil. They're using the misfortunes of others to achieve their own political designs. They're exploiting a sad and sorry situation for personal ambition and agenda, and leaving a wide swath of devastation in their wake. They're determined, they're hard-charging, and they're not going to let the COVID-19 crisis go to waste. They're not going to let it end without having the next chain in place, lined up, and ready to lock. They're evil.

And it's crucial the good people of America understand the depth of the evil forces at work, trying to crumble and collapse the country. Tyrants don't just quit. The power hungry don't just give up the ghost. Wicked people don't just go home and binge-watch a Netflix series and forget about their wickedness. They go home, plot, strategize, and plan more wickedness.

Right now, they're rushing to reset entire economies and whole political systems to usher in a time of total top-down global government control, using the coronavirus as the jumping point, selling the coronavirus as a danger that must be controlled, and positioning themselves as the only ones who can control the danger. And if it means they have to fabricate dangers and create false narratives of red alarm risks to safety, security, and health, so be it. They'll do it. They are absolutely already doing it.

They want a lockdown. They want total and complete lockdowns of individual freedoms, individual rights, individually held liberties so they can stage their reset and reshape a new America, a new world, more in line with their collectivist and elitist beliefs. It's called destroy, then rebuild. What they're destroying is the Constitution; what they're trying to rebuild is cultural Marxism and communist control.

Beware. Be warned. Be armed with the truth to fight. This is the world the Left envisions. This is the America the collectivists are busily building . . .

CHAPTER ONE

The Politics of Fear and the Politicization of the Pandemic

And the angel who talked with me came again, and waked me,
like a man that is wakened out of his sleep. And he said to me,
"What do you see?"

Zechariah 4:1 (RSV)

In December 2019, officials with the Wuhan Municipal Health Commission in China reported a number of cases of pneumonia, later identified as the never-before-seen coronavirus.[1] Health officials in the communist country claimed they were monitoring its spread, and on January 11, 2020, reported the first known death due to the virus—a sixty-one-year-old man, a regular Wuhan market shopper.[2] It was only a couple weeks later that coronavirus cases and deaths began surfacing outside China, specifically in Japan, South Korea, and Thailand. In America, it was Washington that saw the first case: an unidentified man in his thirties who had just returned from a trip to his homeland China.[3]

America was told not to worry. Americans were told not to panic. "This is not a moment of anxiety," said Washington's Democratic governor, Jay Inslee, during a press conference in Seattle to update on the "satisfactory condition" of the Providence Regional Medical Center patient,

Reuters reported. "This is a low risk. It appears to have a transmission vector that really should not prevent anyone from going anywhere in Snohomish County, except maybe the isolation ward at the hospital."[4] In just the span of few short weeks, Inslee was singing a different tune.

That was when a man in his fifties became the first American to die from what physicians at his hospital in Kirkland, Washington, ruled as COVID-19, the illness from the coronavirus called SARS-CoV-2.[5] Granted, the man suffered from other health issues.[6] But with virus case counts on the rise, Inslee wasn't taking chances. He declared a state of emergency and directed Washington's agencies to "use all resources necessary to prepare for and respond to the outbreak."[7] It would be weeks later, in mid-April, when a coroner would find and report that the first two deaths in America due to COVID-19 were actually in Santa Clara County, California, on February 6 and on February 17.[8] That's called hindsight.

Needless to say, in February, just a few weeks into the dawn of coronavirus, fear was already making its mark. On Capitol Hill, President Donald Trump swung into high gear. Among the actions he took in the early months of 2020: He closed U.S. borders to flights from certain high-risk regions, including China and twenty-six European nations, minus the United Kingdom.[9] He supported quarantine procedures and carved out an airport screening system to bring home American citizens from high-risk regions, including China.[10] He sought $2.5 billion from Congress for coronavirus mitigation.[11] He established a coronavirus task force to deal with immediate response issues, and named Vice President Mike Pence as a leading figure.[12]

All along, all at the same time, all to the shame of the Democrats and leftists, he fought critics who saw in the coronavirus a chance to politically ding his administration. All to the shame of Democrats and leftists, he battled those who would use raw emotion and fear to advance an un-American agenda. "[Trump's travel restrictions] may have political value, but has zero public health value," Lawrence Gostin, a global health law professor at Georgetown University, told NPR in March 2020. "Most of Europe has the same or fewer cases than the U.S.

Restricting travel certainly won't make America safer."[13] The heads of the European Union chimed in similarly, announcing displeasure with "the fact that the U.S. decision to impose a travel ban was taken unilaterally and without consultation," and chiding that "the coronavirus is a global crisis and requires cooperation."[14]

Global cooperation, perhaps. Concessions to the global powers—nope. Trump's travel restrictions were meant to keep Americans safe, EU bureaucrats be danged. But it wasn't just foreigners who condemned Trump's coronavirus response. Capitol Hill's Democrats jumped right into the fray.

Senator Chuck Schumer called Trump's $2.5 billion funding request "too little, too late."[15] In February, before America had seen its first reported death due to coronavirus, then House minority leader Nancy Pelosi blew up her Twitter feed with rants against Trump. Among her messages: "Americans need a coordinated, fully funded, whole-of-government response to keep them and their loved ones safe. The president's [budget] request for coronavirus response funding is long overdue and completely inadequate to the scale of this emergency," she tweeted on February 25.[16]

That same day, Pelosi tweeted this:

- "For almost two years, the Trump Administration has left critical positions in charge of managing pandemics at the National Security Council and the Department of Homeland Security vacant."[17]
- "The president's most recent budget called for slashing funding for the Centers for Disease [Prevention and] Control, which is on the front lines of this emergency. And now he is compounding our vulnerabilities by seeking to ransack funds needed to keep Ebola in check."[18]
- "Weeks after the #TrumpBudget called for slashing the CDC budget during this coronavirus epidemic, this undersized funding request shows an ongoing failure to understand urgent public health needs."[19]

- "Our state and local governments need serious funding to be ready to respond to any outbreak in the United States. The president should not be raiding money that Congress has appropriated for other life-or-death public health priorities."[20]

Good Lord. Pelosi's fingers certainly were flying. Flying and lying, that is. Well, maybe not outright lying, but certainly tossing out strategic one-liners that she knew full well would play in the media, and in the minds of fearful Americans, as cause to criticize the president.

Here's the much-needed contextual truths to her hatchet tweets. From FactCheck.org, a project of the Annenberg Public Policy Center, posted March 3, 2020:

Democrats have criticized President Donald Trump for his administration's response to the new coronavirus, making claims about cuts to public health programs and the silencing of government experts. But they haven't always gotten their facts right: It's true that the president's budget proposals have consistently called for reduced funding for the Centers for Disease Control and Prevention, but Congress hasn't enacted those cuts. Some Democrats have correctly said Trump "tried" to implement such cuts, while others wrongly claimed he "slashed funding of the CDC" or "cut the funding," in the words of Democratic presidential candidates Mike Bloomberg and Joe Biden, respectively . . . . Multiple Democrats, including Bloomberg and Biden, have criticized Trump for getting rid of a pandemic response position on the National Security Council. The position was eliminated, although John Bolton, then national security adviser, was the person directly responsible.[21]

Truth, schmuth. As it's been said, truth is the first casualty of war—and in recent years, as socialists become all the more emboldened, politics have been, if nothing else, outright war.

Democrats, leftists, anti-Trumpers in the press, in the punditry class, in the much-maligned deep state, inside the globalist circles of the United Nations, World Health Organization, and European Union, and even within some of the GOP's own ranks—all these entrenched elitists used the coronavirus to mount a well-coordinated, well-orchestrated "danged if you do, danged if you don't" attack during Trump's last year in office. They partnered, paired up, tag-teamed, double-teamed, triple-teamed, and more. Truth was rarely their concern. An example?

For shuttering travel from China, Trump was characterized as a racist. For calling the virus the "Wuhan virus," Trump was labeled a racist. For labeling COVID-19 a "Chinese virus," Trump was blasted as racist. "We are in the midst of a crisis with the coronavirus," then Democratic Party presidential hopeful Joe Biden tweeted, one day after Trump announced the China restrictions. "We need to lead the way with science—not Donald Trump's record of hysteria, xenophobia, and fear-mongering. He is the worst possible person to lead our country through a global health emergency."[22]

Trump, on Fox, fought back. "I had Biden calling me xenophobic," he told host Sean Hannity, in late March. "He called me a racist, because of the fact that he felt it was a racist thing to stop people from China coming in."[23]

Then the Democrats' water carriers in the media quickly sprung to Biden's defense. "But Biden has not directly said that the travel restriction was xenophobic," PolitiFact wrote, a day after Trump's comments to Hannity on Fox. "[Biden] has used that phrase in reference to Trump and his handling of the coronavirus outbreak. Biden's campaign told PolitiFact that Biden's tweets were not specific to the restrictions on people coming from China."[24]

Well, there you have it. Biden's people said—so of course, Biden's people are to be believed. It was a ridiculous argument to make, even by leftist standards. It's akin to a propagandist citing his own study as fact. Democrats get by with it because Democrats in the press let them get by with it. Then fast-forward to October, and *The Washington Post* completes the spastic "Trump's a Xenophobe" theatrical cycle. Yes, spastic.

Trump's criticized for restricting travel from China; Trump's criticized for not restricting travel from China. Trump's criticized for his too-early restrictions of travel from coronavirus-infected regions; Trump's criticized for failing to restrict travel early enough from coronavirus-infected regions. On October 1, 2020, *The Washington Post* wrote:

> During the first presidential debate, President Trump hailed his efforts to restrict travelers from China as evidence of his administration's effective response to the COVID-19 pandemic, saying the "early" decision "saved thousands of lives." . . . The president is incorrect. The United States did not implement its travel restriction early. Nor did it "close" the country to arrivals from China. In addition, there is little evidence that travel restrictions alone saved millions of lives—in this country or any other. On the contrary . . . the widespread use of travel bans in this pandemic have made Americans and citizens of other countries more vulnerable to future pandemic threats.[25]

The writers then go on to note Trump's travel restrictions came about a month "after China first announced its outbreak," after "more than 40,000 travelers from China were estimated to have entered the United States." But in the next sentence, they stated this: "Scientists believe the virus likely emerged and began circulating a month or more before it was first recognized in China, which may have allowed it to spread beyond the countries where cases were initially recognized."[26]

Did you catch all that? If scientists didn't even know when the virus first emerged, how could Trump have prevented it from coming from China anyway? *The Washington Post*, no doubt, included the line to show the utter nonsense of Trump's "xenophobe" targeting of China travelers. But what *The Post* was really acknowledging was that the spread of the virus was hardly Trump's fault. The writers would probably voluntarily lie on a bed of burning brush before admitting that—but that's the truth, regardless.

Still, none of that mattered.

All that mattered was jabbing Trump, destroying Trump, and making him appear as feckless as possible to the American public. The election was right around the corner, don'tcha know. If the attacks were inconsistent and illogical, so be it.

In March, then presidential hopeful Senator Bernie Sanders was asked during a Fox News town hall if he would close the borders to help contain the coronavirus. "No," he said, before launching into an attack on Trump as a "president who has propagated xenophobic, anti-immigrant sentiment from before he was elected."[27] In other words: Close borders to contain the virus, and you're a racist.

In April, a Fox News contributor wrote this: "A Jan. 31 article in *The New York Times* quoted epidemiologist Dr. Michael Osterholm as saying that Trump's decision to restrict travel from China was 'more of an emotional or political reaction.' Weeks later, though, the paper reported that dozens of 'nations across the world have imposed travel restrictions to curb the spread of the coronavirus,' and did not criticize any of them for the move."[28] In other words: closing borders to contain the virus is only racist for certain leaders. Like Trump.

And who can forget Pelosi piping in with this not-so-thinly veiled comparison of Trump to the tyrannical Nero of Rome? "As the president fiddles, people are dying," she told CNN host Jake Tapper, in late March. "We should be taking every precaution. [The president's] denial at the beginning was deadly."[29]

That was after New York City mayor Bill de Blasio, a Democrat, put out a March 2 tweet that soon after went viral: ". . . I'm encouraging New Yorkers to go on with your lives + get out on the town despite Coronavirus . . ."[30] But that was before Anthony Fauci, the director of the National Institute of Allergy and Infectious Diseases under the National Institutes of Health, and the media's go-to expert on all things coronavirus, said this on CNN in April: "I mean obviously, you could logically say that if you had . . . started mitigation earlier, you could have saved lives. . . . I mean obviously, if we had right from the very beginning shut everything down, it may have been a little bit different. But there was a lot of pushback about shutting things down back then."[31]

Come on now. Back, forth. To, fro. Up, down. Left, right. It's enough to give whiplash.

No wonder Trump called out the Democrats for "politicizing" the coronavirus and using it as "their new hoax"—a statement, get this, that in itself, Democrats immediately politicized, weaponized, and used in a deceptive manner.[32] A statement that Democrats immediately pounced upon and exploited for their next coronavirus-tied hoax. "Biden video twists Trump's words on coronavirus," PolitiFact reported, on March 15. "In a video tweeted March 3, Joe Biden's campaign made it look like President Donald Trump called the 2019 coronavirus outbreak a 'hoax.' . . . Biden's video is inaccurate. We rate it False."[33]

Shameless. From there, the left's attacks grew even worse.

- "Trump has 'blood on his hands' over coronavirus, says Nobel prize winning economist," the *Independent* wrote in April, 2020, quoting Professor Joseph Stiglitz, who once served as an adviser to presidents Bill Clinton and Barack Obama.[34]
- "South Carolina: Trump 'Has Blood on His Hands' for Downplaying Coronavirus, Health Experts Say," the Association of Schools and Programs of Public Health reported in September 2020.[35]
- "'Blood on his hands': As US surpasses 400,000 COVID-19 deaths, experts blame Trump administration for a 'preventable' loss of life," *USA Today* reported in January 2021.[36]

Shameless and despicable. Shameless, despicable, and outright evil.

The coronavirus, remember, was an unknown. A complete, total unknown. No matter what moves Trump made, they were bound to be criticized. No matter what steps his administration took, they were sure to be spun as leadership misfires. No matter what Trump did, he was certain to be set in Democrats' targets.

This isn't to say Trump had a perfect record when it came to coronavirus response. In fact, a solid argument could be made that he gave too much White House platform time to the likes of Fauci and fellow medical-bureaucrat-in-chief Deborah Birx, whose dire warnings and daily cautions were constants in the early months of the coronavirus. But almost always, their forecasts came without the oh-so-crucial cooler head considerations and contextual observances of the general progression of viruses. Almost always, they failed in their advisements to strike any balances between health and politics; between health and economics; between health and individual freedoms, individual choice, and individual right to self-determine—or to even consider any such aspects of basic American life and liberty as part and parcel of their medical messaging at all.

Ultimately, Trump let them seize too much of his own administration's policy reins. Ultimately, Trump ceded too much power to the health pinheads.

Some might call that armchair quarterbacking. Some others might acknowledge that as an uncomfortable truth. But look back on the early weeks, early months, and ongoing, never-ending, never-ceasing "war" on the pandemic that played from the White House through the media. It resulted in real-time case counts—meaningless, without context of recovery versus fatality figures—and ultimately, widespread executive orders that completely shut down the country. It's a valid point: Trump could've better balanced the "all fear, all the time" talk with more talk of the Constitution and God-given rights. He could've booted Fauci earlier; he could've yanked his flip-flopping, unscientific self from the national stage—or at the least, kept him away from the microphones, behind closed doors, and as just one voice on a larger coronavirus response committee that included business owners, public school officials, psychologists, and economists.

As it was, the relationship between Trump and Fauci soured, in large part because of the growing conflict between Americans' health and America's future. "The tension between the two men [Trump and Fauci]—who are no longer speaking," CNN reported in July, 2020, "has grown publicly as they have responded to one another through interviews and statements. Trump does not plan to dismiss Fauci, and probably couldn't directly fire him if he wanted to, White House officials have determined."[37] The subtle message? White House officials, for whatever reason, by whatever prompting, had actually investigated the feasibility of firing Fauci, but determined it difficult, at best.

At the same time, Trump, as leader of the free world, and as the man with whom the buck naturally stops, bears at least some culpability for the politicizing of the pandemic. But it's reasonable to say that unlike the Democrats, he is deserving of a bit of a free pass. Trump, after all, was an admitted germaphobe:

- "Donald Trump admits 'I have germ phobia' in Howard Stern interview," the *Independent* wrote in 2017, about the president's 1993 broadcast discussion with the shock jock.[38]
- "Donald Trump says he is a 'germaphobe' as he dismisses salacious activity," CNBC reported in January 2017, on a Russia report, later identified as false, that alleged Trump to have engaged in disgusting sexual play with prostitutes.[39]
- "The Purell presidency: Trump aides learn the president's real red line," Politico wrote in July 2019. The story went on to quote a "former Trump campaign official" as saying, "If you're the perpetrator of a cough or of a sneeze or any kind of thing that makes you look sick, you get that look. You get the scowl. You get the response of—he'll put a hand up and a gesture of, you should be backing away from him, you should be more considerate and you should extricate yourself from the situation."[40]

If the deep state wanted to find the means of exacting revenge on the "America First" president, a coronavirus would certainly have been their kryptonite.

But whatever the basis of the politicizing, whatever the causes of the long-term sufferings of citizens who saw their constitutional rights infringed at every turn, fact is: the American people deserved better. The coronavirus may have been real, but the Democrats took that reality and bent it to their political will.

Their outright lying, their outright gaslighting, their outright exploiting of a health issue that placed innocent American lives in danger—it was inexcusable, and even evil. And every once in a while, a tiny bit of truth would pop up just to show how very, very evil the left's use of the virus was.

"I'd be lying to you to say that [Trump] hasn't been responsive to our needs. He has," said California Democratic Governor Gavin Newsom, about the president's handling of the coronavirus, during a CNN interview with Jake Tapper in April.[41] Oops. How the Democrat handlers must have huddled. On the heels of that interview, anti-Trumpers were quick to do damage control. This is what they came up with: Newsom's cooperative spirit was not aligned so much with honest admiration for the president as with pragmatics. "Let's face it," Democrat strategist and former Newsom mayoral staffer Nathan Ballard said, "[Newsom's] got to be with Donald Trump right now. [Trump] holds the keys to the federal treasury and he is a vindictive and impulsive man."[42]

Right. Because allowing, even for a second, that Trump wasn't the bungler-in-chief the Left was busily making him out to be would prove fatal to the Democrats on Election Day, and even more to point, to the left's long-time, long-term goals to completely shatter the country's political and economic systems, flipping both capitalism and the Constitution on their heads. Never let a crisis go to waste.

That's been the playbook of Democrats for a very long time.

In short order, the leftists in America, and around the world, used the politics of fear to bring to a crushing halt the engines of free markets, free enterprise, free thinking—of freedom in general. The chaos that was generated by all the conflicting opinions, viewpoints, and guidance, along with all the ever-changing recommendations, policy points, and medical suggestions, only exacerbated fears while playing into the designs of the Democrats. Don't wear a mask, wear a mask, don't wear a mask, wear two masks—even the most willingly obedient American couldn't possibly have obeyed such conflicting, fast-changing advice. So where would they turn for clarification and comfort? Why, to the experts, of course. To the doctors, the medical officials, the health bureaucrats on the national stage—the ones who supposedly care nothing for politics but only for the safety of citizens. What a lucky break for Democrats who believe in the might of government.

That is precisely why doctors shouldn't be in charge of policy. Doctors consider solely best health practices—which may or may not be true, which may or may not change with the times. But even if their best health practices were to prove 100 percent true, fact is, humans aren't made to live a standard of best health practices. If that were the case, nobody would drive, eat sweets, watch television, or dare leave their homes. It's too dangerous; too many health risks out there.

Can you say bingo? The same reason why doctors shouldn't be in charge of policy is precisely why the Left wanted doctors in charge of policy—and precisely why the Left wanted doctors to stay in charge of policy, even after their doctorlike policies proved, over the course of weeks and months, devastating to the economic, societal, educational, psychological, and even physical health of Americans. Democrats saw opportunity to control. To expand power. To rule. To crush. To subjugate. To usher in political reforms, economic changes, and societal shifts of such magnitude that even a Trump term two couldn't undo.

Mark these words: The year of COVID-19 will no doubt be remembered as the golden era for socialists, communists, collectivists, globalists. Here's a short list of what they accomplished:

- They shut down America's small businesses—while keeping open the chosen few, like Walmart and Target; marijuana and liquor stores.
- They closed the nation's public schools to all in-person instruction—and then let the unions keep doors closed, at the great detriment to youth, long past the stage of health danger.
- They used the free market to impose mandates they didn't have the constitutional right or political nerve to pass themselves—that is, face masking of free Americans—and then stood by and watched the chaos that came from retail employees having to act as law enforcers for "laws" that weren't law.

- They stood by and watched as bands of police pulled riders without face masks off public transportation, chased runners without masks off empty beaches, arrested pedestrians without masks in city streets, fined citizens without masks who walked in public—all based on randomly targeted, randomly imposed, arbitrarily crafted health-based dictates, policies, and orders.
- They imposed burdensome, tyrannical political will on the people based on faulty, skewed, and outright deceptively interpreted data—via executive orders that far outlived their supposed health emergency basis for being.
- They wrecked national holidays, religious holidays, basic American holidays, by both order and advisement, telling families to stay home, friends to stay away, families and friends to not travel—for Easter, for Thanksgiving, for Christmas.
- They shut down the country's biggest forms of entertainment—movie theaters, professional sports, concerts and venues for music and comedy, national parks, local parks, and more.
- They upset high school graduations, destroyed college and college-bound athletes' scholarships, delayed and halted many a young bride and groom's wedding—and worse, devastated untold numbers of funerals, burials, occasions for grieving loved ones.
- They advanced the cause of government surveillance and tracking of citizens, and called for billions of tax dollars to go toward a nationwide contact tracing system that would forever put Big Brother at the helm.
- They jeopardized the nation's children, causing emotional, behavioral, psychological, and even physical harm to the most vulnerable by forcing them to live lives of hermits, and adopt stay-at-home habits borne by fear.
- They turned a thriving economy and booming job market into a depressed state of uncertainty and constant upheaval—and along the way, pressed the idea into the national consciousness that to work, one needs the government's permission.

- They shut down churches—churches!—by executive order. By the whim of a governor; by the command of a bureaucrat.
- They hypocritically, arrogantly, and with full elitist intent, went about their own business—eating at restaurants, visiting their hair salons, traveling as wished, partying with friends—all the while, demanding the citizens who paid their salaries to refrain from eating at restaurants; getting their hair cut; traveling across community, county, country, and overseas; and meeting with friends and families for food and drinks.

These are not the unfortunate, but natural, by-products of a worldwide pandemic. These are the disturbing outcomes of the government's response to the pandemic. These are the horribly unconstitutional, un-American, dictatorial outcomes of the Democrats' use of the pandemic for political means.

With Joe Biden in the White House, with Kamala Harris at the helm, with Congress held in both houses by Democrats, make way for more pain. The Left is not going to let go the golden goose called *pandemic*. As Biden told the G7 powers in February, during his first formal address as president to the international community: "America is back, the transatlantic alliance is back."[43] The coronavirus clampdowns were simply dry runs for all the socialist, communist, globalist, collectivist designs that are still to come.

CHAPTER TWO

Contact Tracing Lies and the Lying Liars Who Advance Them

> When the righteous are in authority, the people rejoice; but when the wicked rule, the people groan.
>
> Proverbs 29:2 (RSV)

Joe Biden, while campaigning for president, said this in April 2020: "Once we identify COVID-19 infected people, we need to isolate them and identify those to whom they might have unwittingly spread the disease. This is called contact tracing . . ."[1] Remember that while reading this chapter.

On May 1, 2020, Representative Bobby Rush, Illinois Democrat, introduced legislation called the COVID-10 Testing, Reaching and Contacting Everyone (TRACE) Act to create a grant program within the CDC to "fully mobilize coronavirus testing and contact tracing efforts," and to fund it to the tune of $100 billion.[2] Yes, that's billion with a *b*. And that was just for fiscal 2020. The bill allowed for "such sums as may be necessary" for fiscal 2021 and for following years, as "the emergency period" of the pandemic warranted.[3]

Interestingly enough, the bill was numbered H.R. 6666—a quasi-marking of the biblical beast from Revelation: "[L]et him who has understanding reckon the number of the beast, for it is a human number, its number is six hundred and sixty-six." One off, yes. But one off by addition, not omission. And certainly, the bill's intent is evil enough. Why? Think government tracking, surveillance, and power to quarantine citizens, even if the quarantining—as the untangled yarns of H.R. 6666 show—is conducted against citizens' will.

Rush, however, in introductory remarks, described TRACE as crucial to returning to normal. As nothing more than a benign way for America to get back to being America. "Reopening our economy and getting back to normal will be all but impossible if we do not step up our testing efforts and implement robust and widespread contact tracing," he said, in mid-2020. "The COVID-19 TRACE Act . . . [creates] a $100 billion grant program for local organizations to hire, train and pay individuals to purchase supplies to run mobile testing units and door-to-door outreach, as is safe and necessary . . . "[4]

He harped on its bipartisan nature, saying he was "immensely proud to see this bill receive bipartisan support."[5] Please. There was nothing bipartisan about it. ProPublica recorded seventy-three cosponsors, all but one of whom, Representative Jefferson Van Drew, were members of the Democratic Party.[6] Van Drew, a Republican representing New Jersey, was actually elected in 2018 as a card-carrying Democrat, but he switched to the GOP in January 2020, in defiance of the impeachment of President Donald Trump, which he opposed.[7] Seventy-three cosponsors, all but one Democrat—and that sole Republican a former Democrat—does not a nonpartisan bill make.

There's the first spin, now unspun. The second? It deals with what H.R. 6666 does, and more important, where H.R. 6666 leads, or potentially leads. Look first to the text of the legislation:

- The purpose of the bill: "To authorize the secretary of Health and Human Services to award grants to eligible entities to conduct diagnostic testing for COVID-19, and related activities such as contact tracing, through mobile health units and, as necessary, at individuals' residences, and for other purposes."[8]

- Section 2 of the bill: "In general, the [HHS secretary], acting through the [CDC] director, may award grants . . . to conduct diagnostic testing for COVID-19, to trace and monitor the contacts of infected individuals, and to support the quarantine of such contacts, through mobile health units; and as necessary, testing individuals and providing individuals with services related to testing and quarantine at their residences."[9]
- Section 2b clarifies how the $100 billion will be spent—on the hiring, training, compensating of specially trained contact tracers, as well as on the purchase of safety equipment. The section also stipulates priority with funding goes to "hot spots" for pandemic outbreaks, and to "medically underserved" jurisdictions.[10]
- Section 2f defines the "eligible entities" who might apply for and receive TRACE funding. They include: "federal qualified health centers," or those community facilities receiving federal funding; school clinics; hospitals that serve primarily low-income individuals; academic medical outlets; nonprofit groups—"including any such faith-based organization," high schools; colleges, universities, and places of higher learning; and "any other type of entity" the HHS secretary determines "to be an eligible entity."[11] In other words: practically anybody and everybody.

Not only does the bill, as its title makes clear, aim to contact trace "everyone," but so, too, it apparently aims to spread the $100 billion to everyone.

Rush, meanwhile, on his website, goes to great pains to make sure any red flags about the legislation are properly squelched.

Look now to the congressman's own words:

Does the COVID-19 TRACE Act require testing? No. The COVID-19 TRACE Act is about providing testing to those who want/need it. Not everyone has the ability to visit drive-thru testing sites, and many others are unable to leave their homes to get tested . . . This bill would allow testers to come to you through mobile testing units and door-to-door outreach. . . . However, if you don't want to be tested for coronavirus, you won't don't [sic] have to be—but you should![12]

Another Q&A:

If I test positive for coronavirus, will I be forced to quarantine? Absolutely not. Again, these tests would be completely voluntary. The bill does not force you or your loved ones to do anything at all. With that being said, if you or a loved one does ha[ve] the coronavirus, it is advised that you do self-quarantine and maintain social distance from others.[13]

And one more Q&A, from Rush's same web page:

I saw online that the bill allows the government to enter my home and remove my children if we test positive for the virus. Is that true? I've seen these alarming posts as well, but I can assure you that they are completely false. This bill does not authorize anyone to enter your home, for whatever reason, without your permission, nor does it allow the government to remove anyone from your home because of the coronavirus. Again, this bill is about providing access to testing and outreach for medically underserved communities . . . This bill is about helping our country safely reopen the economy so we can get back to normal![14]

Nothing to see here, folks. Go home. Really? How the heck many underserved communities does Rush think America has . . . anyway—$100 billion worth? If that's all this bill is about—"providing access to testing" for the "medically underserved communities"—then look to the windows. Pigs have to be flying.

Still, the deception goes deeper. Rush may technically be telling the truth—that his legislation "does not authorize anyone to enter your home," or "remove anyone from your home," that it does not enforce quarantines, it does not mandate testing, and that, in fact, it "does not force you or your loved ones to do anything at all," as he wrote on his web page. But the bill opens the door for others to do all that. His bill paves the path for other government entities to remove the resistors, to forcibly quarantine the reluctant, to mandate testing. His bill empowers others to turn all the so-called voluntary provisions of the TRACE Act into compulsory measures—and empowers others to take punitive measures when necessary. How so? That's best explained with a comparison.

Beginning in 2008, I spent an entire year researching and writing about the intersection of private property rights and National Heritage Areas (NHAs) as a fellow with the Robert Novak Journalism Fellowship Program. NHAs are congressionally designated land preservation tags that advance the mission of the National Park Service (NPS) by "fostering community stewardship of our nation's heritage," as the NPS puts it. One key facet of the legislation that goes into the making of an NHA is a promise that generally goes like this, again from the NPS: "NHA designation does not affect private property rights."[15]

In fact, NHA legislation makes explicitly clear that nothing contained in the bill will impede the rights of property owners to use their properties as they see fit. But wait for it . . . read on. Coincidentally enough, Rush in February 2021 reintroduced for the second or third time the Bronzeville–Black Metropolis National Heritage Act, aimed at establishing select areas of Chicago as an NHA.[16] And just like most NHA legislation, Rush's, numbered for the 117th Congress as H.R. 670, contained a section speaking specifically to private property rights:

Nothing in this Act—(1) abridges the rights of any property owners (whether public or private), including the right to refrain from participating in any plan, project, program or activity conducted within the Heritage Area; (2) requires any property owner to permit public access (including access by federal, state or local agencies) to the property of the property owner . . . (3) alters any duly adopted land use regulation, approved land use plan, or other regulatory authority of any federal, state or local agency.[17]

Sounds plain enough English, right? That's pretty much the boiler plate property protections' lingo in almost all NHA designation bills.

But here's the loophole: while it's true nothing in the NHA designating legislation strips private property owners of their land use rights, the NHA designation opens the doors for others to strip private property owners of their land use rights. In fact, this is exactly what often happens. The devil's in the details. Also contained in NHA legislation is the establishment of a "local coordinating entity" that will work, supposedly in partnership with pertinent local, state, and federal officials, to establish and oversee a management plan for the heritage site. Rush, in his H.R. 670, named the Black Metropolis National Heritage Area Commission, an organization tied to The Chicago Community Trust, as the "local coordinating entity" of his proposed NHA.[18]

Now the duties of the Black Metropolis National Heritage Area Commission are spelled out in Rush's legislation—just like in all the bills brought forward to propose new NHA sites. The legislation always lays out what will be the responsibilities and powers of the "coordinating entity," usually beginning with the creation of a "management plan" for the properties contained within the NHA boundaries. Rush's NHA legislation gives the commission the power to prepare reports, make grants, enter into agreements with other NHA partnering agencies, to hire and pay staff, to solicit funds, to contract with other groups—and to "prepare a management plan" for the NHA that will propose ways of protecting the property.

Door, meet crack.

This is where the soft and friendly sounding NHA designation begins to move into the realm of regulatory control. NHA management plans, by definition, are aimed at protecting and preserving the newly designated properties from uses that are deemed, by the "coordinating entity," to be threatening or damaging to the site's historical character. Management plans, though developed locally, are ultimately OK'd by the Interior secretary; those that don't meet the fed's approval are turned back to the "coordinating entity" for revisal. A lot of money rides on the submission of successful management plans. In Rush's bill, it's a matter of $10 million over ten years, as well as opportunity to solicit more.

So what we have here is a bill that establishes a boundary of property as worthy of preservation; that sets up a coordinating entity, or land use manager, with the heavy background breathing of the fed to determine how best that property might be preserved; and that dangles to the pertinent local players some serious cash to make that land management plan a reality. And all along, don't forget, private property owners are told not to worry—the legislation contains protections for their interests. For their constitutional rights.

Which it does. But which means nothing when it comes to local zoning laws. Or local comprehensive plans. Or local historic protection rules. Or any number of locally passed permitting policies that come on the heels of NHA designations, by way of "coordinating entity" partnerships with locally elected and appointed members of the Board of Supervisors, Planning Commission, Zoning Commission, Architectural Review Agency, or any number of other local government and citizen groups.

Door, meet open.

This is where the regulation comes; this is where the restrictions to property owners take place. Local government officials, cash-strapped as they are, environmentally conscious as they are, are either happy to work with NHA coordinating entities to protect NHA properties—because they see the tourism potential, for instance, of the newly designated NHA, or they see the green good of protecting the space, or they smell the odor of incoming NHA dollars—or they're not so happy, but politically pragmatic. They see the public relations ding that could come from turning away what seems—on the surface, anyway—an oh-so-worthy endeavor. Who argues against preserving history, anyway?

Working with the NHA coordinating entity means assisting with the implementation of the NHA management plan. What normally occurs are changes to local zoning laws restricting, say, developers' rights to develop, or to local comprehensive plans redefining how properties within the NHA can be used—maybe affecting fishing and hunting, maybe impacting noise ordinances tied to motorbikes, maybe adding layers of bureaucracy for certain home additions. Federal rules regarding what coordinating entities and their partners can do within the bounds of management plans are few and far between—meaning, NHA land management plans can vary widely from jurisdiction to jurisdiction.

But the common denominator is that NHAs bring changes in property rights. The NHA legislation itself contains opt-out language for land owners, but the thing is, how do land owners opt out of local land use laws? Once local zoning laws adjust to the new considerations of the NHA, it's difficult to fight those laws. It's even difficult to make the connection between the NHA and the establishment of new zoning and local land-use regulations. The development of an NHA can take years. So, too, the ensuing changes to local land-use plans. And unless you're someone who happens to follow local politics and attend local government meetings on a regular basis, chances are you'll never see the links between NHAs and private property restrictions.

But they're there. The ties that bind—the regulations that trickle from federal NHA legislation to local regulation—they're there. As the Congressional Research Service wrote in its updated "Heritage Areas: Background, Proposals and Current Issues" report in mid-2020:

> The management entity usually develops and implements a plan for managing the NHA in collaboration with partners and other interested parties. Although the plans' components vary, in accordance with the authorizing legislation and local needs, they often identify resources and themes: lay out policies and implementation strategies for protection, use and public education; describe needed restoration of physical sites; discuss recreational opportunities; outline funding goals and possibilities; and define partners' roles and responsibilities. Once the Secretary of the Interior approves a plan, it essentially becomes the blueprint for managing the heritage area and is implemented as funding and resources are available.[19]

No matter how you slice it, the government—the highest level of federal government, in fact—has a hand in land management of all NHAs. Denying is deceptive. So, too, is including language in an NHA bill that tells property owners their constitutional rights will be respected and that their lands will be safe from regulation. Those assurances are meaningless once all the layers of bureaucracy of the "coordinating entity" and "management plan" overseers are in place. Those promises are destined to be broken by at least one governing board, one agency, one permitting office, somewhere, sometime down the line of NHA management. If not right away, then in the coming years. The promise of otherwise—the assurance of private property protections—is a red herring. It's purposely included in NHA legislation to distract from relevant questioning and to discourage those who would criticize.

And that, ladies and gentlemen, is exactly the same with H.R. 6666. The TRACE Act coughs up massive amounts of taxpayer money to hire, train, and equip contact tracers to come to a neighborhood near you—to a home near you—to your own home, even. And even though the language of the bill promises that all is voluntary, and that nobody can "enter your home," nobody can "remove anyone from your home," nobody can mandate quarantines or even coronavirus testing, for that matter, and nobody can force "you or your loved ones to do anything at all," the fact is the onus for carrying out the provisions of the TRACE Act falls to locals. Just like the onus for carrying out the provisions of NHA management plans falls to locals. 'Round and 'round the tiers of bureaucracy go, and where they stop, nobody knows.

At least with NHAs, the losses are usually contained to property rights—to the Fourth Amendment, for instance. With H.R. 6666, the losses—the could-be losses—are far more encompassing. It's big government surveillance on steroids. It's a police state, such as seen in closed communist societies. It's socialist-communist "government knows best" rule; it's collectivist "for the greater good" dictatorial control.

Consider how the CDC advises contact tracing be conducted locally. On its very own web page, in a section titled "Step 2a: Quarantine/isolation instructions and testing quarantine/isolation instructions," the CDC writes these chilling guidelines for those "contacts," that is, individuals who test positive for the coronavirus or show symptoms of COVID-19.

> Advise contacts to cancel or postpone plans that involve social gatherings, vacations or other planned travel until cleared for these activities by public health authorities . . . Local and state health departments may request federal public health travel restrictions, which prevent listed travelers from boarding commercial airplanes and [which] trigger public health notification if they enter the United States by land or sea . . . Support with federal public health travel restrictions may be requested by public health partners by contacting the CDC quarantine station with jurisdiction for the area. If needed, jurisdictions should refer clients for social support services (e.g., food, childcare, housing, and other services) to help encourage clients to stay at home and comply with quarantine or isolation. **If contacts refuse to comply voluntarily with self-quarantine or self-isolation instructions, jurisdictions should consider what options (e.g., legal order for isolation) are available to them under relevant state or local legal authority.**[20] (Bold added.)

On a different web page, the CDC issued similarly ominous sounding guidance. Read on. And remember, when the government says "contacts," the government means people. The CDC, in this excerpt, is talking about separating people from people.

> Separating contacts from people who are not exposed is critical to the success of any contact tracing effort and requires social supports for individual compliance and medical monitoring. First and foremost is the assessment of an individual's ability to stay home and maintain social distance from others . . . For a portion of the U.S. population this will be a challenge . . . If possible, contacts should be asked to voluntarily stay home, monitor

themselves and maintain social distancing from others. **However, health departments have the authority to issue legal orders of quarantine, should the situation warrant that measure.** (Bold added.)[21]

Well, that's terrifying.

And that's where the fears rear up of forcible removal from home, forcible quarantining, forced compliance with coronavirus dictates. H.R. 6666 opens the door, CDC walks into the room, local health officials pick up the Gestapo stick and go.

There's more. If all that doesn't give pause, then perhaps this excerpted training guide for contact tracers will. It's from Johns Hopkins, it's an online training course—and it's about as Orwellian as it gets.[22] In this section, contact tracer wannabes are told how to deal with those people who insist on making their own health decisions in the face of the pandemic. Hat tip to Eagle Forum for transcribing the text:

Now, let's talk about autonomy. Autonomy legally means the right of a person to make their own decisions. It's also known as the right to self or an agency. And what this really means, is that each person can make their own decisions. This is true unless the decisions they make or the things they do can harm someone else. And we all know that this is true. And in the case of contact tracing, it means that people can make their own decisions. But if they're not isolating themselves or not quarantining themselves, that could harm someone else. It does put other people at risk so they do have some limits on their autonomy, or their ability to make their own decisions within the context of contact tracing.[23]

This is eerily akin to what you'd expect from a trained propagandist from China—not from a supposedly esteemed American medical research university. Note the sly suggestive language that, on one hand, acknowledges individual rights, but on the other, trounces those individual rights when individuals don't voluntarily subject themselves to the desired collectivist outcome. It's the language of serpents. It's the whisper of evil. It's the song of a Pied Piper slowly but surely leading liberty-loving Americans down a path of total government control—but willingly.

"And we all know that this is true"—the snake hissed, its body slithering, its eyes fixated on its victims. If individuals won't voluntarily abide the government's coronavirus mandates, it means their thinking is off, their mental capacities compromised, and therefore, it's incumbent on the government to make their decisions for them. It's the kind thing to do. We know these individuals don't want to harm others. It's the compassionate thing for government to force them to do what's best for all.

"And we all know that this is true"—there are limits to individualism. If that's the case, then imagine where the government could go. That's the language of communists; that's the line of argument of collectivists—that's how America loses its concept of God-given rights.

And that's where H.R. 6666 leads. This is the second spin of Rush's contact tracing legislation, unspun. This is what the $100 billion in H.R. 6666 pays for—trained contact tracers coming to your community, to your neighborhood, to your very door. What's more, Rush knows that. He must. Rush knows how the political game is played. He understands the concept of plausible deniability—of phrasing legislation in a way that accomplishes regulatory control via the trickle-down method.

Rush is a guy who's been both politician and political activist for a very long time, first serving as U.S. congressman in 1992, and winning every reelection campaign since. Prior, he served as alderman for Chicago's Second Ward, ran against Richard M. Daley for mayor—but lost—and formed the Illinois chapter of the Black Panther Party.[24] He knows politics; he knows political strategy and the power of strategic partnerships.

Besides, his office's reaction when I wrote a critical commentary about his bill for the *Washington Times* that then went viral on the *Drudge Report* was so over-the-top, it struck as a real Shakesperean "the [man] dost protest too much, methinks" moment. I wrote, in reference to the bill's stated authority for contact tracers to "support the quarantine" of coronavirus "contacts" "as necessary . . . at [citizens'] residences," this viewpoint: "That means government comes to your home, taps on your door and demands you take a COVID-19 test. And if you test positive, that means the government makes sure you stay at home. How? Good question. Good unanswered question. Good chillingly unclear question." I also wrote of the bill's funding of government bureaucrats to knock on Americans' doors "to enforce compliance with quarantining."[25]

Rush's communications director, Jeremy Edwards, first charged in an email that my interpretation of the bill was "patently false" because the legislation contained "no such language." Then he demanded a correction. Then he demanded I read the bill. Then he pointed to another news organization that apparently had drawn a similar conclusion of the bill to mine, but that "corrected" its "inaccuracies" upon contact. Then he provided links to fact-checking sites that offered a nothing-to-see-here, nothing-to-worry-about, go-home-folks, conclusion of H.R. 6666. The most interesting—that is, revelatory—part of the back-and-forth emails with Edwards is his argument that the bill did not contain explicit permissions for the government to "demand" a COVID-19 test of citizens, or "enforce" quarantining.[26] The serpent whispers. The same serpent selling the innocence of NHAs is the one selling the innocence of contact tracing.

Be not fooled. Contact tracing, in itself, is not nefarious. It's actually been around for a long time. At its simplest, it's when health officials ask patients who've tested positive for a contagious disease to tell where they've been, so as to alert those who've been potentially affected. It's basically a commonsense advance warning to unsuspecting individuals. It's when technology enters the picture, however, that contact tracing becomes more complicated—and it's when technology plus big government enters that contact tracing becomes intrusive and worrisome.

One growing area of contact tracing is in smartphone technology, where individuals download apps that alert them to the presence of people who've tested positive for the coronavirus. Some of these apps simply register the general proximities of positive test case people within a certain time frame, without releasing too much private data. For instance, the least intrusive form of proximity tracing assigns specific labels to devices that tell if you've come into the presence of someone who's tested positive for the coronavirus—but the specific labels assigned to the devices make it impossible to identify the person who's tested positive.

Case in point: Let's say the perfectly healthy Joe Walker enters a store where the COVID-19-carrying Jill Shopper has just exited, after which his proximity tracer pings and lets him know that he has potentially been exposed to the coronavirus. Joe Walker doesn't know the identity of the coronavirus carrier; he only knows that he may want to get tested himself in the coming days to make sure he's not infected. Jill Shopper, meanwhile, goes about her shopping as usual.

Simple enough, yes? Some of this proximity tracing technology has actually been developed into wearable devices, like watches, as well. And it's being marketed to businesses as a COVID-19 safety measure, which is somewhat concerning.

The asset tracking product company Radiant RFID offers "automated social distance and contact tracing solutions to help companies transition their employees back to work, safely, in the wake of COVID-19," the organization's web page states. The web page goes on:

> Utilizing Samsung wearable devices [that look like wrist watches], the Radiant solution allows for anonymous contact tracing . . . Employees receive automated alerts (vibrations and color-coded messages) in near real-time of social distance proximity on their devices while in the workplace; employers receive alerts of any issues and can monitor and review easy-to-use reports on social distancing . . . The data can empower employers to create useful feedback to improve staff training and workflows. It also serves as a non-intrusive reminder to employees to work at safe distances.[27]

That last claim seems negligible, at best. Imagine standing too close to a colleague at the coffee machine, only to hear your name barked over the internal company audio system with the sharp command to, "Stand back! You are too close together!" Or perhaps a more discreet employer might opt instead to call you in for a closed-door admonishment, based on your proximity history that shows several violations of six-foot social distance policies? That might be an exaggeration; proximity tracing, after all, is supposed to be anonymous—and Radiant emphasizes that its devices are anonymous. But then again, maybe not. The proximity data goes from wearer to data collector—in Radiant's case, from employee to employer—in "near real time." Besides, the path of unintended consequences is wide. With technology, it's not just what is. It's what's coming. Either way, such devices send a shiver up the civil liberties pole. And Radiant is hardly the only company using the COVID-19 pandemic to boost its marketing and sales of tracking technology. It's a competitive industry. It's an emerging, growing, expanding, competitive industry. Intrusive must be in the eye of the beholder.

Still, that's not even the most concerning of contact tracing technology. More disturbing are the GPS and Bluetooth types that collect and disseminate more specific location data. Whereas proximity tracing alerts to the nearby status of a test-positive coronavirus person—but without identifying exactly where or when or whom—location tracing provides much more revealing information. "Location tracking is highly invasive because it tracks all your movements such as going to a church, or a birth control clinic, and who you associate with," said Jennifer Oliva, an associate professor of law at Seton Hall University School of Law in Jersey City, New Jersey, to WebMD in September 2020.[28]

Who gets that information? Who stores that information? Who ultimately has access to that information? Who knows.

In the end, contact tracing is data collection, and with all data collection comes those same three questions. It's when the answers aren't evident that problems mount. As the CDC acknowledges on its own contact tracing web page, one drawback of the Bluetooth and GPS methods is that "[h]acking and other unauthorized access or use of data may compromise data security and confidentiality."[29]

That's a heck of an acknowledgment, given the government's own shaky past with securing databases. In June 2015, the Office of Personnel

Management saw 21.5 million records hacked.[30] In May 2006, the Department of Veteran's Affairs saw 26.5 million records breached.[31] In October 2009, the National Archives and Records Administration saw 76 million records compromised.[32] In December 2015, the U.S. voter database saw 191 million records exposed.[33] That doesn't even get into the various states—the South Carolina Department of Revenue, 3.6 million records in October 2012; the state of Texas, 3.5 million records in April 2011.[34] And it doesn't touch on the private companies and their similarly dismal experiences with securing customers' data: Adobe and its 2013 exposure of 153 million records; eBay in 2014, and its breach of 145 million accounts; Equifax in 2017, and its compromise of almost 148 million consumers.[35]

But those frequent trips to the local bar, that appointment at that psychotherapist's office, that three-hour stop at the local Planned Parenthood—all that data, swept as it could be by contact tracing technology, is guaranteed safe from breach?

Remember, the H.R. 6666 plan is to hire $100 billion worth of contact tracers. That's a heck of lot of bureaucracy to trust. The Electronic Frontier Foundation lays out well the problems contact tracing can bring to those who value privacy, to those who cherish liberty, to those who simply think the government has no business nosing about their private medical records. In a list of reasons to oppose contact tracing technology, EFF also highlights the possible dangers of applying the technology to fields other than medical, and the potential for it to expand far beyond what health officials intended, or maybe even imagined.

We oppose dragnet surveillance . . . to identify infected people . . . [including] cameras in public places that use face recognition or thermal imaging, and mounting such technologies on drones. We oppose monitoring quarantine of COVID-19 patients with ankle GPS shackles or compulsion to download tracking apps. We oppose giving police officers access to any COVID-19 public health data, including the addresses of people who tested positive. We oppose immunity passports and verified credentials of test results. Gatekeeping systems that require peoples to present a digital token of supposed health in order to enter various spaces are a worrisome step towards national digital identification.[36]

And like that, the bureaucratic line of contract tracing as safe and effective and benign went up in smoke.

"Six months before the COVID 'plandemic,' Bill Gates had negotiated a $100 billion contact tracing deal with (the) Democratic congressman sponsor of the bill," blared one PolitiFact headline in June 2020, as a teaser about a spreading story on the Internet of two private investigators who claimed Rush worked out the particulars of H.R. 6666 during a meeting in August 2019 in Rwanda, East Africa, months before the pandemic broke.[37]

PolitiFact determined the Gates-Rush deal to be a bit of fake news. So did plenty of other fact-checking news organizations. From PolitiFact:

[The reports] cite an interview given by private investigators John Moynihan and Larry Doyle on a TruePundit podcast in which the investigators said that representatives from the Gates Foundation met with U.S. Representative Bobby Rush, D-Ill., in Rwanda, East Africa, in mid-August 2019 "to hash out who would score the windfall from a government contact tracing program." The article points out that, in May [2020], Rush introduced the $100 billion Testing, Reaching and Contacting Everyone (TRACE) Act to fight the coronavirus. Our searches of Google and Nexis turned up no reports of a meeting in Rwanda between Rush and the Gates Foundation.[38]

True. There are no reports showing a meeting between Rush and the Gates Foundation, or Rush and Gates himself, in Rwanda, to discuss contact tracing legislation. But there is evidence placing Rush and two members of the Gates Foundation in the same Rwandan location at the same time. Pages 37 and 38 of the documentation from an August

12–19 conference on "Africa's Economic, Security and Development Challenges and the U.S. Role," held in Kigali, Musanze and Muhanga, Rwanda, as part of the Aspen Institute Congressional Program in August 2019, contained these "conference participants" names: Representative Bobby Rush and Paulette Rush, Ryan McMaster, "UN Relations Officer, The Gates Foundation," and Kim Webber, "Program Officer, The Gates Foundation."[39] Interesting coincidence.

"There's no evidence Gates worked with . . . Rush on a $100 billion COVID-19 contact tracing bill months before the COVID-19 outbreak occurred," PolitiFact wrote.[40] Yep. Again, true. But that doesn't change the fact Rush was in Rwanda, at the exact same time, at the exact same location, participating in the exact same conference as two key officials with Gates's own foundation. Who can say what's discussed behind closed doors? Who can say what's not discussed in private? It's a conundrum, all right. Here's another: The government's ongoing assurances of the efficacy and even necessity of intrusive, technology-based contact tracing, as well as those promises that privacies will be protected, data completely secured, and civil liberties utterly upheld.

But widespread contact tracing is coming. Sure as sure can be—it's coming.

- "As lockdown measures begin to reduce COVID-19 cases to manageable levels," the World Health Organization wrote in September 2020, citing Stephane Hugonnet, a medical doctor and epidemiologist with the WHO health emergency program, "the epidemiological practice of contact tracing must go into full force."[41]
- "Biden Administration Likely to Leverage Tracing Apps Nationally," Government Technology reported in November 2020.[42]
- "Contact tracing, a critical part of efforts to slow the spread of the coronavirus, has fallen behind in recent months as COVID-19 cases have soared. President Joe Biden has pledged to change that," *U.S. News & World Report* wrote in February 2021. "Biden

proposes hiring 100,000 people nationwide as part of a new public health jobs corps. The corps would help with contact tracing and facilitate vaccination."[43]

Government facilitators coming to a community near you. Coming to a neighborhood where you live. Trained by the best Johns Hopkins and the CDC have to offer; funded by millions—no, billions—of taxpayer dollars; emboldened by layers of bureaucracy that practically guarantee no accountability; schooled in the art of NHA-slash-H.R.-6666-like deceptions. What could go wrong?

They're from the government, and they're here to help.

CHAPTER THREE

Spinning the Truth So Socialism Can Thrive

> . . . yet their voice goes out through all the earth, and their
> words to the end of the world.
>
> Psalm 19:4 (RSV)

Freedom of speech is in danger. Check the year. The U.S. Constitution is still in effect. Yet because of snowflakes, easily offended pinheads, opportunistic politicians, and a general Big Tech clamp on all things conservative, the foundation of America's liberties—the right to self-express—is in danger of crumbling.

Democrats couldn't be happier. Their friends in the progressive, socialist, communist, and collectivist camps are throwing confetti. On wings called coronavirus, censorship is spreading worldwide. The nonprofit Human Rights Watch (HRW) reported in February 2021:

> At least 83 governments worldwide have used the COVID-19 pandemic to justify violating the exercise of free speech and peaceful assembly. Authorities have attacked, detained, prosecuted, and in some cases killed critics, broken up peaceful protests, closed media outlets, and enacted vague laws criminalizing speech that

they claim threatens public health. The victims include journalists, activists, healthcare workers, political opposition groups and others who have criticized government responses to the coronavirus.[1]

On the topic of censorship, HRW found:

- Various governments have passed laws that criminalized the sharing or spreading of health data deemed false.
- Security forces in at least 18 countries have targeted journalists for arrest, and in some cases physically assaulted them, for the "crime" of reporting on coronavirus news that counters government messaging.
- At least 52 governments have implemented arbitrary laws that give authorities the power to block the sharing of certain COVID-19 coverages, even to the point of shutting down media outlets that refuse to toe the official line.
- Another eight governments have outright refused to provide information to the press on COVID-19 statistics that would allow for independent verification of political statements.
- Related to censorship of media: dozens of governments have threatened to fire or otherwise harassed medical personnel who've dared to speak to journalists and give them information and statistics that counter the state-approved messages.[2]

The offending countries include closed societies, tightly controlled societies, and even societies perceived by the West as free. China, for instance, was faulted for arbitrarily arresting and prosecuting journalists, for shutting down media outlets, and for erasing media reports deemed offensive to the government. Hong Kong was faulted for targeting protesters and banning protests. Australia and Israel were faulted for targeting protesters and targeting journalists.[3]

- "In India," VOA news reported, "Prime Minister Narendra Modi petitioned the Supreme Court to have [coronavirus-related] reporting cleared by the government before publication. The request was denied but it sent a chilling message to India's press."[4]

- From the Atlantic Council, this: "The Russian government has been actively engaged in spreading disinformation and misinformation around the pandemic. . . . The government also announced specific punishments for users spreading 'false information' about the coronavirus. . . . Internet platforms remain a key focus of Russia's push to stem the flow of pandemic-related information that authorities deem false."[5]

- And from Tedros Adhanom Ghebreyesus, director-general of the World Health Organization, this: "We're not just fighting an epidemic. We're fighting an infodemic."[6]

Infodemic? Censordemic is more like it. Here's the sad part. It's not just dictatorial, socialist, closed, or otherwise unfree nations that have ushered in chilling censorship atmospheres under the guise of doing some sort of coronavirus greater good. It's in America, too.

America may be land of the free, home of the Constitution, a nation of individualists with rights rooted in God, not government. But once the coronavirus hit, all that flew out the window. Fear-fueled prognostications became the order of the day. Debates about free speech turned quickly into debates about acceptable speech, then quickly after that, finger-wagging debates about dangerous speech. As if. As if founders figured "dangerous speech" into some sort of constitutional exception clause. But none of that mattered.

Suddenly, dissent became criminal. On the coronavirus, there was the government's line of thought—or not. Or nothing, is more like it. Socialists, collectivists, Democrats, and leftists saw their golden opportunity and pounced. From Freedom House, under a headline called, "Dealing with Dangerous Speech," in a 2020 report about the censorship of COVID-19 coverage:

In what has been described as an "infodemic," inaccurate and unscientific posts have contributed to the loss of life from COVID-19, either due to their flagrant disregard for the danger posed by the virus or because they promote dangerous or ineffective treatments. President Jair Bolsonaro in Brazil and President Donald Trump in the United States . . . both suggested at times that the pandemic is no more dangerous than common influenza, and they . . . recklessly promoted unsafe or untested treatments . . . consistent with their administrations' history of rejecting science in making public policy.[7]

Words that kill? The worlds of science and medicine are filled with dissenting opinions, countering viewpoints, opposing research, and spirited, heated data-fueled discussions. At least, they're supposed to be. It's how the truth gets vetted and the facts become clear. Government has no business making the medical and health decisions for U.S. individuals. In that same vein, government has no right in deciding which medical and health information flows to the public, so individuals can make their own informed decisions. "Dangerous and ineffective treatments" indeed. Who is a bureaucrat to decide the ultimate worth of a medical treatment?

More than that: Who is a Big Tech or social media giant? Careful now, America. It's not as if the Left hasn't sought to stifle dissenting opinions in prior times. But this Freedom House excerpt shows how the coronavirus has really focused and moved along their free speech stomping—one bitty step at a time, one careful plant of propaganda after another. Within the span of just a year, questioning natures and critical analyses were turned into enemies of the people. And in America, it wasn't so much the government that ultimately clamped speech, as it was the private market.

- "Twitter penalizes [Donald] Trump Jr. for posting hydroxychloroquine misinformation," *The Washington Post* wrote in July 2020.[8]

- "Twitter removed a tweet by White House coronavirus adviser Dr. Scott Atlas who claimed that face coverings were not effective in stopping the spread of the coronavirus," *Business Insider* wrote in October 2020.[9]
- "Instagram Bars Robert F. Kennedy Jr. for Spreading Vaccine Misinformation," NPR reported in February 2021, in a headline above a story about Kennedy's warnings of the coronavirus shot.[10] A spokesperson for Facebook, the company that owns Instagram, told NPR that Kennedy's account was removed "for repeatedly sharing debunked claims about the coronavirus or vaccines."[11] But debunked by whom?

Regardless, shouldn't the American people have the right to decide for themselves whether vaccines are safe for their personal use, or not?

The pandemic changed that dynamic. The pandemic opened the gate for speech police who used the cause of citizen safety to shutter dissenting thoughts. It wasn't long before the tyrants in the Democratic Party—the socialists, the collectivists, the far leftists, and globalists—saw this opened gate and jumped to exploit. They capitalized on the fear-filled situation to advance the idea that other speech deemed unsuitable, improper, unacceptable, dangerous, ought to be similarly stifled. They capitalized on a situation—COVID-19—that was unusually successful at getting American citizens to accept the idea that some speech was actually dangerous—that some speech could actually cause death. They figured the time was ripe for picking at free speech, and pick they did.

Now, America has entered a danger zone. Once the argument's been made that free speech is great, but some free speech is irresponsible—nay, reckless, nay, dangerous—then it's just a short hop to the conclusion that somebody—somebody!—has to put a stop to this dangerous speech. Somebody's got to fix this. Who? Why, the government, that's who. The experts in government. After all, people are dying. Dying, with a capital D. And if government can't do what needs to be done because of those pesky First Amendment prohibitions against Congress creating laws that abridge the freedom of speech, then government's friends in the media and technology worlds certainly can.

That's what occurred during the pandemic. Democrats, tech giants, social media hounds, mainstream media leftists, globalists, health bureaucrats all worked feverishly to control the flow of information to the people, painting the coordinated censorship activities as best medical practices. They called Donald Trump rallies "super-spreader" events, while turning blind eyes to the violent gatherings of Black Lives Matter and Antifa. They made it seem as if doctors who recommended a return to normal living were quacks who were placing peoples' lives in jeopardy. They erased messages that questioned the safety of vaccines. They pulled videos containing information that countered the federal government's viewpoints—even as the federal government's own best medical practice recommendations kept changing.

Chaos and anger fueled more chaos and anger. Confusion and fear fueled more confusion and fear. Goalposts were moved. Concessions were made. Americans who normally wouldn't stand for burdensome government crackdowns started to accept certain crackdowns out of an overwhelming desire for a return to normalcy.

And all along, free speech was being eroded. All along, the conditioning of a people to accept that some speech is needful of censorship went forth. Suddenly, the debate was not about free speech, but about responsible pandemic recommendations, and then responsible speech in general—and then about the differing degrees of deemed irresponsible speech that ought to be censored.

The pandemic paved a path that leftists have long lusted to lead the country to tread: censorship of dissenting viewpoints. And what's so clever about how the Left is accomplishing this chill on free speech is they're using the free market to bring it about—yes, the free market called social media—along with complicit citizens who have now become properly conditioned to accept that some speech is indeed dangerous, and properly emboldened to call for more free-speech crackdowns.

In 2019, before the pandemic hit, then senator Kamala Harris, campaigning for vice president, said this: "The words of a president matter.

Trump has again shown he is irresponsible and endangering others with his tweets. He should lose the privilege to be on Twitter."[12] Twitter responded days later to Harris with this: "We understand the desire for our decisions to be 'yes/no' binaries, but it is not that simple. We reviewed the tweets you cite in your letter, and they do not violate our policies against abusive behavior, targeted harassment, or violence."[13]

Ian Sams, the national press secretary for Harris, then responded to Twitter with this: "Twitter is not holding Donald Trump accountable for abusing their platform to threaten people and incite and inspire violent behavior. . . . As Donald Trump uses his tweets to incite violence, threaten witnesses and investigators, obstruct justice, and inspire mass shooters and pipe bombers, this response is inadequate."[14]

There's that whole "speech is dangerous and must be regulated" line of thought. Coming from the camp, no less, of the woman who shortly after became America's second-in-charge of defending the Constitution. And of course, we all remember how this story ended:

- "Twitter bans President Trump's account," CNN wrote on January 9, 2021.[15]
- "Twitter to uphold permanent ban against Trump, even if he were to run for office again," NBC News wrote a few weeks later.[16]

In the span of just a few short weeks, Twitter reversed its decision on Trump and took the path of despots. At the pressing of one of the nation's highest ranking and most influential politicians. This is a depressing turn of events, one that aptly demonstrates the speed by which America's freedoms have fallen—first, from the pandemic; then from changing political and cultural landscapes.

Liberty is a delicate thing. How can liberty-loving Americans successfully wage war against the leftists and globalists in government who've aligned themselves with the leftists and globalists in the tech world to curb speech they've deemed offensive—without calling for government crackdowns on free speech themselves? It's a rock-and-a-hard-place argument to make. Parler was supposed to be the free market alternative

to Twitter. But look what happened to Parler; Amazon pulled its platform plug. Whoosh, Parler was gone.

Yes, the company rebounded. "Parler returns online after monthlong absence," CNET wrote in February 2021. "The right-wing Twitter
clone had been down after Amazon stopped providing services in early
January."[16] But the message sent free speech's way was frightening just
the same. It said: mess with the tech giants, and the tech giants will mess
with you. It also was a head thump on how far behind the curve conservatives have fallen in terms of competing with the leftists who dominate
social media and the world of technology.

Make way for even more stifling of speech. If the pandemic cracked
the gate, the months since the pandemic have flung wide the doors. For
those who think the coronavirus, more than a year after the coronavirus,
is about curing Americans of the coronavirus, wake up. This is about the
left's use of the coronavirus for greatest maximum gain, to inflict the
greatest political damage, to bring about the internal destruction of the
greatest country on earth: America.

Let the cancel culture go forth. In early 2021, Loudoun County Public
Schools, a Northern Virginia district with a $1 billion annual budget
and more than eighty thousand students, canceled its celebrations of Dr.
Seuss because "research in recent years," spokesman Wayde Byard said,
"has revealed strong racial undertones in many books written/illustrated
by Dr. Seuss."[17] As an interesting aside, a little more than 61 percent of
this county voted for Biden in the November 2020 presidential election.[18]

But the research to which Byard referred was a 2019 publication
called, "The Cat Is out of the Bag: Orientalism, Anti-Blackness, and
White Supremacy in Dr. Seuss's Children's Books."[19] Among its findings:

- That "white supremacy is seen through the centering of whiteness
  and white characters, who comprise 98% of all characters," or
  2,195 of the characters.
- That "every character of color is male," and these male characters
  are "only presented in subservient, exotified, or dehumanized
  roles."

- That there is a "most startling" absence of "women and girls of color" across the entire spectrum of Dr. Seuss books.
- That some of the "most iconic" Dr. Seuss books include characters that are "animal or non-human" in form, but that nevertheless "transmit Orientalist, anti-black and white supremacist messaging through allegories and symbolism."[20]

My goodness. One doesn't know whether to laugh or cry.

Still, it's tempting to dismiss this entire report as nonsense, the stuff of overly intellectualized scholars seizing on an opportunity to leave a mark on the culture—or, more to point, the stuff of pinheads with too much time on their hands. But coming as it does on the heels of a free-speech, pandemic-induced chill, and showing, as it does, as influential enough to push a Virginia school district to drop its annual Dr. Seuss birthday book celebration, shrugging it off would be folly.

Besides, it's not just one school district. It's not just one flash-in-the-pan study. It's a social justice crusade started by a couple of far-leftists whose entire careers were dedicated to digging out racism. In 2017, researchers Ramon Stephens, a black PhD candidate at the University of California, San Diego, and Katie Ishizuka, a woman whose grandparents had been detained in the Japanese internment camps in America, endeavored to find and flag instances of racism and damaging stereotypes in books by Theodor Geisel, better known as Dr. Seuss.[21] They sent their findings to the National Education Association, requesting the union stop using certain Dr. Seuss stories as the focus of its reading program, particularly during the annual Read Across America day that coincided with the author's birthday. The NEA complied.

"In 2018," the *Los Angeles Times* wrote, "the NEA removed all of Geisel's books from its Read Across America resource calendar, replacing them with diverse books and authors. When asked what prompted the NEA to end its partnership with Dr. Seuss Enterprises, a spokesperson said: 'We shifted to focus on celebrating a nation of diverse readers by featuring books in which all students can see themselves.'"[22]

Never mind that Stephens, a black man whose UC San Diego bio states that he "holds more than 15 years of experience in social justice work," may not be the most unbiased when it comes to color-blind research.[23] Never mind that Ishizuka, a woman with a civil rights activist background and a familial tie to Japanese internments, might not be the most open-minded or forgiving of historical contexts when it comes to cartoonish images of Asians. From a 2017 interview with Ishizuka, published by This Picture Book Life, come these additional bios:

Katie Ishizuka is a researcher, activist and social worker with a decade of experience working with youth and adults of color involved in the criminal justice system and advocating for community-based alternatives to incarceration. She is [a] published author on Anti-Oppressive Practice for Oxford University Press (2015) and the School-to-Prison Pipeline for the Justice Policy Institute (2013).

Ramon Stephens is a . . . long-time proponent of student voice, retention and resilience for marginalized youth [and] has developed & run student-driven, culturally relevant curriculums & after-school programs for students of color in D.C. Public Schools, Long Beach Unified, San Diego Unified and U.S. San Diego.[24]

Never mind that Stephens and Ishizuka actually have a company, The Conscious Kid, that is dedicated to helping parents root out racism in their homes—meaning, their livelihoods depend at least, in some part, on finding the racism to root from these homes.[25] Never mind, too, that Stephens and Ishizuka have two sons of mixed race, and therefore have inherent sensitivities to cultural biases, both real and imagined. "Our sons are two and four [in September 2017] and it is very important for us to be intentional about surrounding them with narratives and images that center, affirm and celebrate their identities," Ishizuka said in an interview with This Picture Book Life. "When I went to our nearest public library to request every children's book they had featuring black characters, the librarian came back with a list of three."[26] Never mind all that.

The end result was this: their hurt feelings, their sensitivities to possible hurt feelings, were enough to sway an entire school district. And then some. "Given this research, and LCPS' [Loudoun County Public Schools] focus on equity and culturally responsive instruction, LCPS has provided guidance to schools in the past couple of years to not connect Read Across America Day with Dr. Seuss' birthday exclusively," Byard said in his statement.[27] They swayed the NEA, the nation's largest union. They seemingly swayed even the president of the United States. "At some schools, including in L.A. County, educators have cut ties with the work of Geisel," the *Los Angeles Times* wrote. "President Joe Biden omitted any mention of Dr. Seuss from his Read Across America message [and] the author's estate announced it would no longer publish six books deemed to contain offensive material."[28]

This is how cancel culture works. It seeks to erase the offensive, simply because of the hurt feelings the offense produces. It works to wipe out the viewpoints that are labeled as problematic, simply because they cause problems for some. It moves to clear pasts and reset histories and recalibrate positions, simply by rubbing them from the public consciousness, from the public arenas. And here's the real kicker of the cancel culture movement: it pretends as if it's doing a good for society, as if it's only maturing the society—as if it's only helping the culture progress to new levels of awareness and to heightened senses and sensibilities. But its way of maturing society is to erase history. Its method of maturating is to cancel what seems offensive by modern standards.

Moreover, the cancel culture fails to reconcile the fact that all history, all culture, all politics, all works of art and humor and entertainment, and even whimsy and fancy, are all offensive to somebody. Where does it end? Who decides the end?

In the case of Dr. Seuss, it certainly wasn't a groundswell of opposition that brought about the author's cancellation. Rather, it was a couple whose entire beings were wound up with the social justice causes of the Far Left; it was a man and woman with an arguably oversensitized sense of what constitutes racist versus what could simply be harmless stereotype—or whimsy. That's not to say Stephens and Ishizuka didn't perform a public service by pointing to perceived racist overtones or offensive stereotypical undertones in one of America's most-loved children's authors. It's not even to say their company, The Conscious Kid, doesn't play an important role in helping parents navigate the crowded field of children's literature and make choices that are in line with their tastes and moral compasses.

But it is to say: Shame on the NEA for listening. Shame on certain public school districts for listening. Do you think the NEA would have a problem hanging up the phone on petitioners who want the recently deceased Rush Limbaugh celebrated during Read Across America events for his Rush Revere children's books on patriotic Americanism? Do you think if a couple of scholarly conservatives presented the NEA with a study showing the anti-American, anticapitalism, anti-Founding Father teachings that take place in so many of today's public school systems, and suggested Rush Revere readings as a curriculum-adopted counterpoint, that the teachers and their union representatives would welcome the texts with open arms? Of course not. The NEA would have no trouble telling these scholarly researchers to take a hike. Neither would any of the school districts around the country presented with the same research.

When it advances a leftist viewpoint, it's called diversity. When it advances a conservative viewpoint, it's called hateful. That's the problem with the cancel culture. It's being driven in large part by leftists, by snowflakes, by easily offended and angry un-American types who not only think their hurt feelings ought to be taken seriously by their closest friends and family members, but by an entire nation. They feel their hurt feelings ought to translate into national policy, national apology, and a bureaucratic redress of grievances. And they care little for traditions, norms, history, historical contexts, or even facts.

It's all about their personal, and often petty, petulant emotions. Rather than stage teaching moments, rather than expand the public discourse, rather than add to discussions and debates, rather than present uncomfortable discoveries in manners that stoke reflections and genuine heartfelt reconciliations—they'd rather boot stomp on the cause of their offenses and rip it from realities. They'd make great Winstons—the character in George Orwell's novel of dystopian society, *1984*, who served as a records editor at the Ministry of Truth, completely rewriting media and textbook histories to bring them in line with government views. Haven't read it? At spots in time, in spots around the nation, *1984* itself has been challenged, targeted for banning, even banned.

But Dr. Seuss? If Dr. Seuss is the standard, then certainly all of America's history, culture, arts, entertainment, educational systems—all these systems and more—face the chopping block.

* *Little House on the Prairie* has been faulted for its portrayal of Native Americans.
* *The Adventures of Huckleberry Finn*, for its use of the N-word—the same n-word, interestingly enough, that's still slung with abandon by modern musical artists in certain musical communities, where exceptions are freely made.
* *To Kill a Mockingbird*; *Gone With the Wind*; *Roll of Thunder, Hear My Cry*; *Little Black Sambo*—all targeted for banning for themes deemed offensively racist.
* Television sitcoms, both past and present, have irked ire—from the stereotypical *Jeffersons*, and the big-nosed and gluttonous *Alf*, to the all-white casts of *Sex and the City* and *Beverly Hills, 90120*, to the old-timey stereotypical characters of Buckwheat and Sunshine Sammy on the 1950s *Little Rascals* series. Even *The Simpsons* has raised hackles with cartoon characters that spark criticisms—for some—of abject racism and negative stereotypes.
* Hollywood movies are just as rife with problematic depictions. *Breakfast at Tiffany's*, the 1961 classic Hollywood film, has been attacked as discriminatory against Asians. So, too, the 1984 Hollywood teenage classic, *16 Candles*, for its portrayal of the foreign exchange student Long Duk Dong. Then there are all those

Pink Panther films, with character Cato Fong playing martial arts sidekick to Inspector Clouseau.

- Even *Star Wars: The Phantom Menace* has been criticized for its fantasy character Jar Jar Binks, as being too offensively akin to a minstrel show star of long ago.
- Then comes the whole *1619 Project* versus *1776 Project*, and the question of when America became . . . well, America. If the former date, then the door opens to harping on America's roots as racist. If the latter date, which is how tradition has dictated in schools both public and private, then American exceptionalism reigns.

That's but a drop in the bucket of offense that almost expectedly compromises American society—and it's almost expected because the country, after all, is a melting pot. By design, there are bound to be culture differences.

But certain principles are supposed to unify us as one. One of those principles? The concept of American exceptionalism. Another? The idea that in this country, individual rights come from God, not government. That God-given right of free speech is being chipped away at daily, though, thanks in large part to pandemic panic and opportunistic leftist politicians and their minion friends who are corralling the fear to wrest control. They're using feelings to cancel a nation. And that previous list doesn't even get to the perceived offensiveness of long-standing memorials, monuments, and historical markers, or to the school, building, highway, and bridge names, some of which have already been torn down, already replaced, already erased. More will follow. The Left isn't letting go of this chance to change the country any time soon.

At this rate, America, within just a very few years, will stand for nothing at all—which is, of course, where the Left wants to lead. A nation that has no solid foundation, a country without a firm sense of history and culture, is one that is ripe for shaping.

It starts small. It starts with a Dr. Seuss. Then a Muppet. Then a Potato Head. "Disney slaps 'The Muppet Show' with 'offensive content' disclaimer," the *New York Post* wrote in early 2021. "The disclaimer shown prior to each episode warns viewers that the show features 'stereotypes' and 'mistreatment of people or cultures.' It's unstated precisely what Disney considers to be offensive . . . but some characters depict Native American, Middle Eastern and Asian people."[29] That, plus country singer Johnny Cash, in one episode, performs in front of a Confederate flag.

"Mr. Potato Head is going gender neutral," CNN wrote, also in early 2021. "Hasbro is dropping the honorific 'mister' from the 'Mr. Potato Head' brand, renaming the shapeshifting plastic spud to the gender-neutral 'Potato Head.'. . . 'Hasbro is making sure all feel welcome in the Potato Head world by officially dropping the Mr. from the Mr. Potato Head brand name and logo to promote gender equality and inclusion,' the company said."[30] That's a bit of spin. If Hasbro were truly interested in "making sure all feel welcome," the company wouldn't cater to a teeny segment of society—the LGBTQ community—at the expense of alienating the much larger traditional family values communities. Do Christians "all feel welcome" with a Potato Head that advances a narrative that conflicts with biblical teachings and Bible-based morals? Doubtful. But out of the seemingly small and minute come the bigger deals.

Intercollegiate Studies Institute is an organization committed to advancing the causes of individual freedom, such as put forth by the Founding Fathers' visions. The group holds an annual seminar for student journalists, and in early 2021, this Collegiate Network Editors Conference, as it's formally called, was set for a facility in Alexandria, Virginia. "But it [had to be moved to] a new location because of an eleventh-hour maneuver by bureaucrats—and maybe some people with an agenda," ISI reported on its website. "Without warning, and less than 72 hours before the event began, bureaucrats from the city of Alexandria, Virginia, shut down the conference. The supposed reason is public health, but cancel culture could be the real culprit."[31]

In a Fox News interview with host Tucker Carlson, ISI president Johnny Burtka told how the local department of health, "in response to an anonymous health complaint . . . allegedly expressing concern about the safety of attendees at our conference"—how local health bureaucrats reclassified the educational program as a social event, which meant, according to Virginia COVID-19 restrictions, only ten people could attend. Curiously enough, there were plenty of other conferences being held in the same community, in the same month, Burtka said. "This had nothing to do with public health," Burtka told Carlson. "What it had to do with is there was someone who clearly did not want this event to happen, they didn't want our young, courageous student journalists interacting with some of the editors of some of the most major conservative publications in the country, so they went out of their way to get us canceled."[32]

That interview took place just a short time after Fox News itself was a victim of cancel culture—along with One America News and Newsmax TV. U.S. Representatives Jerry McNerney and Anna Eshoo, both Democrats from California, sent a letter to twelve cable, satellite, and video streaming companies in February 2021, requesting they explain why they allow these news organizations a platform. "Experts have noted that the right-wing media ecosystem is 'much more susceptible . . . to disinformation, lies and half-truths.' Right-wing media outlets, like Newsmax, One American News Network (OANN) and Fox News all aired misinformation about the November 2020 elections . . . These same networks also have been key vectors of spreading misinformation related to the pandemic," portions of the letter stated.[33] McNerney and Eshoo then asked such questions as, "What steps did you take . . . to monitor, respond to and reduce the spread of misinformation . . . ?" and "Are you planning to continue carrying Fox News, Newsmax and OANN . . . If so, why?"[34] Can you imagine the gall? These are political operatives—taxpayer-funded public servants of the people. And they sent not-so-thinly veiled threats to private market companies for the crime of carrying conservative speech.

Brendan Carr, a Republican commissioner with the Federal Communications Commission, railed. Rightly so. "Two senior Democrats on the House Energy and Commerce Committee selectively targeted a handful of news media outlets for their coverage of political events," he said. "By writing letters to the cable providers and other regulated entities that carry these news media outlets, the Democrats are sending a message that is as clear as it is troubling—these regulated entities will pay a price if the targeted newsrooms do not conform to Democrats' preferred political narratives."[35]

It's the socialist way; it's the communist way. Shut down dissenting opinions; stifle all opposing rhetoric. But call it something else, characterize it as something else, so people don't recognize the tyranny—label it, for example, a health and safety matter for society at large. But take a memo. Heed this warning. Cancel enough of the small things, and it becomes all the easier to go after the big things.

And here's one be-all and end-all of a big thing for the Left: canceling Christianity.

"The Rise of Christian Nationalism," the Council on Foreign Relations blasted in one February 2021 ominous-sounding headline, above the printed text of a conference call held by the organization. The text goes on to explain: "These are Americans who . . . believe that the U.S. was or still is a Christian nation and that we need to reestablish that connection in order for the United States to flourish."[36] So what? Sounds about like founding principles of America, right? Yet it's painted as a negative. Plenty more media outlets around the nation are picking up that phrase, Christian nationalist, and equating it with domestic terrorism. "Christian nationalism is a threat, and not just from Capitol attackers invoking Jesus," one *USA Today* opinion contributor wrote. "Christian nationalists inside our government are working quietly to take America for Jesus."[37] "Militant Christian Nationalists Remain a Potent Force, Even After the Capitol Riot," NPR wrote in January.[38] The NPR piece went on to critically report on a pastor who posted on his Facebook page of the Black Robed Regiment, the small but powerfully influential band of religious leaders who, at the time of the American Revolution, would preach to the congregation, then pull off their robes and join the armed battle against the British. That's history. That's America's history. That's truthful, verifiable, recorded American history. But to today's leftists—that's something to cancel and erase.

This is not a game. This is not a frivolous, silly fight for a Dr. Seuss read-a-thon. This is about the left's use of a multitude of tools, from the pandemic to the Potato Head to everything in between, to crumble the Constitution and upset the democratic-republic—to remove God permanently, if possible.

Take away the Judeo-Christian roots of our country, and you take away the core facet of our nation's greatness: that of rights coming from God, not government. Strip away God, and what's left is government. Government, big government, bigger government, ever-growing, ever-expanding government; Democratic, socialist, communist, collectivist government. Do that, and America itself is cancelled.

Do not make the mistake of thinking cancel culture is a natural morphing and beneficial maturing of a people who have recognized mistakes and now wish to move past those mistakes into a more tolerant, more diverse, more welcoming future. Don't make the mistake of misreading the cues of cancel culture and believing that government has only the best intentions when it censors information, and that social media giants are actually performing a positive public service by shutting down dissenting—dangerous—views. Don't make the seriously flawed error in believing that speech, in a free country like America, is "dangerous." The slippery slope toward authoritarianism is fast-moving. Remember, founders didn't carve out exemptions in the First Amendment for pandemics. Neither, then, should the free market. Neither, then, should the free American citizen.

Let the voices of liberty go out through all the earth, and their words to the end of the world.

CHAPTER FOUR

Exploiting COVID-19 Is Fun! So Is Exploiting Youth

Train up a child in the way he should go, and when he is old he will not depart from it.

Proverbs 22:6, KJV

In February 2021, more than a year into the pandemic, a student at Colby-Sawyer College in New Hampshire complained of losing $8,000 in housing money because she violated newly implemented coronavirus safety policies by failing to self-quarantine when returning to campus, and instead went grocery shopping. "In the campus emails," student Sam Mohammed said, in an interview with WMUR-9, "it says to stock up before you start your quarantine."[1]

Makes sense. A student's got to eat, right? The logic didn't matter. The school had just implemented specific safety procedures to get students back on campus for in-person learning, and one of those procedures required all returning individuals to self-quarantine for two weeks. Because Mohammed violated the terms of that agreement, she was stripped of her housing and sent packing. Moreover, the school refused to refund her money. Mohammed's roommate, who visited the grocery, too, was also booted from housing.

Aside from the obvious eyebrow raisers about coronavirus regulations and policies that hardly seem in line with science, another curiosity about these students' punishment is this: How did school officials know? Well, school officials knew because there was a tattler in the midst. What's more, the school encouraged such tattling. Colby-Sawyer officials actually created a form that students could submit—anonymously—whenever they saw violations of COVID-19 safety policies.[2] That's how Mohammed was ratted out, along with her roommate. By a secret source who used the cover of a campus-wide "for the good of the community" secretive alert system. Hardly seems American, does it?

Truly, this is the stuff of the Stasi.

But thanks to the coronavirus, and the government's constant harping on the need to protect the youth—the very population that's least likely to contract COVID-19, by the way—America's schools have become breeding grounds for tattle-tales, government informants, and secret spies serving as spinmeisters and operatives for the administrative class.

In Mohammed's case, sympathetic members of the student body started a petition to pressure the school to reverse the decision and relent. The petition, in part, at Change.org read:

> I understand COVID-19 is causing a lot of anxiety for all of us, but this should not mean that our student body turn[s] on each other. The "COVID-19 Concerns—Community and Individual Behavior Report Form" is causing more harm than good for our school community. Asking students to police each other is not encouraging unity to help us all get through this pandemic. Inconsistency, mis-use and mis-trust have resulted.[3]

Well said.

Sadly, too few schools are considering the ramifications of pitting student versus student, child versus child, and with alarming frequency, making such scenarios part and parcel of their campus culture. Laughably enough, they're calling it a return to normalcy.

James Madison University, a Division I public school with a student body that hovers around twenty-thousand, and that's located in the Shenandoah Valley region of Virginia, touts on its website its "#1 most recommended public university in the U.S." ranking by both *The Wall Street Journal* and *Times Higher Education*, as well as its "#2 public university in the south" label from *U.S. News & World Report.*[4] It's also high up on the surveillance-of-students list—though there's no official ranking of that category.

In a document entitled, *COVID-19 Stop the Spread Agreement*, that was issued for the Spring 2021 session, JMU administrators required all students, as a condition of returning to campus, to obey a list of demands, including:

- Eight days of quarantining
- The wearing of face masks "at all times when indoors, in classrooms, in public and outdoors when in the presence of others, except while eating or drinking"
- Social distancing of six feet, unless "the university provides another guideline for a specific space on campus"—meaning, the rules could change at any time
- No hosting or attending social gatherings with more than 10 people
- The practicing of good personal hygiene, including frequent hand washing[5]

Then came Big Brother with a big, threatening stick. The agreement, to be signed by all returning students, went on to state:

I will honestly answer health screening questions in the LiveSafe App. I will do this every day prior to coming onto campus or leaving my residence hall this Spring. I will show my Green Check when requested on campus. . . . I will participate in the University's COVID-19 entry testing program. If I do not complete entry testing by [required deadline date], I understand that I must vacate my on-campus room . . . If selected, I will respond and participate in the University's COVID-19 surveillance testing program . . . If I am told that I am a close contact to someone what has tested positive, I will follow all directions I receive and quarantine/isolate for the entirety of the time directed. I will continue to adhere to the expectations set forth in this agreement even if I have previously tested positive for COVID-19 and am considered fully recovered. I will support the health and well-being of the community by speaking up when other students are not complying with this Agreement, and ask that they do their part to protect this community. I will also submit reports of violations through the LiveSafe app.[6]

Talk about a police state. Violators were subject to fines, suspension, expulsion, and the forfeiture of previously paid monies to the school.

At the same time the school was sending out the agreement, its campus health department was providing updates on the numbers of COVID-19 cases. And in March, amid the spring session, the news was this: "The university observed 14 new positive cases of COVID-19 at the University Health Center . . . putting the total number of active cases at eighty-six. The number of open quarantine and isolation beds is 307 out of 434."[7]

For 86 cases, students who wanted to live on campus—who wanted to experience a taste of true college life—were forced to participate in the university's technological contact tracing program via cell phone app or browser link; display, as a condition of entry to an assortment of school buildings, a "green check" that supposedly showed good health; quarantine on demand; and tattle on COVID-19 policy violators. Anonymously, via the immediacy of an app, if desired.

For eighty-six cases, students were transformed into obedient little COVID-19 soldiers, doing their part and forcing others to "do their part to protect this community," as JMU put it. Eighty-six cases of "test positives"—which means, literally, nothing significant; after all, the only COVID-19 cases that really count are the ones that show how many contracted the virus versus fully recover, and how many contracted the virus versus die. And on that note, even before 2021 it was generally accepted that most people who tested positive for the virus were (1) either surprised they tested positive because they showed no symptoms or (2) able to fully recover and return to normal activities.

"Experts," WebMD reported, citing August 2020 sources, "don't have information about the outcome of every infection. However, early estimates predict that the overall COVID-19 recovery rate is between 97% and 99.75%."[8] Didn't matter. With COVID-19, facts were often shoved to the side—first, for fear; later, for political reasons. Schools played right along with the fear-fueled politicization of a virus that was hardly as deadly as the fearmongers would have believed. Why? For control. For power. At best, for political correctness—to go along to get along so as not to become the next target of power-hungry, control-freak government officials. Whatever the reason, the stomping of an entire nation of youth's abilities to self-determine is both outrageous and detrimental to the fate of America.

What a way to teach the next generation to comply, obey, and carry out government orders, without thinking. What a way to mold the emerging nation's leaders, movers, and shakers to put the needs of the collective before the needs or rights or desires or constitutional authorities of the individual. This is how a democratic-republic falls, one uncritically thinking generation of sheep at a time. This is how a communist and collectivist class conquers, one properly herded group of youth at a time.

Free thinkers unite! Better for the government to smash them as a single body, than weed out and whack-a-mole them as individuals, spread as they could be throughout all of society: this is what college, amid coronavirus, post-coronavirus, has become. Open the doors for easy government funding, watch the masses take the loans and pour on to campus, then train them over the next four or more years how great government is, how trusted government should be, and how outdated the Constitution, capitalism, and those silly, selfish notions of individualism have become. Graduation day brings on the next batch of cultural Marxists, trained in the ways and manners of near-communist collectivists.

Colby-Sawyer. JMU. Rather than educating, administrators, using the coronavirus as cause, moved more into the roles of overseeing and enforcing and threatening. "It has been one full year since we started managing the COVID-19 pandemic," wrote JMU in a March 2021 health update.

> Despite the warmer weather and restrictions lessening, the majority of students have not yet been vaccinated and are still able to spread COVID. It is crucial for students to continue to wear a mask (even outdoors) . . . Already this semester, we have had a large number of students responsible for violating the Stop the Spread agreement. . . . [Those who] choose to host or attend social gatherings with more than 10 people, to not use the LiveSafe App, to not wear a face covering, to not participate in surveillance testing . . . are choosing to accept consequences.[9]

And once again, if you missed it in the first "Stop the Spread" document—or any number of similarly intimidatingly toned correspondences that were subsequently sent by JMU authorities to the student body, on weekly, twice-weekly, thrice-weekly, even daily basis—these "consequences" included probation, forced participation in COVID-19 compliance "educational programs," suspension, fines, and expulsion.

Get the message? How could anyone miss the message? Obey, abide, and get others to obey and abide, too—else, comrade, you will pay. The lingo of all these documents, reminder memos, website postings, warnings, and so forth better belong with the agents of propaganda than with the supposed stewards of maturing American minds.

Colby-Sawyer and JMU were not alone:

- "Colleges crack down on student behavior as virus threatens more closures," Politico wrote in August 2020.[10]

- "Colleges continue to crack down on students defying coronavirus safety measures," Higher Ed Dive wrote in November 2020.[11]
- "Providence College cracks down following uptick in COVID-19 cases," WPRI.com Channel 12 wrote in February 2021.[12]

Few of the crackdowns were based on scientific reasoning. "We are experiencing more positive COVID-19 cases than we would like," read one email from Providence College authorities to the student body, local WPRI.com Channel 2 reported, in February 2021. "While increased testing is a factor, these additional steps are necessary to ensure that the overall positivity rate stays below the approximately 2% we are currently seeing."[13]

Why the 2 percent threshold? In a flippant phrase: Why not? The 2 percent is as good a rule of thumb as anything else authorities have put out there. Look at this, from Johns Hopkins Bloomberg School of Public Health in August 2020:

The higher the percent positive is, the more concerning it is. As a rule of thumb, however, one threshold for the percent positive being "too high" is 5%. For example, the World Health Organization recommended in May that the percent positive remain below 5% for at least two weeks before governments consider reopening.[14]

Now consider this, from the *Intelligencer* in December 2020:

On November 18, Mayor Bill de Blasio announced he was temporarily closing the nation's largest public-school system on the basis of one coronavirus statistic: the positivity rate. The city's average rate exceeded 3 percent for the first time since June, which was taken to indicate that the virus's spread could soon spiral dangerously out of control. Now, on December 7, de Blasio will reopen public elementary schools regardless of the fact that the city's average positivity has climbed above 5 percent.[15]

Then there was this bit of information, gleaned from the CDC website postings in 2021: In the early part of the year, the agency combined categories of risk levels for schools to use as determinations of reopening. Prior to February 2021, the CDC used a five-category system, broken into: "lowest risk of transmission in schools," "lower risk of transmission in schools," "moderate risk of transmission in schools," "higher risk of transmission in schools," and "highest risk of transmission in schools." The more government-created coronavirus recommendations the school abided, the lower the deemed risk factor for reopening for in-person instruction, the greater the chance the school reopened. Get it? In February 2021, the CDC combined the first two categories—"lowest risk" and "lower risk"—into a single "low transmission" category. And whereas the CDC recommended RT-PCR test positivity rates of less than 3 percent as the ideal for returning students to school, the newer February 2021 standard, using the four-category system, was less than 5 percent positivity.[16]

That's a lot of garble. But what it means is this: The test positivity rate is in a constant state of fluidity, and it changes with both time and source. Providence College worries about 2 percent; New York City's mayor worries about 3 percent one day, 5 percent another; so, too, the CDC. That's not fact-based science. That's best-guess, anybody's guess coin-flipping. Yet it was just this kind of coin-flipping that was used to shut down nearly all of America's schools, K-12 and higher learning, in the early part of 2020.

At the K-12 level, more than 55 million in about 124,000 public and private schools were affected, with most either ordered or advised to stay shut until the end of the 2020 semester.[17] By March, at least 300 colleges and universities shut down campuses, moving students to an online class format.[18] It wasn't long before hundreds more joined the shutdown. When fall rolled around, the freshman of 2020 saw their hopes for on-campus living and in-classroom study dashed, at least for the most part. According to The College Crisis Initiative, fall 2020 plans called for students at more than 1,300 colleges to attend their classes either entirely or mostly online, and students at another 622 to attend some courses online, some in person.[19] The National Conference of State Legislatures, meanwhile, reported in early 2021 that "44% of institutions developed fully or primarily online instruction, 21% used a hybrid model and 27% offered fully or primarily in-person instruction" for the fall 2020 semester.[20]

But did the science justify such shut downs? For so long into 2021? No. Not in the least. Not even as a "just in case" kind of safety measure.

Look at Providence College. Based on the worries of the 2 percent positivity rate, the entire student body was forced to limit attendance at class, limit travel to pick up food, limit travel to pick up medicine or go to medical appointments, limit travel to and from work, and limit travel to pretty much all campus facilities—including those that provided outdoor recreation.[21] On top of that, students were prohibited from having visitors, prohibited from visiting friends living off campus, and "discouraged" from going home or going anywhere off campus for more than two nights.[22] Why two nights, rather than three? Why two nights, rather than any other number of nights? Again—who knows. The measures were all "for their own safety and for the safety of those with whom they would come into contact," as local WPIR.com reported.[23]

Additionally, the restrictions came with no deadline. They came only with demands for obedience, along with threats of punishments and additional regulations—the latter of which would only cease in direct relation to the level of achievement of total obedience. After all, this was the college blamed by the governor of Rhode Island, Democrat Gina Raimondo, for increasing the coronavirus test positivity rate in September 2020 from 1.1 percent to 1.4 percent, resulting in new quarantine regulations for citizens traveling to several nearby states.[24] "These are college students doing what college students do—hanging out with their friends. It's not safe this year," Raimondo said then, of the rise in coronavirus cases at Providence College and also at the University of Rhode Island. "This is hurting people's businesses in Rhode Island. It's not a joke. We're hurting people because of our selfishness. Following the rules matters."[25]

Sure, following rules matters. But when rules are based on made-up and ever-changing science and randomly applied, randomly selected, randomly decided best management health practices, maybe following rules doesn't matter so much as making up one's own mind. Maybe it's time to question those rules.

Regardless, after Rhode Island's governor blamed Providence College and the University of Rhode Island for its students' "selfish" insistence on gathering in groups larger than ten, all schools in the state but those two were allowed to go back to in-person learning, so long as certain provisions were abided. One provision was mandated testing. And from that mandated testing came a particularly fascinating little fact. As *The Boston Globe* reported in September 2020: "The mandatory testing of students and staff revealed something interesting: The majority of positive cases were found among those who were in remote learning."[26]

That's not just interesting. That's cause for tar and feathering of all the health bureaucrats, politicians, education unions, school administrators, and others who fought—who continue to fight—to keep America in a state of chaos and closure based on coronavirus health and safety fears.

How many do-overs do schools get before they're forced to admit the whole coronavirus shutdown debacle was just that—a huge debacle? At a certain point, even the most ardent union supporter, even the loudest of cheerleaders for the public school system, even the most enthusiastic defender of government-run programs—even they have to admit the coronavirus crackdowns that kept children out of school for so many months, for so many semesters, were suspiciously random, suspiciously prone to change, and sourced on suspiciously weak science. At a certain point, it has to be acknowledged that the so-called solution was worse than the virus.

In a March 2021 webinar hosted by *U.S. News & World Report* that was called, "Managing Children's Mental Health: A Pediatric Hospital Imperative," various medical experts weighed in on the state of America's youth, since the onset of the coronavirus and the crackdowns that left them mostly isolated, and they concluded: the situation's dire.[27] As *U.S. News & World Report* wrote, the "loss of the daily school routine," combined with reported COVID-19-tied deaths and illnesses and the "economic and housing instability" from forced business closures and government-pressed stay-at-home orders "have been especially hard for many children."[28] There's an understatement. Youth have been traumatized. "Society," the news outlet went on to write, "will likely be grappling with the after-effects for decades to come."[29] We're from the government and we're here to help.

Among these medical panelists' findings, presented during the webinar:

- Dr. Karin Price, chief of psychology at Texas Children's Hospital in Houston, reported that in 2019, before the pandemic hit, her facility conducted fewer than 500 telehealth visits for youth seeking either psychology or psychiatry services. In 2020, amid the coronavirus, "we did more than 25,000" electronic sessions for children, Price said.[30]
- Dr. Abigail Schlesinger, chief of child and adolescent psychiatry and integrated care at UPMC Children's Hospital of Pittsburgh and Western Psychiatric Hospital, reported that her facility conducted fewer than 1,000 telehealth visits in all of 2019. In 2020, that number soared to "76,000 in one year," she said.[31]

What of the children with poor Internet connections in their homes, or with limited—or zero—online access?

- From Dr. Ukamaka Oruche, associate professor and director of global programs at the Indiana University School of Nursing: "We have kids who are failing school [due in part to technology issues]. We have kids in households where you have one iPad and you have four kids sharing it," or in households where Wi-Fi signals are weak "so the parent has to drive to the school parking lot to get Internet access. This is a major problem."[32]

The findings aren't all that shocking, given the numbers of other reports put together and published in the wake of the pandemic that showed similarly—and not just in America, but around the world. The Global Fund for Children, for example, reported in early 2021 that due to government's response to the coronavirus, "more than 1.6 billion students in over 190 countries" experienced "disruptions" in their schooling, leading to the potential for 24 million of them to drop out of school—in part because two-thirds of students around the world have no Internet access and no ability to participate in online learning.[33] The nonprofit also found that in the months after the pandemic struck, an additional 150 million children around the world were thrown into poverty. Another global agency, Save the Children, found the COVID-19 crackdowns brought "more than 8 in 10 children report[ing] an increase in negative feelings," and higher cases of violence in the home, due to school closings.[34]

Then there was this, an even sadder and sorrier post-pandemic reality, from the Global Fund for Children: "Around the world, the community-based organizations we partner with at [the] Global Fund for Children . . . reported higher rates of early marriage and pregnancy, sexually transmitted infections and HIV, child labor and exploitation, child abuse and trafficking."[35] The information, in other words, was there. It was out there for all to see.

Perhaps some Third World countries with poorly funded governments and education systems and subpar health care facilities could be excused for failing to act immediately on the reports of student suffering, on the data on youthful mental and behavioral risks due to COVID-19. But America? America's supposed to be a world leader in education, in health care, in civil rights, and in protections for the youth. Simply put, America failed her youth. America failed to protect her most vulnerable from long-term and needless psychological harm during the coronavirus. History won't be kind on this point.

What's even more disheartening is the lack of anger and outrage over this failure.

In a sort of summary of what all the findings presented during the *U.S. News & World Report*'s seminar, medical expert Oruche said, "We have a lot to learn yet."[36] Medical expert Schlesinger said, "We've got probably decades worth of learning to do there."[37] *U.S. News & World Report* wrote this: "Indeed, all the panelists expressed hope that the lessons learned over the past year can help inform a more thoughtful and lasting discussion on how to better support children and families in the future."[38] How better to support children during future pandemics? My gosh, how about not treating them like they're the stuff of petri dishes? That's one recommendation. Another? Tell the teachers' unions to stick it where the sun don't shine.

The reason America's youth suffered so despicably—and so needlessly—during the shutdown months of 2020 and beyond was due to the leaders of the teachers' unions driving the opinions, talking points, actions, and policies of their leftist friends and allies in government, in the education system, in the big bureaucracies of the health and medical worlds. Frankly, they exploited the children for personal and political gain. They ought to be ashamed. They probably aren't.

"Twin Cities teachers unions demand schools stay closed this fall," ran one headline from Pioneer Press in mid-2020.[39] Why? According to the story, educators said "the risks of reopening schools during the coronavirus pandemic [were] too great." St. Paul and Minneapolis teachers' unions organized a protest and marched to Governor Tim Walz's mansion, some carrying signs with hyperbolic messages like, "I can't teach from a grave," or "Exactly how many dead kids is acceptable?"[40] They wanted money to hire more staff, to make facilities' improvements to the schools, and for unspecified reasons to help families and schools struggling financially due to the coronavirus.[41]

"The Teachers Unions Are Keeping the Schools Closed," wrote the American Institute for Economic Research (AIER) in December 2020.[42] Why? According to the story, educators were insisting on closures out of "fear that a new wave of infections will occur from holiday travel and more people staying indoors."[43] That was months after *The Journal of the American Medical Association* (*JAMA*) wrote: "Most children with COVID-19 presented with mild symptoms, if any, generally required supportive care only, and typically had a good prognosis and recovered with 1 to 2 weeks."[44] That was also months after the American Academy of Pediatrics called for a return to in-person learning as soon as possible, given the known mental and social negatives that come with forcing youth to stay home and study online for extended periods of time.[45] "The data makes apparent that school closures are not a matter of public health," AIER wrote, in its December 2020 essay. "Instead, lobbying groups—who sway government officials to support their special interests—are central to the matter. They are teachers unions. In a study aimed at understanding the external influences of school closures during the pandemic . . . [researchers] discovered that school districts are less likely to reopen when there is a strong union presence."[46]

The Fairfax Education Association in northern Virginia wanted schools to remain closed until a vaccination was developed and all teachers vaccinated. In a tweet later deleted, the FEA said a "safe return to schools [meant] 14 days of no community spread, PPE, cleaning equipment, full-time nurses in all schools, as well as staff & student vaccinations."[47] The Washington Teachers Union in Washington, D.C., wanted schools to remain closed unless teachers had the right to teach remotely if they chose, no matter what the data and science and medical experts advised.[48] The Baltimore Teachers Union wanted schools to remain closed until all the buildings were deemed safe—whatever that meant.[49] "In Chicago and Other Big Cities, Teachers' Unions Are Delaying School Reopenings," *Education Week* wrote in February 2021.

All along the path of the pandemic, as businesses closed, businesses reopened, as churches closed, churches reopened, as stay-at-home orders were issued, stay-at-home orders were rescinded, a one true constant was the fight from unions to keep schools closed.

Money seemed a sticking point. As *The New York Times* wrote, paraphrasing the concerns expressed on behalf of teachers by Randi Weingarten, the leader of the 1.7 million-member American Federation of Teachers, the second largest teachers' union in the country: "[Teachers] don't trust soap and running water will always be available in schools, because they sometimes haven't been. They don't trust that extra funding will materialize for masks, hand sanitizer and nurses, because in so many other years, budgets were cut."[50]

Money. The AFT, in June 2020, actually affixed the price tag for schools to reopen at $116 billion, including $35 billion for "instructional staff," $7.6 billion for "children's social and emotional needs," and $36 billion for the unspecific "additional academic supports to students."[51] That was in June 2020—not even halfway through the pandemic. "If schools can't get the money they need to safely reopen," Weingarten said then, "then they won't reopen, period."[52]

Pay up, or shut up. Pay up, or stay home. Pay up—or children will suffer. "On Dec. 30, 2020, Gov. Gavin Newsom announced a $2 billion 'Safe Schools for All' plan to encourage more schools to reopen for in-person instruction," EdSource wrote in December 2020. "Shortly thereafter, he called for an additional $4.6 billion in his January budget to address the impact of the pandemic on schools."[53]

What a racket. What a lucrative, money-making, revenue-raising racket for the unions, for the schools, for the educators. As for the children? Oh well. Salt Lake City schools reported the level of students who were below grade level jumped from 23 percent in 2019, to 32 percent in 2020. Fairfax County, Virginia, schools reported the number of students who failed more than two subjects during this same time period rose by 83 percent.[54] McNary High School in Oregon reported 38 percent of grades in late October 2020 were F's, compared to 8 percent during non-COVID-19 virtual learning times.[55]

At Jespersen's school in the Salem-Keizer Public School district [in Oregon], hundreds of students initially had not just Fs, but grade scores of 0.0%, indicating they simply were not participating in school at all. In New Mexico, more than 40 percent of middle and high school students were failing at least one class as of late October [2020]. In Houston, 42% of students received at least one F in the first grading period of the year. Nearly 40% of grades for high school students in St. Paul, Minnesota, were Fs, double the amount in a typical year.[56]

If the science doesn't justify keeping schools closed for so long, in so many communities, across so many states, impacting oh-so-many students and parents and caretakers and families—then why all the shutdowns? Money, for sure. But more than money—think of the potential to change an entire generation of American citizens. Think of the potential to instill obedience through fear and reliance on government—again, by fear—into an entire generation of looming American leaders.

After all, in the eyes of the Left, what's wrong with this country is this dang country. The individualism, the self-government, the limited government, the rule of law Constitution, the capitalist system and free market and entrepreneurial spirit, the concept of rights coming from God—all these and more go into making America such a great, exceptional, free country. Simultaneously, all these and more go into making the Left nuts, because all these and more are what prevent the Left from bringing about its leftist, anti-American, socialist, collectivist, globalist vision.

The pandemic not only padded the pockets of the school systems' leftist overseers. The pandemic also gave occasion for the Left to toss kids out of school, force them to face fearful and uncertain futures, and in so doing, use the chaotic atmosphere that came to move goalposts a little bit more to the side of big government. Want to go back to school? Agree to take the vaccination. Want to return to campus for a real college experience? Accept the terms and conditions of government's contact tracing; say yes to government surveillance. Want to play sports and compete in high school and college-level athletics once again? Agree to wear face masks at all times, inside class and inside locker rooms, even outdoors and on the field—and agree to pay the fines, suffer the probation, or accept the suspension and expulsion that comes as consequences to violators.

The goalpost moves an inch. The goal post moves a foot. The goal post move a field length. Soon enough, America's schools have become breeding grounds for the next generation of leaders trained in the leftist, big-government, government-knows-best, collectivism-trumps-individualism way to go. "Give me just one generation of youth, and I'll transform the whole world," Vladimir Lenin said.

"Train a child in the way he should go, and when he is old he will not depart from it," the Bible said. Train a child to depend on government, and that child will abandon critical thinking, independence, and individualism for the sake of the State. That's the vision the Left has for America.

CHAPTER FIVE

Patriotism Is
Unpatriotic—and More
Pandemic Puzzlers

> . . . while evil men and imposters will go on from bad to worse,
> deceivers and deceived.
>
> 2 Timothy 3:13 (RSV)

In February 2021, WRAR.org, the public news organization at Michigan State University, blared this alarming headline: "President Biden: Getting COVID Shots a 'Patriotic Duty.'" The story below the headline was about President Joe Biden's visit to the Pfizer COVID-19 vaccine manufacturing plant in Kalamazoo, Michigan, and his call to arms for the American people to please, please, please get the shot—it's safe. "But if there's one message to cut through to everyone in this country," Biden said then, "it's this: the vaccines are safe. Please, for yourself, your family, your community, this country—take the vaccine when it's your turn and available."[1]

He called it a "patriotic duty" that would help families, communities, heck, even the nation at-large. That came after Biden, in December 2020, vowed to make mass face-masking of American citizens a mandate wherever he lawfully could—on federal properties, for instance—because, as he said, wearing facial coverings in a time of COVID-19 was

71

"not a political statement," but rather "a patriotic duty."[2] It's all for the good of the people, don'tcha know.

Biden wasn't the only one making these arguments. "Defeat COVID-19 by requiring vaccination for all. It's not un-American. It's patriotic," wrote three opinion contributors, in *USA Today* in August 2020. The piece went on to state: "Do not honor religious objections. The major religions do not officially oppose vaccinations. Do not allow objections for personal preference, which violate the social contract."[3] The trio went on to liken the vaccination to war, arguing that while a "refusal to obey rules one considers unjust is an American tradition," another is the ability of the nation to come together in times of crisis, such as during World War I and World War II. Those are two times when "everyone contributed, no one was allowed to opt out merely because it conflicted with a sense of autonomy," they wrote. The writers were Dr. Michael Ledermanis, a professor of medicine at the Case Western Reserve University School of Medicine; Dr. Stuart Youngner, a professor of bioethics at the Case Western Reserve University School of Medicine; and Maxwell J. Mehlman, a professor of law at the Case Western Reserve University School of Law.

And in their piece, they also wrote:

How can government and society ensure compliance with pro-tective vaccines? Vaccine refusers could lose tax credits or be denied nonessential government benefits. Health insurers could levy higher premiums for those who by refusing immunization place themselves and others at risk, as is the case for smokers. Private businesses could refuse to employ or serve unvaccinated individuals. Schools could refuse to allow unimmunized children to attend classes. Public and commercial transit companies— airlines, trains and buses—could exclude refusers. Public and private auditoriums could require evidence of immunization for entry. . . . .How then should immunizations be documented? A registry of immunization will be needed with names entered after immunization is completed. . . . [I]mmunized persons will need to receive expiration date-stamped certification cards, which should be issued to all who are immunized in the country, whether here legally or not.

Show me your papers, comrade. It's the patriotic thing to do.

This is the stuff of police states, of Nazis in Germany patrolling for Jews, of blackshirts in fascist Italy rooting out the dissenters. This is the slick propaganda talk of despots and tyrants and holier-than-thou intellectuals who regard themselves as elites, born to rule the peons. And scarily, this is what leftists truly want to bring to America's shores, by rebranding patriotism as collectivism and using the coronavirus as the launching pad. Without vigilance, we will fall.

"The winter of our discontent: The patriotic duty of taking the COVID-19 Vaccine," wrote another trio of medical and legal pundits, in the *Tennessean* in December 2020. "Get vaccinated. Not just for your own health, but for the health of our neighbors, friends and family. For the young and the old. The sick and the healthy."[4] In other words: It's the patriotic thing to do. "I received the vaccine today," wrote Ohio Democratic senator Sherrod Brown, in December 2020, "and want the public to know that it is safe, and getting immunized is critical to protecting all Ohioans. Getting this vaccine isn't a partisan issue—it's patriotic."[5] There's that word again.

From a columnist in Virginia's leading newspaper, the *Richmond Times Dispatch*, in March 2021:

It's time to reclaim the word *patriot*, as Merriam-Webster defines it: "one who loves and supports his or her country." Americans who revere the right to keep and bear arms also should bare their arms for COVID-19 vaccinations. Getting vaccinated is a patriotic act because people are taking responsibility not only for their own health and well-being but for that of their community, state and nation.[6]

Again, the "P" word.

And from Ford Motor Company—a #FinishStrong campaign to pressure all Americans into taking the vaccination. The tone of the campaign? Optimistic. Upbeat. An appeal to patriotic duty. Marketing Dive described Ford's public relations push this way:

> The vehicle maker's #FinishStrong campaign debuted with a 30-second spot during the Citrus Bowl on ABC and the Peach, Rose and Sugar Bowls on ESPN and during Fox NFL games . . . Actor Bryan Cranston narrates the spot, which shows portraits of frontline workers and people who survived their bouts with COVID-19. The commercial aims to "appeal to Americans" shared sense of patriotism and what's right—rather than preaching at people or using fear as a motivator."[7]

Let's remember we're talking about a vaccination here. We're not talking about a nation coming together to battle a common military enemy. We're not talking about a people joining forces against an armed insurrection threatening the homes, families, and safety and security of the nation. We're not talking about a terrorist attack on domestic soil; we're not talking about an uprising of violent anti-American hostels intent on destroying the country, enslaving the people, and stealing all the resources from the land. We're talking about injecting chemicals into the bodies of individuals. We're talking about the injection of a foreign substance into a human body at a time when the foreign substance hasn't even been studied for long-term effects—at a time when its injection was still classified as an "emergency use authorization" by the Food and Drug Administration. EUAs are not approvals; as part of the EUA process, drug companies agree to monitor the safety and side effects for a set period, and report back to the feds what they find. That's a kind way of saying the people are the guinea pigs.

Not all EUAs are created equal. In late March 2021, AstraZeneca made moves to bring its COVID-19 vaccine to the United States via an emergency use permission slip from the FDA. That was at a time when several European countries suspended use of the AstraZeneca vaccine due to patients' reports of blood clots and other negative health reactions. "The safety of all is our first priority," AstraZeneca said in a statement sent to CNN in March. "Around 17 million people in the EU and UK have now received our vaccine, and the number of cases of blood clots reported in this group is lower than the hundreds of cases that would be expected among the general population."[8] That's hardly a comfort if you happen to be one of the people who experienced blood clotting, or another medical reaction, from the shot.

That's what happens, though, when a medical treatment has not been fully vetted for both the short term and long term. Not one of the COVID-19 vaccines issued EUA by the FDA—not the Johnson & Johnson, not the Pfizer, not the Moderna, not any of them—can be truthfully packaged and promoted as safe for the long term. That's just a calendar reality; they only came to market in 2020. Typically, it takes years for vaccines in the United States to be approved by feds for manufacturing, sale, and distribution.

According to the website HistoryOfVaccines.org:

- First comes the exploratory stage: "This stage involves basic laboratory research and often last 2-4 years," the site reported.[9]
- Then comes the preclinical stage: "Pre-clinical studies use tissue-culture or cell-culture systems and animal testing to assess the safety of the candidate vaccine and its immunogenicity, or ability to provoke an immune response," the site reported. And here are the money quotes: "Many candidate vaccines never progress beyond this stage because they fail to produce the desired immune response. The pre-clinical stage often lasts 1–2 years and usually involves researchers in private industry."[10]
- Then comes the IND Application stage, when application for an investigational new drug is made to the Food and Drug Administration. That's when a sponsor, most frequently, a private company, submits a report to the FDA describing all the previous lab findings and detailing the manufacturing process. The FDA has 30 days to respond to this application. And once this

application is approved, another three phases of testing begins, this time around, involving humans—involving the vaccine trials in humans.[11]

- Phase One: Vaccine Trials: "This first attempt to assess the candidate vaccine in humans involves a small group of adults, usually between 20–80 subjects," the site reported. The timeline on this phases varies; the primary goal is to assess the safety of the vaccine.[12]

- Phase Two: Vaccine Trials: "A larger group of several hundred individuals participate" in this phase of testing, the site reported. The task here is to further assess the vaccine's safety, as well as determine its ability to provide immunity, in what dosage, by what schedule, and by which means of delivery.[13]

- Phase Three: Vaccine Trials: This phase involves thousands and thousands of people, some of whom are given placebos. This is where the vaccine's efficacy is fully tested. And it's where safety gets a thorough vetting. The sited reported: "One Phase III goal is to assess vaccine safety in a large group of people. Certain rare side effects might not surface in the smaller groups of subjects tested in earlier phases. For example, suppose that an adverse event related to a candidate vaccine might occur in 1 of every 10,000 people. To detect a significant difference for a low-frequency event, the trial would have to include 60,000 subjects, half of them in the control, or no vaccine, group."[14] It's statistical truth; it's mathematical. It's impossible to know the safety of a vaccine if it's not tested in large groups of people—and for a certain element of time.

- Then come the final phases of vaccine development: the approval and licensing, and the "post-licensure monitoring" stages, including the Phase Four trials, which are basically optional safety and efficacy studies conducted by the company that developed the drug, and VAERS. VAERS is the acronym for the Vaccine Adverse Event Reporting System, a database created by the CDC and the FDA to monitor health and safety issues that may or may not have been tied to the vaccines. Roughly 30,000 complaints of vaccine-related issues are lodged each year on the VAERS site; between 10 percent and 15 percent allege the vaccines led to hospitalization, serious illness or even death. Not all reports lead to the CDC's determination of negative health impact from a vaccine. But some do. One VAERS complaint led feds to identify a link between a rotavirus vaccine and intestinal problems; another, to a link between the yellow fever vaccine and certain gastrointestinal and neurologic diseases; yet another, a possible connection between blood clotting and the MMR vaccine.[15]

The years of vaccine development can really rack up, can't they?

But that's all a long way of saying that painting those who are reluctant to take the vaccine as unpatriotic, rather than, say, concerned, uncertain, or otherwise possessed of questions, is astonishing. After all, in America, not only do Americans have the right to decide what goes into their bodies, they also have the right to decide what does not. And Americans who think they know better ought to rethink and get with the constitutional program.

Here in America, individual rights rule. Not pinhead bureaucrats with medical degrees. And patriots—true patriots—defend that concept, first and foremost. Even when a pandemic hits. As William Barr, the former U.S. attorney general under President Donald Trump, put it, Americans don't give up their civil rights just because of a coronavirus. Neither do Americans give up their critical thinking skills in times of challenge, chaos, and crisis. In fact, that's when critical thinking is most needed.

"Be a patriot," four contributors wrote in an op-ed to MedPage, in July 2020. "Wear a mask."[16] They went on to opine, "We are medical professionals from diverse backgrounds. The American flag holds a distinct meaning for each of us. We are proud to serve this country . . . But we are also tired of fighting senseless infections and deaths from the novel coronavirus. To us, in 2020, patriotism is not just waving the flag or voicing our support for the Constitution—it is wearing a mask to protect ourselves and our entire nation, no matter our political party or persuasion."[17] It's patriotic to wear a face mask? By that logic, staying home when sick with the flu is patriotic. We need to be careful with our words.

"Wearing a face mask is patriotic," *Popular Science* also wrote in July 2020. And then the author went on to compare the so-called patriotic practice to China.

> In China, wearing face masks during times of illness has been en vogue since a 1910 outbreak, and many other Asian countries adopted the practices after SARS struck in 2003. Because masks primarily serve to prevent you from transmitting a disease to other people, wearing one when you have the sniffles (or when a global pandemic is afoot) is considered a sign of high civic responsibility—otherwise known as patriotism. Wearing a mask is not a symbol of weakness or fear; it's a sign that you want to minimize the pandemic's impact on your country and the people in it.[18]

Do we all see what's happening here?

Slowly but surely, the definition of patriotism is being changed from an American one that's rooted in rugged individualism, self-determination, and bottom-up governance—where those at the top can, yes, have an opinion and even a recommendation, but not issue orders, a la king-like—to a definition that does like China: groupthink. Collectivism. Coerced concern for neighbors over self.

Here in America, the notion of caring for neighbors comes from God, church, biblical teachings, and moral standings based on rights versus wrongs. In China, the notion of caring for neighbors is dictated by the government. In America, it's voluntary. In China, it's compulsory. In America, love for others is a choice—just like the choice God gives in the Bible; the gift of free will. In China, in secular China, in communist China, it's tough to discern: How much of the public shows of so-called concern for others comes by way of free choice versus government dictate? It's not really love when it's done in fear, out of fear of punishment.

The wearing of face masks has nothing to do with patriotism. And let's not let the socialists, communists, and collectivists turn mask-wearing into a sign or show of patriotism. They're doing that to move the goalpost. They're pushing to make face masks a physical show of patriotism so they can point to the offenders and shame them into complying, so as to move the cultural posts a little bit farther down the field toward collectivism. They're doing it to silence those who might resist their Marxist takeover. After all, these face masks aren't just symbols of obedience or of fear; they're material coverings of the very means of most political dissent: the mouth—that is to say, the voices of the loud and proud and righteously indignant. They don't exactly scream "Give me liberty or give me death" in matters a modern day Thomas Paine might deem worthy to scream "Give me liberty or give me death." Do they?

This is not to say that Americans who want to wear face masks shouldn't wear face masks. Just don't pretend that wearing a face mask is a sign of patriotism—or that refusing to wear a face mask is a show of treachery.

Wearing a face mask is a sign of many things—a sign of believing in the power of the cloth to filter out a virus, a sign of believing in the might of the medical community, a sign of obedience to government, a sign of faith in government, a sign of apathy and willingness to go along to get along, a sign of fear, a sign of obedience, a sign of heartfelt and genuine concern for others, even. Yes, on that last—some people in America truly do wear face coverings because they truly do believe they're truly saving others from the virus. That's their choice. That's their individual choice. But wearing the face mask as a sign of patriotism? No. Not even close.

Words matter. Words count. Let's not hand the socialists an easy win by allowing them to redefine noble patriotism, in all its American individualistic glory, as dark sheep-bleating collectivism. If they didn't want it believed so badly—that face masks are shows of patriotism—they wouldn't have tried so hard to twist Trump's own words and actions on face masks.

In the early months of the pandemic, Trump refused to wear a face mask. In April 2020, he even remarked that "somehow, sitting in the

Oval Office behind that beautiful Resolute Desk . . . I think wearing a face mask as I greet presidents, prime ministers, dictators, kings, queens—I don't know, somehow I don't see it for myself. Maybe I'll change my mind."

His advisers, his political insiders, his White House insiders reportedly pressed Trump to don a face mask, however. In July, he tweeted a photo of himself wearing one, along with this message (widely reported, but no longer available because his Twitter account has since been permanently suspended): "We are United in our effort to defeat the Invisible China Virus, and many people say that it is Patriotic to wear a face mask when you can't socially distance. There is nobody more Patriotic than me, your favorite President!"[19]

He didn't exactly call the wearing of face masks "patriotic." He called himself "patriotic" and reported how "many people" regard face mask-wearing as "patriotic"—and added the caveat, "when you can't socially distance." But he never directly referred to the wearing of face masks as a show of patriotism. That didn't stop the dishonest leftists in the media from crowing that he did.

- "Trump tweets photo of himself in a face mask and calls it 'patriotic,'" Axios blared in July 2020.[20]
- "Trump, who dismissed and refused to wear a face mask for months, now says wearing one is 'patriotic' like him," *Business Insider* wrote, also in July 2020.[21]
- "Trump says face masks are 'patriotic' after months of largely resisting wearing one," CNBC wrote, also in July 2020.[22]
- "Trump Calls Mask Wearing 'Patriotic,' Tweets Photo Wearing One," wrote *Forbes*, also in July 2020, in the news category of "Breaking."[23] Seriously, breaking news?

There's a reason members of the media were so obsessed with Trump's personal and federal policies regarding the face mask. In July, during an interview with Chris Wallace of Fox News, Trump made clear he believed in the potential of face masks to stop the spread of the virus, but he believed more in the rights of individuals to choose.

Among Trump's remarks:

- This: "Everybody who is saying don't wear a mask—all of sudden, everybody's got to wear a mask, and as you know, masks cause problems, too. With that being said, I'm a believer in masks. I think masks are good."[24]
- And this: "But I leave it up to the governors."[25]
- And this, responding to then CDC director Robert Redfield's quip that "all Americans have a responsibility to protect themselves and their families and their communities" by wearing the face mask: "I want people to have a certain freedom," he said, and then added, "And I don't agree with the statement that if everybody wears a mask, everything disappears."[26]

The message from Team Trump was individual choice, individual responsibility, individual decision-making, individualism. Wear the mask if you want; wear the mask if you choose. The media, the mouthpiece for the collectivists of the country, couldn't leave that message untouched, unchallenged—unchanged. So as soon as Trump donned a mask, it became national news—"breaking" headline news, even. As soon as it was possible, Trump was recast as a believer in the patriotic duty to wear a face mask.

But the reports were deceptive: Trump never did directly make the case that he personally believed wearing a face mask was a sign of patriotism. Trump never did do the left's bidding by leaving behind his own views of individualism to come on board with the left's all-courts-press for collectivism.

That's why the brouhaha over the face masks, though. The anti-American left is actively using the coronavirus to rebrand what it means to be an American, one redefining of "patriotism," one reimagining of values, one reshaping of cultural traditions, truths, teachings at a time. The key to understanding how the socialists fight, and why they pick the causes they do, is to keep in mind the larger war that's always being waged: that of God-given rights versus government granted.

Once you see that field, once you look through that telescope, everything the Left does falls neatly into a clarified, easy-to-understand place. And that makes the fight against these evil collectivists all the more effective.

"Military vets were among the Capitol Hill rioters, protesters," CNN reported in a headline in mid-January 2021, days after extremists rushed Congress, leading to the death of four. But why such a story in the first place? The clues were in the story's opening paragraphs. "Among the mob of extremists and Trump supporters that invaded the US Capitol last week in a deadly riot were former members of the very institution that is supposed to protect America from invasion: the US military," the CNN piece began.[27] It's a ridiculous insinuation. Likely, there were far more members of the military who attended the Capitol rallies and protests who were not in any way, shape or form tied to the violence that erupted. After all, as Statista reported in 2019, almost 44 percent of American males over the age of 75 were veterans; so were nearly 30 percent of those between the ages of 65 and 74, as well as roughly 13 percent of those between the ages of 55 to 64, and just over 8 percent of those between the ages of 35 and 54.[28] Another 3-plus percent of males between 18 years old and 34 years old were also veterans in 2019, according to this same Statista survey.[29] Chances are good there were far more veterans at the now-famous pro-Trump rally on Capitol Hill who were entirely peaceful, than not. But that doesn't meet the narrative the press is trying to paint about members of the military, both past and present. So the media reshapes and reimagines.

As CNN went on:

The radicalization of military veterans has long worried experts who monitor extremism online and elsewhere. And though it isn't known whether soldiers and veterans are disproportionately vulnerable to radicalization, their association with extremist groups has been enough of a concern over the years for hate-group watchers to study the matter and lobby Congress to take action to counter it. In February, the Southern Poverty Law Center [SPLC] and other groups urged the US House Armed Services Committee ensure the military branches vet enlistees for signs of white nationalistic beliefs, such as reviewing their social media accounts, creating a tattoo database and performing psychological screenings.[30]

What exactly constitutes "signs of white nationalistic beliefs," in the eyes of the SPLC? There's a broad brush. This is the nonprofit that actually listed the Center for Immigration Studies (CIS) as a hate group in 2017, twisting its calls for legal and sensible migrant policy into something akin to a Ku Klux Klan hanging. "CIS has a long history of bigotry, starting with its founder, white nationalist John Tanton," SPLC's director of the Intelligence Project, Heidi Beirich, wrote in 2017.[31]

The problem with the term *nationalist* is that it doesn't exactly or always mean what those who sling it as a negative spin it to mean. A nationalist is simply someone who loves one's country. The left's overuse and misuse of this term, however, has implanted its definition in the minds of too many as one and the same as a supremacist.

Kudos to the *Columbia Journalism Review* (*CJR*) for getting this right a few years ago: "Almost every American is a 'nationalist' of one kind or another," *CJR* reported, in "The key difference between 'nationalist' and 'supremacist,'" published August 2017.

A "supremacist" believes a particular race (or sex, or other genetic or cultural characteristic) is naturally superior to others . . . A "nationalist," though, is at heart merely someone who strongly believes in the interest of one's own nation, however "nation" might be defined. President Trump is a "nationalist," as are most liberals, populists, and everyone to the right and left. But adding an adjective to indicate what "their" nation is can turn "nationalism" into a polarizing term.[32]

And bingo, that's how the Left turns something that's normal and traditional—like love of country, defense of country, fight for country—into something divisive that can then be exploited for political gain. This is how socialists and cultural Marxists operate: by creating schisms where few schisms previously existed, and then swooping to bring the big government guns to solve what has become a fight for equity, for fairness, for just treatment. The elephant in the room is that the fight itself was fabricated by the Far Left on purpose to ultimately redefine societal concepts of equality, fairness, and justice.

Nationalism, with or without the qualifying adjective, is soon enough a label of shame. Nationalism, soon enough, becomes interchangeable with supremacism, with racism, with patriotism—with Trumpism. In a news world that's run by cycles of seconds, not hours, with social media headlines and Twitter snippets leading and shaping some of the most powerful debates of the day, it's irresponsible, even dangerous, to dicker with definitions. What's patriotic in truth quickly and often irreversibly turns racist, whether by laziness, ignorance, or strategic political deception—it really doesn't matter. What matters is the results. What matters is when the Left scores wins by selling, through the media and into the minds of Americans a "woke" sense, that all that was once respected, revered, and admired should now be regarded as radical, reactionary, and disgraceful—or at the very least, suspiciously along those pejorative lines.

In January, Senate Armed Services Committee member Richard Blumenthal, a Democratic from Connecticut, joined with more than a dozen other Democrat senators in asking Pentagon inspector general Sean O'Donnell to investigate "white supremacist and violent fringe extremist activity" in the military.[33] Citing the January 6, 2020, election-fueled violence on Capitol Hill, the Democrats wrote, "The issue of white supremacy and extremist ideology within the ranks of our military is not new, but the attack on the Capitol makes clear this alarming trend must be immediately addressed." They asked for the watchdog to "identify recommendations for each of the services to prevent, address, and neutralize extremist ideology within the Armed Forces." And they called for the Pentagon to provide military members who were transitioning to the civilian sector certain support services to make them "less vulnerable to recruitment by extremist organizations, and more resilient in the face of misinformation and conspiracy theories—the perpetuation of which the FBI has deemed a domestic terrorism threat."[34]

From "white supremacist" to "extremist ideology" to "conspiracy theories" to "domestic terrorism" all in one letter. As if those who engage in discussion of conspiracies, including discussions about whether something is actually conspiracy or real, are one and the same as extremists, who are one and the same as white supremacists, who are one and the same as domestic terrorists? As if Americans who join the military out of a patriotic sense of duty to country are at substantially higher risk of becoming crazed conspiratorial white-supremacists-turned-terrorists? It's bad enough Democrats want to divide the nation, as a means of conquering. Dividing the military would be devastating.

"A slide used in a Department of Defense (DOD) training manual identifies Catholics and evangelical Christians as 'religious extremists,' along with members of the Ku Klux Klan, al-Qaeda, and Hamas, according to a Marine Corps officer," *Epoch Times* reported in March 2021.[35] Come again?

First Liberty Institute, a nonprofit law firm in Plano, Texas, obtained a screenshot of a training slide taken from a U.S. Army manual that was entitled, *Religious Extremism*. Marine Corps Reserves officer Michael Berry, who also serves as general counsel to First Liberty, presented the contents of the slide during a House Armed Services Committee hearing on March 24, 2021. "Included among those listed [on 'Religious Extremism' slide] are al-Qaeda, Hamas, and the Ku Klux Klan as groups that use or advocate violence to accomplish their objectives and are therefore rightly classified as extremists," Berry said, the *Epoch Times* reported. "But also included are Evangelical Christianity and Catholicism, who most assuredly do not advocate violence. Surely, the fact that Evangelical Christians and Catholics hold fast to millennia-old views on marriage and human sexuality does not make them extremists who are unfit to serve."[36]

It shouldn't, anyway. But COVID-19 has given the Left an opportunity to discuss what it means to be a patriot, and that discussion has opened all kinds of doors to degrade and reshape the meaning of that word—to America's great detriment. With socialists, with far leftists, with collectivists who want to turn America into something that it was never meant to be, and who want to root out the Founding Father's emphasis on individual rights over government powers, it's crucial to pay attention to the narrative. Their words are not aimed so much at explaining, as exploiting. Their rhetoric is not aimed so much at clarifying, as reconditioning. They seek to use words to control—really, as weapons of a larger and strategic communications war.

Nowhere is this exploitation more dangerous than when hits on the Judeo-Christian foundation of this nation. "Christian Nationalism Is Worse Than You Think,"[37] ran a January 2021 headline in *Christianity Today*, a religious-based news outlet that makes national waves for its open hostility against President Donald Trump, as captured in its December 2019 piece: "Trump Should Be Removed from Office."[38] But Christian nationalism—worse than you think?

This is where the Left is leading on this label, as written in *Christianity Today*:

As crowds lined up in front of the Capitol [on January 6, 2020], Christian imagery was on display amidst the Trump/Pence 2020 and Confederate flags, QAnon memorabilia and Viking helmets. People held crosses, "Jesus saves" signs and "Jesus 2020" banners. As protesters crowded onto the Capitol steps, across the street, someone blew a shofar while a woman sang, "Peace in the name of Jesus. The blood of Jesus covering this place." In the aftermath of the Capitol attack, many saw a clear connection between the violence and Christian nationalism.[39]

Many did—from the Left—that's true. But the reason many from the Left saw this "connection" was that it was a "connection" the Left itself was trying to foster.

The ultimate takedown of America will occur when all evidence of God is stripped from society, when all references to God are yanked from the public stage, when all those who believe in God and the moral compass set forth in the Bible are successfully stifled and cowed into silence. If America, after all, is a nation made great by the idea of individual rights coming from God, not government, then it only stands to reason that the biggest enemy of those who see government as their personal means to power and control is, in the end, God.

People who worship God aren't worshipping the State. People who view God as the leader of their lives aren't viewing government as the sole provider, the sole comforter, the sole solution to what ails. This is why communists cannot suffer Christians. This is why the founders warned about the inextricable link between religion and morality, and between morality and liberty. This is why the framers appealed to divine providence for His hand in keeping the newly formed colonies, and by subsequent and logical extension, the states, then the country, "free and independent." This is why the Left is trying oh-so-hard to degrade the notion of Christian nationalism—a basis upon which our nation was established—that is to say, Judeo-Christian principles.

From Phillips Seminary and the Center for Religion in Public Life, was a summary of the book *Taking Back America for God: Christian Nationalism in the United States* by Andrew L. Whitehead and Samuel L. Perry, that included this paragraph:

Christian nationalists believe either that the nation was founded as a Christian nation and must be taken back for God, or that the U.S. was at least supposed to be a Christian nation but no longer acts like it. In either case, declension is part of the story. In Christian theological terms, there was a time in America that was better than now. Currently, the nation is "fallen." And for the "true believer" Ambassadors, God's people are authorized agents of God's holy violence to take America back.[40]

The spin is the part about the holy violence. Christian nationalists do indeed believe what the Bible teaches—that God judges nations, that God will not be mocked, that God is sovereign, that America has gone down a path of moral decay that in many respects, no doubt, angers and saddens God. But Christian nationalists aren't clamoring for blood. Neither Christians nor nationalists want to behead Bible-offenders. That's another religion entirely.

Then there was this, from a nonprofit called Christians Against Christian Nationalism:

> Christian nationalism seeks to merge Christian and American identities, distorting both the Christian faith and America's constitutional democracy. Christian nationalism demands Christianity be privileged by the State and implies that to be a good American, one must be Christian. It often overlaps with and provides cover for white supremacy and racial subjugation.[41]

Best to refute all that by bullet points.

- Christianity was indeed merged with America at the nation's birth. Read the Mayflower Compact. Read the Declaration of Independence. Read the framers' own words on the roots of liberty, and recognize that the Creator, divine Providence, and Supreme Judge to which the founders' frequently referred was the God of the Bible.
- America's constitutional democracy? America is a republic with a Constitution. It's not a democracy—at least, not a direct democracy—and the founders didn't want one because they worried the government might turn into a wishy-washy whim of mob rule or the peoples' passions.
- Neither Christians nor American nationalists are pressing for a state-created Christian church. The First Amendment makes clear religious freedom is a God-given right, not government gift. But Christians would like it recognized that since Judeo-Christian

principles founded the country and largely keep this country free, Judeo-Christian principles must ultimately be preserved and maintained—not attacked and driven from the public.

* One doesn't have to be a Christian to be a good American. One need only recognize that the notion of God-given rights is what keeps America both great and free, and that to fight against this principle makes you a terrible American—in fact, anti-American.

And if you're anti-American, well then, please go ahead and leave.

But it's that last sentence from the "Christians Against Christian Nationalism" site that makes clear what the Left is really doing here: they're trying to lump God-fearing Christians, Bible-believing traditionalists, America-loving patriots, and the like into the hateful, vile, and vicious categories of white supremacists and racists. They're trying to make it seem as if Bible thumpers are one and the same as white supremacists. They're trying to rope in the church-going, flag-waving, Fourth of July celebratory types as little more than racists. They're trying to make godly, virtuous, patriots feel ashamed. Why? What for? What's the endgame here?

Because it's the Christians, the Judeo-Christians, the American nationalists, the patriots, the hard-charging, flag-carrying, National-Anthem singing, Bible-believing, principled-from-above citizens of the country who are the staunch, determined, and unyielding enemies of the socialists. It's these who represent the final wall for the collectivists and globalists to crumble—the defenders of God, family, country. The fighters for the American spirit. The rugged individualists who not only know their places in God's kingdoms of heaven and earth, but who dare denounce those who would intrude.

So when someone says to put on a face mask—no wait—two face masks—no, wait—three; when someone says to take a coronavirus vaccine and obey all the government's other orders on health, and COVID-19, and on whatever new variant viruses may come; when someone says to do all this because it's the "patriotic" duty to do, the proper response, the American response, the patriotic response is this: Sorry.

No. It violates my Judeo-Christian nationalist beliefs. And best to say it loudly and proudly so all the other socialists in the room can hear. Send them slinking off; send them slithering away. They're the ones who don't belong.

CHAPTER SIX

The Free Market, in Free-Wheeling, Frenzied Freefall

Why do the nations conspire, and the peoples plot in vain?

Psalm 2:1 (RSV)

In mid-March 2020, President Donald Trump notified Americans of updated CDC coronavirus safety guidelines that stated, in part: "In states with evidence of community transmission, bars, restaurants, food courts, gyms, and other indoor and outdoor venues where groups of people congregate should be closed."[1] The coronavirus was novel; states took that guidance and ran with it via executive orders and mandates to shut down doors on businesses everywhere—with a few notable exceptions.

In June 2020, with some businesses still closed, others opened, and still others operating on a restricted but partially opened basis, the World Economic Forum came out with a mid-coronavirus message that went like this: now is the time to reform capitalism. It was the time to pounce, the globalists at the WEF decided. In the words of WEF founder and executive chairman, Klaus Schwab:

COVID-19 lockdowns may be gradually easing, but anxiety about the world's social and economic prospects is only intensifying. There is good reason to worry: a sharp economic downturn has already begun, and we could be facing the worst depression since the 1930s. But while this outcome is likely, it is not unavoidable. To achieve a better outcome, the world must act jointly and swiftly to revamp all aspects of our societies and economies, from education to social contracts and working conditions. Every country, from the United States to China, must participate, and every industry, from oil and gas to tech, must be transformed. In short, we need a "Great Reset" of capitalism.[2]

And that, ladies and gentlemen, is why the elites of both America and the world will never let the COVID-19 crisis come to an end.

They want a complete overhaul of the means of making money, of the system of doing business, of the buying, selling, and exchanging of goods, products, services, and creations. And they want their select few to be at the top of the economic chain—and the 99 percent of the world's workers, producers, industrialists, entrepreneurs, and inventors feeding their hands. They want the total in top-down control. They want worldwide socialism. They want worldwide dominance.

The coronavirus in all its lockdown glory is their means of resetting the entire nature of the globe. Among the principles of this reset? There are four "building blocks" outlined by WEF: mindset, metrics, incentives, and connection:

- **Change the mindset of humanity.** One writer with the WEF cites two books as examples of what this transformation should bring—the first, *Capital and Ideology* by Thomas Piketty; the second, *Humankind,* by Rutger Bregman. Piketty argues that the free market is outdated and flawed, and breeds inequality. Bregman argues that economies and governments that are based on the idea that humanity is inherently selfish and aggressive are built on a false premise, and that it's far more accurate to construct societies that start with a presumption that "we are in reality hardwired to be kind, cooperative and caring," WEF wrote. The first, from Piketty, is tired leftist ideology. The second, from Bregman, is a particularly damaging notion that directly conflicts with a basic principle of American freedom: that being the recognition of all humanity as sin-filled at birth, needful of and reliant upon a higher power for moral leadership. Remove God from the equation—turn humans into inherently goodly creatures rather than sinful by nature—and the doors are open wide to determine and define, and redefine, and redefine again, what is good versus what is evil, in the eyes of man. This is called worship of mind, or in a word, self-worship.[3]

- **Create new standards and measurements of success.** In the economic realm, a key standard of measurement is the GDP, the gross domestic product, the total monetary value of goods and services that are produced by a country in a given year. It's clean, it's clear, it's pure, it's honest. GDP cuts through all the political and social clutter, and affixes a simple dollar and cents value to a country's output as a means of determining how much the economy has grown, or stalled, and in that vein, how reliable, trustworthy, and sustainable that nation seems, economically speaking, for the foreseeable future. The World Economic Forum wants to do away with GDP as a measurement, and instead institute a standard that measures happiness. Or environmental protections. Or feelings of well-being of the people. Here's the pertinent quote from WEF's site: "Dissatisfaction with GDP is widespread, and there are many alternatives being [tried out] that focus on the well-being of people and planet: for example the UN's Human Development and Social Development Indexes, WellBeing metrics, Genuine Progress Indicators, a Happy Planet Index and an initiative to use Gross National Happiness. 'What gets measured gets managed' is the old adage. The Great Reset needs to take that lesson firmly to its heart and start the transformation by refocusing on what really matters."[4] The problem with using happiness as a measurement of national economic success, of course, is that it's highly interpretative—generally meaningless. It's not a provable measure of success. What it does do, however, is allow the bureaucrats at the top to constantly shift resources here, change policy there, redistribute finances from here to there at whim, based on some sort of haphazard, best-guessed strategy to spread contentment around the world. And what that does is feed the power lusts of the bureaucrats who get to define happiness and then dictate how that happiness will be best accomplished. "What gets measured gets managed"—and voila, happiness becomes a tool by which policymakers exert control.

- **Create new incentives, different from normal revenues' streams.** Move over, shareholders. Step aside, profit and loss statements. The WEF wants a new method of compensating corporations that relies less on the tangibles—that is, money— and more on judgment calls. The logic is sound, if not conflicting with the commonly understood principles of capitalism. From WEF: "About every five years, there is another big initiative somewhere saying . . . that shareholder value as the only indicator of company success was damaging [to] both the companies and to society . . . But in the real world, it has been business as usual on incentives all this time."[5] In other words, corporate types talk the talk but rarely walk the walk. So what does the WEF want? A new venture capital system, for one. Do not gloss over the details on this; it's imperative to see the big anti-American picture with this plan. Again, from WEF: "Venture capital companies—and even mainstream institutional investors—rarely included even the most basic questions about social and environmental risks in their investment criteria . . . Those sorts of tricky questions are left to environmental and social governance (ESG) funds."[6] WEF wants venture capitalists to start including social justice measures, environmental impacts, concepts of equality, and the like as part and parcel of the investment determination process. This would bring a massive shift in funding; most venture capital these days flows into projects already developed by governments and corporations, under the category of follow-on funding. In other words, a good portion of today's venture capitalists primarily enter the game after innovation, during commercialization, when companies are trying to grow but need the necessary infrastructure to support that growth. They're bigger than angel investors; they take on higher risks than banks—and so demand a larger share of the company rewards, often in terms of equity. But they're quite the American way. As *Harvard Business Review* wrote in the late nineties: "The U.S. venture-capital industry is envied throughout the world as an engine of economic growth."[7] And the WEF wants these cowboys of capitalism, as they're often perceived, to start demanding the hopeful recipients of their money first prove, for example, they have a plan of growth that's in line with the UN Sustainable Development goals—the global body's radical of all radical environmental agenda? This is sheer interference in America's gold standard system of economic growth, designed by intent to bring the domestic GDP down to "equalize" the playing field with poorer nations.[8]

- **Create new bonds among all of humanity.** One of WEF's core beliefs with its Great Reset is that humans the world over share common traits, and that bringing people together is the means of making over capitalism and global economies. In WEF's words: "Finding ways for technologies to harmonize, not polarize, and for us all to make deeper, more meaningful connections with each other and with the natural world will reduce the distance that allows us to see our fellow human as we truly are: not 'other,' but just like us. This is probably the most important building block of all to make the Great Reset the transformation our generation can look back on with pride—and probably amazement."[9] WEF then cites the rather bizarre example of the cease-fire called on Christmas in 1914, at the outset of World War I, as evidence of humanity's all-in-this-together spirit, while making the case that if it weren't for those mean ol' generals, peace would've thereafter prevailed. In WEF's words: "Bregman [in his book *Humankind*] shows the heartbreaking consequence of the distance between leaders and the lives of the rest of us, and how that is the biggest problem of all. He finishes his book with a look at the 1914 Christmas Day truce . . . [when] over 100,000 troops laid down their arms on the front line to play football, share stories, photos, food and drinks. But it wasn't just a Christmas Day thing; in some places, this lasted a number of weeks, with many servicemen remembering it as the highlight of their lives. It could easily have escalated into full-scale peace . . . Only the dogged perseverance of generals far away who used propaganda to stir hate and [who] instilled obedience through orders to court-martial anyone for 'friendly gestures' toward the enemy managed to kickstart the war again. These leaders' distance from the people was the critical factor."[10] This is classic leftist logic about war—that diplomacy always trumps engagement, and that the key to ending battle is understanding the enemy's needs—like education, or comfortable housing, or job opportunities—and then providing them. With tax dollars, no less. The problem with this logic is that it's egregiously flawed. Humans may share certain common traits—like the need for food, housing, clothing, and certain standards of living. But humans certainly deviate when it comes to religious beliefs, cultural norms, gender roles, family values, and a host of other characteristics. Could you imagine a 1914 war with, say, Muslims and a call for a Christmas Day ceasefire? Different god. Very different values. Already, Bregman's book, along with WEF's insistence that the peoples of the world are "just like us," all just the same at heart—falls apart. Creating bonds with others is a terrific idea, so long as those bonds don't stomp out individualism, as well as truths about humanity, to make way for a forced, largely faked collectivism.[11]

But those are the building blocks of the Great Reset. That's what WEF has in store for the economies of the world, for the governments of

Correctly? America will take established free market for $800, Alex. But apparently, that's not a Schwab-approved option. He went on:

> Generally speaking, we have three models to choose from. The first is "shareholder capitalism," embraced by most Western corporations, which holds that a corporation's primary goal should be to maximize its profits. The second model is "state capitalism," which entrusts the government with setting the direction of the economy and has risen to prominence in many emerging markets, not least China. But, compared to these two options, the third has the most to recommend it. "Stakeholder capitalism," a model I first proposed a half-century ago, positions private corporations as trustees of society, and is clearly the best response to today's social and environmental challenges.[18]

To Schwab, U.S. capitalism, reliant as it is on pure profits, is outdated. So, too, China's method of state-regulated "capitalism"—and that's "capitalism" in quotation marks, because an economy that's regulated and controlled by the government is not an economy that's capitalistic in nature. The better economic method, he said, is to construct a system that puts the corporate leaders as the "trustees of society"— which, in American-speak, means that businessmen and businesswomen would become the unelected leaders of government, of the economy, of all. Business leaders would become America's policy-makers. America's elected policy-makers, in turn, would become figureheads, offering policy guidance for the actual policy-makers to put into practice; offering policy guidance and potentially tax dollars, either directly or by lucrative tax loopholes, to support those businesses that take revenues dives due to social justice programs that alienate some consumers.

That's not a democratic-republic. That's not a constitutionally run society. That's an oligarchy.

And for a stark example of how this would play in America, it's not necessary to go back any further than 2021. When talk swirled about potential for a coronavirus vaccine passport to be part and parcel of the nation's return to normalcy, President Joe Biden issued an executive order that called on the federal agencies to look into linking vaccines to vaccine "certificates"—or, in the bureaucrat-speak of the Federal Register, to "assess the feasibility of linking COVID-19 vaccination[s] to International Certificates of Vaccination or Prophylaxis (ICVP) and producing electronic versions of ICVPs."[19] A few weeks later, Biden's White House issued a statement that said, in effect, his administration would not mandate, or try to mandate, vaccine passports, but rather leave the matter to the private sector to decide. This is not exactly comforting.

At least if the government were to try to mandate vaccines as a condition of moving about freely, citizens would sue, courts would gasp—at least, some would—and the idea would die on the rock of the Constitution. But private business gets a free pass on much of what constrains government. "We expect," said White House press secretary Jen Psaki, when asked in March 2021 about the vaccine passport:

> that a determination or development of a vaccine passport or whatever you want to call it will be driven by the private sector. Ours [our role] will more be focused on guidelines that can be used as a basis. There are a couple key principles that we are working from—one is that there will be no centralized, universal federal vaccinations database and no federal mandate requiring everyone to obtain a single vaccination credential. Second, we want to encourage an open marketplace with a variety of private sector companies and nonprofit coalitions developing solutions. And third, we want to drive the market toward meeting public interest goals.[20]

How about the public interest goal of upholding the limited government constructs of the Constitution? How about a solution that states: *Government, leave me alone to determine my own health?* Governance by executive order is a no-go in America. The president is not a king. Governance by committee is a recipe for big government disaster.

Governance by guidance that is then implemented by private business is tyranny in the making. This is where the Great Reset leads.

This is where Biden and his band of merry Great Reset advocates is taking America. It's the weaponizing of the private sector against private citizens, on behalf of government's wishes. More than that, it's cowardly. Politicians who pretend like they're allowing the private sector to decide a matter, while simultaneously issuing guidance, encouragement, and a pressurized public relations campaign aimed at "meeting public interest goals" are not only brazenly skirting accountability and sidestepping the voters who pay their salaries, they're also liars. They're presenting as if they're hands off, all the while pulling the strings of policy, regulation, and enforcement.

Either politicians introduce legislation—or they don't. Either presidents sign bills into laws, or perhaps use their platforms to press Congress to pass bills they want to sign into law—or they don't. But enough of the doubletalk, enough of the forked-tongue talk. Enough of the government using the private market to do the dirty work it wants done, but can't get done because of that thing called the Constitution.

Bureaucratic "guidance" should stay as guidance, with the final decision-makers being the individual. That's freedom. That's individualism. That's how a country where rights come from God is supposed to operate. Where are the laws backing up the signs in storefront windows demanding face masks as a condition of entry? Where's all the legislation giving the private sector the constitutional right to make such demands?

Right. So will go the vaccine passport—if Americans allow it. Lawmakers who go on record and introduce bills requiring citizens to take a vaccine, or to show proof of vaccine as a condition of, say, driving from one state to another, could be easily voted from office. But how to vote out the CEO of Walmart, who requires customer to show a green-lighted medical app on their smartphones before they enter and shop? Evil, meet genius. Tyrant, meet private sector. "We want to drive the market toward meeting public interest goals," Jen Psaki said.[21]

That's the same as what the WEF wants with its Great Reset, too. "[We want] stakeholder capitalism," said Schwab, of the WEF. "[This] positions private corporations as trustees of society, and is clearly the best response to today's social . . . challenges."[22] The corporation with the biggest and best social justice plan wins.

Not all the signers of the Business Roundtable's newly defined corporate purpose statement are necessarily advocates for WEF's Great Reset. But just as the face-masking of Americans laid the groundwork for the vaccine passport—just as Action A, wittingly or unwittingly, prepared and conditioned the public for Action B—a CEO's willingness to commit, by signature, to the U.S.-based Business Roundtable's repurposing of corporations as more social justice, less money-making could similarly condition them to then accept the global WEF's agenda. At the very least, it shows who's a possible player, and who's not. It gives Schwab and his ilk a starting point of corporations to target.

Among the chief executive signatories of the Business Roundtable's updated corporate purpose statement: Jeff Bezos, Amazon; Doug Parker, American Airlines; Gail Kozaria Boudreaux, Anthem Inc.; Tim Cook, Apple; Brian Moynihan, Bank of America; Eric Foss, Aramark; Philip Blake, Bayer USA; John Stankey, AT&T Inc.; Corie Barry, Best Buy Inc.; Robert Dudley and Bernard Looney, BP.[23]

Other companies on board with the Business Roundtable: Caterpillar Inc. Bristol Myers Squibb. Cigna. Cisco. Citigroup Inc. Chevron Corporation. Chipotle Mexican Grill. The Coca-Cola Company. Dell Technologies. Deloitte. Comcast Corporation. CVS Health. Delta Air Lines Inc. The Walt Disney Company. Dow. Eli Lilly and Company. Exxon Mobil Company. Ford Motor Company. FedEx Corporation. Fox Corporation—yes, Fox News, signed by Lachlan Murdoch.[24]

Still others? Gap Inc. The Home Depot. Johnson & Johnson. Land O'Lakes Inc. Mastercard. Mattel Inc. McDonald's. Lockheed Martin. Nasdaq. Northrop Grumman Corporation. PepsiCo. Target. UPS. USAA. United Airlines. Visa Inc. Walgreens Boots Alliance. Walmart. Wells Fargo. World Wide Technology. Xerox. Zoetis Inc. 3M.[25]

There are more. But it's interesting, the news some of these companies have generated in recent times regarding their turns toward social justice—in some cases, at utter risk of alienating scores of angry consumers.

Coca-Cola and Pepsi, for example, have seemingly cast aside their battle for soda dominance in the profit world for a fight to win first place on the racial equity front.

In June 2020, there was this, from Pepsi CEO Ramon Laguarta:[26]

As people around the world demand justice for George Floyd, Ahmaud Arbery, Breonna Taylor, Rayshard Brooks, and far too many others, we have been thinking hard about how PepsiCo can help dismantle the systemic racial barriers that for generations have blocked social and economic progress for Black people in this country . . . I am announcing the next step in PepsiCo's journey for racial equality: a more than $400 million set of initiatives over five years to lift up Black communities and increase Black representation at PepsiCo. These initiatives comprise a holistic effort for PepsiCo to walk the talk of a leading corporation and help address the need for systemic change.[27]

Also in June 2020, there was this, from Coca-Cola Chairman and CEO James Quincey:

George Floyd. Killed. A senseless tragedy for him and his family. Ahmaud Arberty. Breonna Taylor. Philando Castile. Sandra Bland. Freddie Gray. Michael Brown. Eric Garner. Tamir Rice. Trayvon Martin. All Killed. All Black Americans, predominantly male. Black Americans. All of whom should be alive today. I, like you, am outraged, sad, frustrated, angry. Companies like ours must speak up as allies to the Black Lives Matter movement. We stand with those seeking justice and equality. . . . Today we are announcing $2.5 million in grants from The Coca-Cola Foundation for the Equal Justice Initiative to assist advocates and policymakers in the critically important work of criminal justice reform; the NAACP Legal Defense Fund in support of the "Policing Reform Campaign," and the National Center for Civil and Human Rights to deliver a platform to bring people for powerful conversations that matter and inspire social change . . . In addition, we will match employee donations to these initiatives, as well as contributions to the 100 Black Men of America and the National CARES Mentoring Movement. Starting with me.[28]

In November 2020, there was this announcement from RISE about PepsiCo:

PepsiCo Beverages has partnered with RISE to harness the unifying power of sports to combat racism, advance equity and inclusion and inspire enduring change. RISE is a national nonprofit that educates and empowers the sports community to eliminate racial discrimination, champion social justice and improve race relations. . . . "Pepsi is proud to join RISE to combat racism and engender meaningful change through the power of sports," said Justin Toman, who leads PepsiCo Beverages Sports Marketing. "We're excited to join our partners in the NFL, NBA and NHL to work collectively to bring impactful programs to life that deliver on our shared mission of advancing equality and understanding."[29]

In December 2020, there was this report from Business Insider about Coca-Cola:

Coca-Cola held a "Together We Must" virtual dinner event series in October and November, in partnership with the National Center of Civil and Human Rights, Civic Dinners, and Equitable Dinners, around the topics of social justice . . . Each dinner was helmed by a different notable figure with a presence in social justice . . . Coca-Cola Brand Director Erica Tuggle said the dinner series was the company's "next step" after announcing $2.5 million in grants from the Coca-Cola Foundation for the Equal Justice Initiative, the NAACP Legal Defense Fund, and the National Center for Civil and Human Rights.[30]

And who can forget Coca-Cola's widely reported online staff training seminar urging employees to "try to be less white" to combat racial discrimination? Among the tips to white workers: "Be less arrogant, be less certain, be less defensive, be more humble, listen, believe, break with apathy" and "break with white solidarity.[31]

But this is the WEF way. It's not about making money. It's about making people feel good—about making certain segments of society feel good—even if what they're feeling good about is pure bunk, based on deceptive narrative, based on far-leftist agenda.

"Between Floyd's death and the end of October, about one-third of Fortune 1000 companies responded by making a public statement on or commitment to racial equity, and the private sector pledged a total of $66 billion towards racial justice initiatives," wrote Melisande Kingchatchaval Schifter, with the WEF's diversity and equity project, in *Forbes* in January 2021.[32]

Yep. The floodgate's been opened. Home Depot's CEO, Craig Menear, pledged $1 million to the Lawyers' Committee for Civil Rights Under Law after making this statement in June 2020: "We are all confronting deep pain and anguish over the senseless killing of George Floyd, Ahmaud Arbery and other unarmed Black men and women in our country. We cannot ignore that their deaths are part of a pattern of racism and reflect the harsh reality that as a nation we are much too far from fulfilling the promise of equal justice for all."[33] Citi pledged more than $1 billion for its "Action for Racial Equity" campaign to expand credit and banking opportunities for minorities, and to invest more in "Black-owned businesses" and "homeownership for Black Americans."[34] Ben & Jerry's kicked off a podcast looking at racism in American history, to include "the lingering racism still embedded in many US institutions."[35] The American Institute of Architects pledged to fight "racial injustice," and put out a statement that included this call-to-arms: "America's list of racially motivated murders demand action."[36]

The competition is on. Pepsi, Coke, Home Depot, and more—they're all business players in a global race for recognition as the corporation that cares most about minorities, about racial justice, about equality and tolerance, and that cares about these social issues far more than about money, revenues, and profits. "New Scorecards Compare 250 Largest S&P Companies on Racial Justice and Workplace Equity Disclosure," Globe Newswire reported in November 2020. Among the scorecards' key findings? That "soft drink giants Pepsi and Coca-Cola are in the top 10" while "competitor Monster Beverage is in the bottom 10."[37]

Where are the companies supporting, say, police officers or law enforcement, or those serving to protect communities from the criminals, thugs, and violent offenders of the streets? Underground. Staying quiet. Staying hidden, if possible. "These Six Oil Companies Are Funding the Police (and Must Be Stopped!)" ran one Greenpeace headline in October 2020.[38] It doesn't meet the narrative. To the Left, police are racist—police are always racist. Police are always on the prowl for their next young black male to unnecessarily halt for questioning—or shoot to kill. So when company CEOs do want to donate to the boys in blue? Shh. "How Target, Google, Bank of America and Microsoft quietly fund police through private donations," *Guardian* reported in a June 2020 headline.[39] They have to do it on the sly so nobody notices. So nobody boycotts. So nobody targets their business for protests, uprisings, and worse. What a shameful shame. That's the Great Reset.

And it's a reset that's moving along at a rapid pace, systematically sowing the seeds of free market change in America so that corporations are becoming, as Schwab wanted, "the trustees" of society, and corporate CEOs, the policymakers. This is not a natural segue of American business; at this point, it's not even a wholly voluntary shift for many companies. If company chiefs truly wanted to give up profits to push some societal good, then by all means, they have that choice—they don't need the permission from the WEF to cede profits for social justice causes. But that's not what's going on here. This Great Reset, in its own words, by its own admission, is about changing the definition of capitalism to be something that's not capitalism—while still deceiving the masses by calling it capitalism, only in a new form.

It's a highly orchestrated, highly pressured campaign from the WEF to turn businesses into the enforcement arms for globalists and elites.

It's a strategic move of the world's wealthiest to use governments and the markets for best selfish gain. The Great Reset, at root, is a power grab by the independently operated WEF, on behalf of the independent ambitions of the world's most power hungry. The fallout for America will be massively destructive. What difference will elections make if the Great Reset is successful? What difference will entrepreneurial dreams of spirited Americans make if the Great Reset reaches its final stages?

America is not a country of, by, and for the corporate community. It's a country of, by, and for the people—a country of individualism, not collectivism; a country of free market entrepreneurship and innovation, not spread-the-wealth, limit-the-growth campaigns. It's a country that exceeds by doing, excels by striving, prospers by driving to be the best— and that has led the world in economic ventures, scientific inventions, creative endeavors, and yes, monetary accumulations for decades. And it's a country that has voluntarily taken those gains and given back to communities of lesser ability and to peoples of depressed and suppressed societies because of a moral compass that emphasizes charity and good-ness. It's America's recognition of God as the giver of rights, and of God as the granter of freedoms, that have led to so many American individual achievements over the years—and then, to just as many occasions of sharing those achievements and blessings with others.

The Great Reset will kill that spirit. "Does capitalism need some Marxism to survive [this] Fourth Industrial Revolution?" Jem Bendell wrote for the WEF, in 2016. "[T]he cross-pollination of ideas between capitalism and Marxism is worthy of serious discourse."[40] That tells everything that's needed to be known about the Great Reset. It's Marxism—cultural and economic Marxism—masked as "better" cap-italism. It will be the end of America as we know it. The pandemic is being used to shutter business, stifle entrepreneurship, and usher in a new era of corporatism where CEOs serve as enforcers for the farther leftist government agendas imaginable. Pay attention to the campaigns of corporations in the coming months, in the coming years, and make your purchases accordingly.

CHAPTER SEVEN

Control the Health Care, Control the People

. . . my God, in whom I trust. For he will deliver you from the snare of the fowler and from the deadly pestilence . . .

Psalm 91:2-3 (RSV)

The announcement rocked media headlines. New York, circa March 2021, was going to open for business, at least for limited business, and get back to hosting public sporting events at Madison Square Garden— so long as those entering the facility first showed their Excelsior Pass to ticket takers or to security personnel, that is. It was Democratic Governor Andrew Cuomo's way of pushing a vaccine passport onto the people, without having to call it a vaccine passport. "Similar to a mobile airline boarding pass, individuals will be able to either print out their pass or store it on their smartphones using the Excelsior Pass's 'Wallet App.' Each pass will have a secure QR code, which venues will scan using a companion app to confirm someone's COVID health status," the official website of the governor of New York stated in April 2021.[1]

Nothing to see here, folks; go home. Certainly, nothing like a vaccine passport to see here. No. Nope. Not at all. Rather, it was simply the good government's way of making sure "as many New Yorkers as possible" get vaccinated, as Cuomo said. So as to do their part of "keeping the infection rate down," Cuomo said. So as to foster the "reenergizing" of the economy, "in a safe, smart way," Cuomo said. So as to get "one step closer to reaching a new normal," Cuomo said.[2]

How nice. The way of the future, the path toward new normalcy: government working with private business to make sure private citizens have their shots—in a way that lets government claim it's not doing any such thing. "I'm not saying that [the federal government] should or that they would [mandate the coronavirus vaccine], but I'm saying you could foresee how an independent entity might say, 'Well, we can't be dealing with you unless we know you're vaccinated,'" said Anthony Fauci, the federal government's go-to on all things coronavirus, in an April 2021 interview. And then he was quick to add this: "But it's not going to be mandated from the federal government."[3]

Of course it won't be mandated from the federal government. The federal government doesn't want to be tied up in all kinds of nasty court cases questioning the constitutionality of its powers to put chemicals into peoples' bodies—only to be told, Hey, you can't do that. Instead, the federal government will boot it to the states to decide—to do the dirty work—and ultimately, even better, to the private companies that aren't held to the same legal standards as the public sector. Fauci pretty much stated the plan. So, too, White House press secretary Jen Psaki, who said, around that same time frame, that the idea of a "vaccination credential"—note the language; not passport, but "credential"—would be driven by "the private sector."[4]

And drive, the private sector did. Drive, the private sector has begun.

- In March 2021, Las Vegas Sands Corp. announced it was putting into effect a mobile application called Health Pass that displays the user's personal medical information, including coronavirus test results and vaccination status.[5]
- In New York, it was first Barclays Center, then Madison Square Garden, then—the state? This headline, from the governor's office: "Proven, Secure Technology Will Confirm an Individual's

Vaccination or Recent Negative COVID Test; Will Help Fast-Track Reopening Theaters, Stadiums & Other Businesses as More New Yorkers are Vaccinated."[6]

- American Queen Steamboat Company, which operates tours along the Mississippi River, the Ohio River, and other noted waterways of historical importance, announced that beginning July 1, 2021, the "COVID-19 vaccination is required for all guests and crew for all sailings."[7] Interestingly, the company also stipulated that even with the vaccine requirement, and as based on CDC guidance, that all guests would still have to take a coronavirus test as a condition of boarding; all guests would still have to socially distance and wear face masks while on board; and all guests would still have to fill out a medical questionnaire and subject themselves to temperature checks before boarding.[8]

- Then there was this, from Arkansas Governor Asa Hutchinson, in April 2021: "If an employer wants to have everyone vaccinated in their workplace," he said, "they have the prerogative to do that. That's the private sector and their right to protect their workplace."

Say what? By that logic, employers should've—could've—been requiring employees for decades to show, in addition to their driver's license and Social Security card, their shot records as condition of employment. Employers haven't, because it's intrusive. But this is the direction America's headed. This is the Pandora's box the coronavirus has opened. This is the next boot the Left will be lacing. "Could Vaccination Records Be Part of an Employment Background Check?" the blog Verifirst asked in December 2020. And the answer, in the same post? Yes. "Many news outlets, SHRM [the Society for Human Resource Management], and employment lawyers are saying yes," Verifirst wrote. "If employers view the lack of immunization as a threat to current employees or customers, or if the employer faces future liability, it could be a potential requirement, pending medical or religious exemptions."[9]

So says a blogger. So say some human resources people. So say some legal minds. But that's doesn't necessarily make it so. The final word in America on the rights Americans retain rests with—da-dum-dum, drumroll please—the American citizens. But American citizens need to be both vigilant and strong in order to keep those rights. Unfortunately, citizen vigilance and strength haven't really been part of the American picture over the course of the coronavirus, so much as obedience and fear.

If America's not careful, the Left will push the country into a system of health care that has the government peering into all aspects of citizens' most private affairs, deeming who's safe to roam the streets, who's safe to stroll the beaches, who's safe to attend college, visit museums, board buses, trains, and trolleys, and who has to stay inside, indoors, away from the vaccinated elites. And the government will do it all in a way that allows them to wash their hands of any sense of elitism, because the blame will fall on the private sector; the responsibility for enforcement will rest with the businesses; the crackdowns, clampdowns, separations of one segment of society from another will come from the corporations—working hand-in-hand with their behind-the-scenes puppet-string pullers in government. It'll be the socialist-slash-collectivist-slash-Marxist takeover of all individual rights, all individual choices, all individual liberties, without having to fire a shot.

Get this clear. This is coming. If the coronavirus, with a recovery rate, depending on whom is asked, of somewhere in the vicinity of 97 percent, or even upward of 99 percent, can condition Americans into believing in not just the necessity of a vaccination, but also the public good of allowing private businesses to serve as the enforcement arm of the vaccine program, the potential for additional health-related regulation onto the people is endless.[10]

Endless. The media's working overtime to make sure those who raise red flags are dismissed. From *Time* magazine, "The U.S. Has Had 'Vaccine Passports' Before—and They Worked," an article printed in April 2021—this excerpt:

Introduced to the western world in the 18th century, the smallpox vaccine was the first of its kinds. It was administered not with a syringe but by scratching pustular material on a person's arm. Typically, the vaccinated area would form a blister, scab over, and leave behind a distinctive scar. Because of its unique appearance, Americans treated the smallpox scar as a documentation of vaccination, or a sort of early vaccine passport.[11]

A sort of vaccine passport. Been there, done that. Today's vaccine passport idea is nothing different. The article went on to note:

- At the end of the Civil War, Union Brigadier General Ralph Pomeroy Buckland ordered doctors to vaccinate anyone in Memphis "found without well marked scars."[12]
- Between 1898 and 1903, several states mandated small pox vaccinations on all its citizens, and political leaders turned to both public and private facilities to pressure reluctant Americans to take the shot.[13]
- Both medical professionals and private employers tried to make the vaccination compulsory. "A Chicago physician wrote in 1901 that 'Vaccination should be the seal on the passport of entrance to the public schools, to the voters' booth, to the box of the juryman, and to every position of duty, privilege, profit or honor in the gift of either the state or the nation.' Employers across the country acted to make smallpox immunity a condition of employment," *Time* wrote.[14]
- In Maine in 1903, political leaders barred anyone working in lumber camps who couldn't first prove they were vaccinated against smallpox. In Minnesota, meanwhile, in 1901, the State Board of Health tried to force smallpox vaccines onto loggers by mandating they show the telltale scars as a condition of receiving pay. It didn't go so well; in that case, timber companies themselves fought the health board's order, saying it was not their jobs to serve as the enforcement wing of the government.[15]
- Factories, mines, railroads, and other places of industrial work were particularly successful in demanding employees obtain the

vaccination as conditions of employment—"and though workers sometimes resisted, corporations and governments usually ensured that they took the vaccine in the end," *Time* wrote.[16]

The messaging was widespread; the pressure was powerful.

As *History* also reported, students couldn't attend public schools without showing their scars or presenting papers from qualified physicians stating they were medically unfit to take the shot.[17] Predictably, forgeries presented a problem. Just as predictably, government squeezed tighter.

The mandatory vaccination orders angered many Americans who formed anti-vaccination leagues to defend their personal liberties. In an attempt to dodge public health officials, who went door-to-door (often with a police escort) to enforce vaccination laws, some anti-vaccination activists would forge certificates of vaccination. Unable to tell if certificates were legitimate, health officials fell back on physical evidence: they demanded to see a vaccination scar. . . . In the overcrowded tenement districts of cities like New York and Boston where smallpox spread with deadly speed, health officials enlisted policemen to help enforce vaccination orders, sometimes physically restraining uncooperative citizens. Frustrated with the widespread resistance to vaccination, these vaccine squads began to ignore certificates altogether and go right to the source [and demand citizens show the scar].[18]

All these historical accounts of America's priors with so-called vaccine passports are interesting—enlightening, even—particularly the parts where police were called to the scene to forcibly vaccinate the unwilling. But there are notable differences.

There are notable differences between smallpox and the coronavirus—and even bigger and more notable differences between the two vaccinations. And it's these differences that make the dismissal of concerns about the coronavirus vaccine and the coronavirus vaccine passport all the more eyebrow raising. As if to say: What's going on here, anyway?

In a lengthy article entitled, "The Smallpox and Coronavirus Vaccines: 30 Facts From 'The Vaccine Vault,'" *Forbes* reported that COVID-19 was "nowhere near as deadly as smallpox," which carried a 30 percent mortality rate and "decimated populations from the third century B.C. until 1977."[19] Ultimately, some 300 million deaths in the 20th century alone were blamed on smallpox.[20] In April 2021, the World Health Organization reported a total 2.84 million deaths due to coronavirus around the globe.[21] Vastly different. Also of note is the numbers of COVID-19's fatalities were roundly criticized as inaccurate, mismatched, and in some cases, overinflated. "'Head-spinning discrepancy': Why numbers for state and local COVID-19 deaths don't match," *San Antonio Report* wrote in August 2020.[22]

Then there was this, from News 6 out of Orlando: "News 6 has discovered a discrepancy in COVID-19 deaths reported across the state of Florida. . . . Here's the issue: If someone dies anywhere in Florida, the medical examiner in that county counts that death. If someone dies of COVID-19 in Florida but their primary residence is somewhere else— perhaps they're 'snowbirds' or were visiting the state for another reason—the state of Florida does not include that death in its count."[23] Bam. The numbers of coronavirus-related deaths could vary widely, depending on where they're sourced. That's not even nefarious; that's just differing systems.

Here's another interesting factoid of the comparisons of smallpox to COVID-19 and the push for modern vaccine passports: on eradication, one of these things is not like the other. Three days after Pfizer and BioNTech announced the early results of their vaccine showed it to be at least 90 percent effective in preventing coronavirus, David Heymann, the World Health Organization's leader of the infectious disease unit during the 2002–2003 SARS epidemic, said this during a webinar hosted by the think tank Chatham House: "What needs to happen is a new way of communication that people can understand. Political leaders have political ambitions and the public health leaders and the technical leaders have ambitions on stopping the outbreak, and the two of those have to be reconciled in some way. The public doesn't understand all about vaccines . . . including that this disease may, even with vaccines, become endemic."[24] Endemic. That's doctor lingo for "never go away."

In fact, Anthony Fauci acknowledged similarly during this same November 2020 webinar: "I doubt we are going to eradicate this. I think we need to plan that this is something we may need to maintain control over chronically. It may be something that becomes endemic; that we have to just be careful about."[25] For those who saw the pandemic as a tool of exerting long-held political controls on the people, Fauci's remark was music to their ears. A coronavirus that never goes away? Think of all the time that will buy the WEF for its Great Reset. Think of how socialists and collectivists could use such never-ending fear for a "new normalcy" shredding of constitutional rights and individual liberties. An honest media—a media in it for the people, not the government—would double down, triple down, quadruple down, and bend over backward to assuage citizens' fears about the coronavirus by putting the pandemic in truthful contexts and telling, for example, that most diseases are not eradicated.

Most diseases never completely disappear. Smallpox, for example, is a rare exception—and that's why comparisons of smallpox vaccines to coronavirus vaccines make absolutely no sense. That's why they're deceptive. Read this, from *Forbes*: "SARS-CoV-2, like most viruses, has animal 'reservoirs.' If public health efforts succeed at pushing it out of human populations, it will likely live on in fruit bats and ferret populations (at least), only to return to infect humans again."[26] Now read this, from the Food and Drug Administration: "During the smallpox era, the only known reservoir for the virus was humans; no known animal or insect reservoirs or vectors existed."[27] So once the smallpox vaccines did their work in humans, the virus had no other place to live. It was eradicated. And eradication is, in fact, so difficult to achieve that in addition to smallpox, there is only one other disease that is considered completely wiped out from the world—rinderpest, also known as cattle plague, for its near-100 percent fatality rate in certain animals.[28] Rinderpest didn't even infect humans, but it caused widespread hunger because of its ability to devastate entire cattle herds in just a few days.[29]

Here are some more enlightening, illuminating facts about viruses and diseases:

- Eradication is not the same as elimination. Eradication means it's gone, or at least considered gone, on both "permanent and global" scales. Elimination is a zeroing out of infections in a specific geographical location. So a virus can be eliminated from a certain spot, without being eradicated around the globe. Just because a virus has been eliminated doesn't mean it can't be transmitted elsewhere; actions to prevent its spread are still required.[30]
- Not all diseases can be eradicated. In fact, most cannot. Even the World Health Organization (WHO) acknowledges that. More than that, the world's health experts don't even agree on which diseases can be eradicated, versus which cannot. In 2018, for example, the International Task Force for Disease Eradication (ITFDE) considered these diseases to be potentially eradicable: polio, Guinea worm disease, lymphatic filariasis, cysticercosis, measles, mumps, and rubella.[31] That same year, the WHO, on the other hand, only considered polio and Guinea worm disease to be eradicable, and the other five on the ITFDE's list to be potentials for elimination at certain spots around the globe.[32]
- There are more viruses on planet earth than stars in the sky, and they're constantly mutating—meaning, it's really no surprise when new variants emerge.[33] These two facts are huge, given the left's use of the coronavirus to clamp freedoms, as well as leftists' intent to continue to use the virus, and its variants, to clamp freedoms.

From *National Geographic*:

An estimated 10 nonillion (10 to the 31st power) individual viruses exist on our planet—enough to assign one to every star in the universe 100 million times over.[34]

From *Air & Space* magazine:

Their total number is staggering. It is estimated that there are 10 viruses for every bacterium on Earth.[35]

From *National Geographic* again:

Viruses infiltrate every aspect of our natural world, seething in seawater, drifting through the atmosphere, and lurking in miniscule motes of soil. Generally considered non-living entities, these pathogens can only replicate with the help of a host . . .[36]

From *Air & Space* magazine again:

The diversity of viruses is just as impressive. Some use DNA to pass on genetic information, some use RNA, and some use both during their life cycle . . . Viruses are like a natural lab seemingly playing around with genetic permutations and combinations. . . . Viruses also have benefits. Most of the genetic information on Earth probably resides within them, and viruses are important for transferring genes between different species, increasing genetic diversity and ultimately enhancing evolution and the adaptation of various organisms to new environmental challenges.[37]

There's power in them there viruses, in other words.

Enough power that it could be said, à la mad scientist like, that the one who controls the viruses controls the human race. The one who understands to the point of being able to manipulate viruses is the one who holds the key to understanding to the point of manipulating DNA—at least in some cases; at least to some degree. And that circles back, once again, to the previously posed question: So what's going on here, anyway?

If the coronavirus is just one of billions of viruses out there, and the coronavirus vaccine can't possibly eradicate the disease, then why the utter, absolute, total, near-despotic shutdowns of society, and for so many months on end?

Well, this virus was new; we didn't know what we were dealing with; we had to take precautions to save lives—we were told. That's both true and not true. Coronaviruses are "a large family of viruses named for the crown-like protein spikes on their outer surface" and there are actually "seven well-described coronaviruses that infect humans" and cause respiratory ailments like SARS (the severe acute respiratory syndrome) and MERS (the Middle Eastern respiratory syndrome), and most recently, COVID-19."[38]

Well, this virus was deadlier than other coronaviruses, and other diseases; we had to stop the spread quickly to save lives; and the only way to stop its spread was to isolate, wear face masks, socially distance, and stay home—we were told. Again, that's both true and not true. Yes, COVID-19 has been blamed for more deaths than SARS in 2002–2003 and MERS in 2012.[39] But the test kits for COVID-19 were faulty, the death counts due to COVID-19 were flawed, and compounding the problem was the fact hospitals and medical professionals were actually financially incentivized to report higher cases and fatalities tied to COVID-19. "Officials Knew CDC Coronavirus Test Kit Was Prone to Failure," NPR wrote in November 2020.[40] "Early CDC COVID-19 Test Kits 'Likely Contaminated,'" WebMD wrote in June 2020.[41]

From the Associated Press, in May 2020:

> Many people who died of coronavirus were older and already fragile, weakened by heart disease or some other malady. So ascribing a single cause [proved] challenging. . . . [Then] the CDC told states to include probable COVID-19 cases in their reports to the agency. Probable coronavirus deaths don't have positive test results but in which other evidence—like the symptoms and course of their disease, and exposure to infected people—points to the infection.[42]

Call it a doctor's choice. Call it a best-guess medical opinion.

And finally, on the financial payouts to hospitals for COVID-19 case counts, this fact-check piece from *USA Today*, from early 2020:

> We rate the claim that hospitals get paid more if patients are listed as COVID-19 and on ventilators as TRUE. Hospitals and doctors do get paid more for Medicare patients diagnosed with COVID-19 or if it's considered presumed they have COVID-19 absent a laboratory-confirmed test, and three times more if the patients are placed on a ventilator to cover the cost of care and loss of business resulting from a shift in focus to treat COVID-19 cases. This higher allocation of funds [was] made possible under the Coronavirus Aid, Relief and Economic Security Act through a Medicare 20% add-on to its regular payment for COVID-19 patients . . .[43]

So. What do you think about the coronavirus now? Or more important: What do you think about the government's response to the coronavirus, which was simply to shut down business, shut down travel, shut down schools, shut down churches, shut down beaches and parks and all forms of recreation—shut down freedoms and liberties and normal, natural, human interactions and activities? For our own health and well-being?

Then came the "variants." Just as restrictions were starting to subside—or more to truth, just as Americans were starting to resist the restrictions and insist on returning to some semblance of normalcy—then came government's concerns about the coronavirus variants:

- "Fauci Sounds Alarm Over Coronavirus Variant First Found in U.K.," *U.S. News & World Report* wrote in March 2021. The story went on to state, "Leading infectious disease expert Anthony Fauci . . . warned that the COVID-19 variant first documented in the United Kingdom is a "growing threat" in the United States.[44]
- From WebMD that same month: "Variants of Variants Seen in COVID-19 Ravaged Brazil."

- From the CDC that same month: "CDC director warns COVID variants could spark another avoidable surge as travel numbers reach high," ABC 6 Action News wrote in a late March 2021 headline.[45]

That story went on to report:

> Dr. Rochelle Walensky, director of the Centers for Disease Control and Prevention, said . . . she's worried the US could see "another avoidable surge" of COVID-19 if mitigation measures—such as mask-wearing, physical distancing and avoiding crowds or travel—are not followed. "As I've stated before, the continued relaxation of prevention measures while cases are still high and while concerning variants are spreading rapidly throughout the United States is a serious threat to the progress we have made as a nation," Walensky said at a White House briefing.[46]

And yet, the CDC—Walensky's own CDC—acknowledges that variants of viruses are nothing new, nothing especially alarming, nothing especially surprising. "Viruses," the CDC wrote on its "About Variants of the Virus That Causes COVID-19" web page in April 2021, "constantly change through mutation, and new variants of a virus are expected to occur over time. Sometimes new variants emerge and disappear. Other times, new variants emerge and persist. Multiple variants of the virus that causes COVID-19 have been documented in the United States and globally during this pandemic."[47]

Are Americans supposed to simply sit in their homes and wait it out until doctors determine that all the coronavirus variants are the kinds that disappear, rather than persist? And then what? Are Americans then supposed to wait until all the other viruses—until all the other billions upon billions of viruses in the world—are eradicated, or controlled, or deemed harmless, or eliminated? What's the endgame here, anyway? Once upon a time, it was to flatten a curve. "The U.S. Has Flattened the Curve," *Time* wrote, way back in April 2020. "Next Up Is 'Squashing'

It—and That's Not Going Well."[48] Hmm. Next up, squashing? More like, next up, more exploitation.

Wake. Up. America. The lines of logic—safety, health, preventing COVID-19 deaths—that the government, in partnership with some in the corporate sector, are using to keep control of entire societies and economies don't add up. They don't. They simply lead to more questions, more red flags, more puzzling contradictions in terms, more ever-changing nonscientific standards that are couched in scientific-sounding terms.

The only line of logic that does add up is self-interest. Someone, a select group of someones, is purposely fueling fear over the coronavirus to bring about a world where medical decisions aren't made so much by the individual as by the state, and where health choices are based on what's good for the collective. Look at the messaging in America about face-masking. Look at how the vaccine is being presented as a duty to others, duty to country. Look at how the whole system of health care in America is being switched from one of personal privacies and individual choice to one of obedience to the government for the greater good, for the protection of neighbor, for the safety of fellow citizens—even when those protections aren't based on sound science or irrefutable fact.

Control the borders; control a country. Control the health care system; control the entire population. From coronavirus to coronavirus variants to vaccines to vaccine passports to—what? That's the big open question. The possibilities truly are limitless. In the meanwhile, there's lots of money to be made in vaccines, in vaccine development, in vaccine transport and delivery—in essence, in keeping the populations of the world in fear of dying from diseases.

From the *Guardian*, in March 2021:

The arrival of Covid-19 vaccines promises a return to more normal life—and has created a global market worth tens of billions of dollars in annual sales for some pharmaceutical companies. Among the biggest winners will be Moderna and Pfizer—two very different US pharma firms which are both charging more than $30 per person for the protection of their two-dose vaccines. While Moderna was founded just 11 years ago, has never made a profit and employed just 830 staff pre-pandemic, Pfizer traces its roots back to 1849, made a net profit of $9.6bn last year and employs nearly 80,000 staff.[49]

Pfizer developed a coronavirus vaccine in collaboration with BioNTech, a German company, and the two share profits from its Comirnaty shot, the first messenger RNA, or mRNA, vaccination to be approved for emergency authorized use by the FDA. The companies' joint profits have been driven by orders from governments desperate to stop the spread of the coronavirus. According to the *Guardian*, by March 2021, various governments had purchased about 780 million of the Pfizer/BioNTech shot; of that, the United States bought about 200 million doses at a cost of $3.9 billion.[50] The two companies expected to share somewhere in the vicinity of $15 billion for its first-year sales of the coronavirus vaccine, though analysts said that number could soar as development and delivery contracts expand.[51] Moderna, meanwhile, estimated its first-year sales of its own mRNA vaccine to bring in $18.4 billion—again, from orders from governments.[52] In February 2021, the United Kingdom ordered 17 million shots from Moderna; the European Union ordered 150 million doses—added to the already ordered 160 million doses; the United States ordered another 100 million doses, above the previously ordered 200 million doses.[53] Not bad for a company that just a year or two earlier had been on tough financial times. Over the course of the first coronavirus year, Moderna's share price jumped from $19 to $155, resulting in a company value of $60 billion and the opening of offices in eight countries, with plans for even more expansions.[54] Meanwhile, if the revolutionary mRNA vaccines go over well, Moderna is prepared to develop almost two dozen more for viruses, ranging from HIV and Zika.

Then there was AstraZeneca and the Joe Biden administration's announcement to send 4 million doses of that company's vaccine—which at the time, were not approved for use in the United States—to

Canada and Mexico.[55] It was to be a loan, White House press secretary Jen Psaki said. But the terms that were released were definitely unfavorable for America, or more to truth, for American taxpayers who picked up the tab. Per Reuters in March 2001:

> The "releasable" or ready-to-use vaccines [were] being lent under a deal in which the United States expects to be paid back with doses in return. [America] is getting prepared to roll out the AstraZeneca vaccine domestically if it gets authorization from the U.S. Food and Drug Administration, the White House said. . . . The United States does not need the AstraZeneca shots to meet its target of having enough doses for all U.S. adults by the [White House stated goal of] the end of May.[56]

That means U.S. taxpayers footed the bill for vaccines they didn't even need, only for the Biden administration to turn around and give them to Mexico and Canada supposedly on loan—but the terms of repayment were for doses of vaccines the United States didn't even need, and ostensibly, for doses from a company, AstraZeneca, that weren't even approved by the FDA for distribution in America. It's great to be charitable with other people's money.

There's a larger point to be made with this glance at coronavirus vaccine financials, and it's about the breakdown of health care choice and simultaneous big government takeover of the medical industry: Vaccine developments are not based on free market needs. They're massively manipulated and controlled by government, at taxpayer expense, in partnership with a few elites in the private market who've recognized the potential of this field, and who've swooped to capitalize on the coronavirus.

The relationships are incestuous. And cloaked in bureaucratic favoritism. Take a look at one example: Bill Gates.

- The Bill & Melinda Gates Foundation has owned shares in Pfizer since 2002.[57]

- The Gates Foundation also owns shares in BioNTech. "It invested $55 million in the biotech, with the potential for total funding to reach $100 million," the Motley Fool reported in September 2020. "The foundation's goal with this investment was to work with BioNTech to develop vaccines and immunotherapies for preventing HIV and tuberculosis (TB) infection."[58]

- In 2015, the Gates Foundation "committed to investing $52 million in CureVac," a German biotech firm, as well as provide additional funds to "develop vaccines based on CureVac's messenger RNA (mRNA) platform," the Motley Fool wrote.[59] In April 2021, CureVac announced an EU approval of its coronavirus vaccine was imminent; the UK and EU, meanwhile, announced preorders of 455 million doses of the mRNA shot.[60]

- Moderna's money, prior to turning revenues from its coronavirus vaccine, came primarily from grants from the U.S. government, via the Defense Advanced Research Projects Agency (DARPA), and once again, the Bill & Melinda Gates Foundation.[61]

But vaccine development is only one part of the equation. The vaccines still need to get into the arms of the people. And that requires more partnerships.

- The Coalition for Epidemic Preparedness Innovations launched in 2017 at Davos, Switzerland, as a means of matching financers with vaccine developers. "CEPI is an innovative global partnership between public, private, philanthropic, and civil society organizations launched in Davos in 2017 to develop vaccines to stop future epidemics. Our mission is to accelerate the development of vaccines against emerging infectious diseases and enable equitable access to these vaccines for people during outbreaks," the website wrote.[62] Among the founders? The Bill & Melinda Gates Foundation and the World Economic Forum.[63]

- Gavi, the Vaccine Alliance, based in Geneva, Switzerland, "is an international organization that was created in 2000 to improve access to new and underused vaccines for children living in the world's poorest countries," the Gavi-supporting International Finance Facility for Immunization website stated.[64] The Gavi website also predicted banner years during 2021–2025. "In the 2021–2025 period, our work together—leveraging donor financing, powering countries, shaping sustainable markets will allow us to achieve the Alliance's goals and reach a further 300 million children between 2021 and 2025 and, through the full protection of the broadest vaccine portfolio in history, save an additional 7–8 million lives," the website went on.[65] That's a bold prediction for broadening the business of vaccinations—but couched in terms of saving lives. How do they know? Anyhow, once again, among the founders of Gavi: Gates. The Bill & Melinda Gates Foundation gave seed money for the group with an initial pledge of $750 million in 1999, along with the World Health Organization, the World Bank, and UNICEF.[66] Among the funders? The American taxpayer. "We were thrilled to see the United States include $4 billion for Gavi in its latest COVID-19 relief package," Bill and Melinda Gates wrote in their January 2021 annual letter.[67]

- COVAX is a group launched during the coronavirus as a global "portfolio of COVID-19 vaccines" dedicated to "acting as a platform that will support the research, development and manufacturing of a wide range of COVID-19 vaccine candidates, and negotiate their pricing," its website stated.[68] Basically, COVAX works as a clearinghouse for emerging vaccines to speed up the distribution process, and as a funding source for manufacturers. Among its program coordinators? Gavi, the Vaccine Alliance, and CEPI, the Coalition for Epidemic Preparedness Innovations, groups once again tied back to Bill Gates. But COVAX is multifaceted—as well as its partnership with Gavi. "To make all this a reality, Gavi has created the COVAX Facility through which self-financing economies and funded economies can participate. Within this also sits an entirely separate funding mechanism, the Gavi COVAX Advance Market Commitment (AMC), which will support access to COVID-19 vaccines for lower-income economies. Combined, these make possible the participation of all countries, regardless of ability to pay."[69] Countries that pay into the facility are guaranteed of receiving enough vaccines—both coronavirus and ones that come in the future—to provide for up to 50% of their populations. The facility also facilitates beneficial development and disbursement deals with vaccine manufacturers and—this is a biggie—"incentivize[s] them to expand their production capacity in advance of vaccines receiving regulatory approval.[70]

What a lucrative racket that could be, yes?

Basically, COVAX is sort of one-stop vaccine shopping—or one-stop vaccine investing, depending on which side you represent, the tax-paying citizen or the Bill Gates partner. That's a simplification, of course. And it's a simplification that admittedly doesn't take into consideration the fact that some in the world of vaccine development truly, genuinely, absolutely believe in the philanthropic mission of helping others through medicine, and saving lives and quality of lives through research, development, and miraculous pharmaceutical innovations.

But this coronavirus vaccine ain't that philanthropic miracle. It's actually a platform for global takeover of much of the health system, with America, and America's free market, as the crowning glory of conquest for the global elites. If Gates and his vaccine partners were working within the boundaries of the free market system, there wouldn't be any red flags—not even with the raking of millions and billions of dollars in profits. That's how a free market works: the innovators reap their rewards because the innovators take the risks. But that's not what's taking place here. That's not where this coronavirus platform is leading, either.

With this coronavirus vaccine, governments are using tax dollars to pay private firms to develop a vaccine the governments insist is necessary—or people will die! And the private firms are providing the vaccines to the governments in exchange for tax dollars. And in between come the nongovernmental groups who are creating more partnerships between governments and private firms to develop not just the coronavirus vaccine, but even more vaccines, ever more vaccines, more and more and more vaccines—to cure even more and plenty of other viruses, and then to take additional tax dollars to help deliver all these vaccines to less stable, less financially solvent nations. Peel back the curtains and it's seen: most of these separate nongovernment groups are actually tied to the same people, to the same government entities, crying about the dire need for all to take vaccines in the first place. It's a big cycle of behind-the-scenes—incestuous—vaccine development, vaccine money-making relations.

The cash cow is the opened door to more mRNA vaccines. The cash cow is the opened door to more mandated vaccines, whether by government compulsion or by private sector conditions. The cash cow of all cash cows is the complete takeover of health care; the complete destruction of any system that lets patients choose.

"On March 16, the National Institute of Allergy and Infectious Diseases announced the launch of the first test in humans of an experimental vaccine for COVID-19 made by Massachusetts-based biotechnology firm Moderna, Inc.," Johns Hopkins wrote in its March 2020 newsletter. "Moderna's vaccine is RNA-based. RNA vaccines introduce a mRNA sequence into the patient. . . . Although no mRNA-based vaccines have made it to the market, there have been successful clinical trials."[71] Well, isn't that special. There have been some trials. But there have never been, in all of American vaccine history, any mRNA-vaccines that have been approved for market use—until the coronavirus. Until the coronavirus, with its 95 to 99 percent recovery rate. Until the coronavirus, with its government-insistent calls to get the shot, take the shot, everybody needs to get the shot quickly to get back to post-coronavirus normalcy. Until the coronavirus, and all its worldwide shutdowns of economies, schools, businesses, places of worship, and so forth and so on—and government promises of ends in sight, based on how well citizens obeyed governments' commands. Until the coronavirus, with all its curious uncomfortably cozy conflicts of interests with the vaccine developers.

It's always worth an investigation when the ones who foster the fear are the same ones who profit from the fear. Remember Al Gore and his polar bears? Climate change is big business when the emotional triggers are just right. Now remember this: Moderna's got "23 other mRNA drugs and vaccines in its portfolio," the *Guardian* reported.[72] Gates has partnerships around the world, ready to go at a moment's notice, to purchase, deliver, and administer the next round of vaccines, post-coronavirus. The global elites are on board; the World Economic Forum has a Great Reset to realize. And it's all being billed as the way to save lives. Perhaps Gates truly is the philanthropic savior of humanity his supporters want to believe he is. Perhaps the WEF and its Great Reset, Gavi, CEPI, and COVIX and all the other conflicted-of-interest groups with government truly are trying to put an end to all the world's ills, all the global diseases that plague.

But is that feasible? Is that possible? Viruses are as many as the stars in the sky. Meanwhile, the rush to inject a world's worth of arms with an experimental vaccine that's never ever before been used in humans, of a type, mRNA, that's never ever before been approved for human inoculation, goes forth.

Fear fueling fear, fueling more endless fear. Where does it end? When will it end?

"The E Tattoo Is the Future of Healthcare Technology," wrote Now, an online communications arm of Northrup Grumman, in January 2020. "Medical tattoos can monitor important biomarkers such as heart rate, blood pressure, hydration, or blood sugar levels. . . . Healthcare wearables . . . continuously monitor patients. They could even send alerts to medical systems."[73]

Sure. They could also monitor who has taken vaccines, and who hasn't. They could also serve as handy-dandy vaccine passports. They could also serve as easily transportable medical record storage devices— quick checks for private businesses, say, to ensure all who enter are up to date, with the latest government-issued medical guidance. They could also serve for other agencies, for other safety and security reasons, as proof of the wearer's noncriminal background, for instance, or as evidence of the tattooed individual's clearance for flight, boarding, or interstate travel. Coronavirus today. The world of health care tomorrow. Police and law enforcement and travel authorities and private business next week.

The coronavirus, rightly or wrongly, wove itself into Americans' minds as a justifiable reason to cede individual rights, to give up individual decision-making rights, to shrug off individual privacies tied to personal health choices. Where it ends is anybody's guess. Individualism or collectivism? God-given liberties or government-granted rights? The choice is upon us. The twelfth hour has arrived.

CHAPTER EIGHT

From Pandemic to Climate to Capitalism, Oh My!

But false prophets also arose among the people, just as there will be false teachers among you, who will secretly bring in destructive heresies . . .

2 Peter 2:1 (RSV)

Bill Gates said in a February 14, 2021 post on his blog: "there's nothing wrong with using more energy as long as it's carbon free."[1] And lucky for us, he's got the answer. He's kind of like God's gift to humanity that way, isn't he? (Insert sarcasm here.) But seriously, when Gates speaks, America ought to listen—and not just to what he says, but how he says it and what he doesn't say. He's an egomaniac who masks his egomaniacal tendencies as philanthropy, taking full advantage of all the cushy tax advantages that come with leading a foundation as he pushes policy into governments around the world. Don't believe it? Go back in time to the Justice Department's antitrust suit against Microsoft, the company Gates cofounded, and the deposition that showcased the then CEO's utter contempt for, well, anyone and everyone. Dan Goodin wrote in *Ars Technica*, in a 2020 look back on his journalistic coverage of the case:

The strategy during the three-day deposition was classic Microsoft. Obstruct. Paint the government as out-of-touch policy wonks who had no idea how tech and real markets worked. And above all, deny even the most basic of premises in the government's case. The plan from Gates' army of lawyers and PR handlers seemed to be to wield his image as a software wunderkind who dropped out of Harvard to bootstrap his company and [who] went on to become the world's richest man. . . . By day 2, it became clear that strategy was failing spectacularly. . . . Publicly lauded as the wise sage, consummate businessman, and industry visionary, Gates was accustomed to being treated with obsequious deference from all but a small number of peers. As such, he had little or no experience tolerating—let along encountering—dissent, criticism, or challenges to his authority.[2]

That's probably true of most billionaires. They're used to getting their way. Tell them no and watch their true characters emerge.

Others covering the famous antitrust suit, which included eighteen states and the District of Columbia as plaintiffs, painted Gates in similarly arrogant form. The *Guardian*'s John Naughton, in a 2020 piece entitled, "Let's Not Forget, Bill Gates Hasn't Always Been the Good Guy":

The most striking things I remember from the case were the recordings of Gates's depositions under oath in which he was consistently truculent, evasive and non-responsive—to the point where his sheer obstructiveness sometimes made the trial judge laugh. They show a mogul who is incredulous that the government would dare to obstruct his route to world domination.[3]

That was Gates at the age of forty-three. As a mature adult. So what's changed in him all these many years later, when he's now regarded as the supposed defender of the poor and downtrodden? In a phrase: public relations. "Gates's [Bill & Melinda Gates] foundation was originally cooked up as a feel-good gloss to cover up his shredded reputation during Microsoft's antitrust trial, putting him in the long tradition of obscenely rich people using the occasional generous gift to try justifying their enormous wealth and power," Rob Larson wrote in *Jacobin*, in April 2020.[4]

Never underestimate the power of the buck to soothe hurt feelings. Between the time of the widely watched antitrust trial against Microsoft, and the verdict, Gates gave billions of dollars to his foundation. *Jacobin* reported he "contributed $20.3 billion, or 71 percent of his total contributions to the foundation . . . during the 18 months between the start of the trial and the verdict."[5] Knowledge Ecology International reported that less than four months after giving depositions, and just eight days before Sun Microsystems filed a complaint about Microsoft's "refusal to provide interoperability information," Gates, through the Gates Foundation, provided $100 million of seed money to the Bill & Melinda Gates Children's Vaccine Program.[6] And then:

- In May 1999, the Gates Foundation gave a $25 million grant to the International AIDS Vaccine Initiative.[7]
- In January 2000, Gates stepped aside as Microsoft's chief executive officer.[8]
- In February 2000, the European Commission kicked off an investigation into Microsoft's competitive practices.[9]
- In February 2000, the Gates Foundation gave the first of what became many grants to National Public Radio.[10]
- In April 2000, a judge finds that Microsoft did indeed engage in monopolization practices in violation of the Sherman Act, and as redress, suggests breaking up the company.[11]
- In July 2000, Gates promises $50 million to Botswana to combat HIV.[12]
- In October 2000, the Gates Foundation grants $1 million to the World Health Organization.[13]
- In December 2000, the Gates Foundation sets up an annual $1 million award for groups working on behalf of citizens' health around the world.[14]

- In May 2001, the Gates Foundation awards its $1 million Gates Health gift to the Global Health Council.[15]
- In June 2001, the U.S. Court of Appeals for the District of Columbia remanded the antitrust suit against Microsoft to the District Court for reassignment to a new trial judge—in effect, tossing out the recommendation of the judge from April 2000, who recommended breaking up the company because of unfair monopolistic practices.[16]

All that's to say: the philanthropic giveaways worked their PR magic.

"The trial was a terrible black eye for Bill Gates," said Ken Auletta, author of a 2001 book about Microsoft, *The New York Times* reported. "[Back then, Microsoft's public relations arm was] desperate to counter the growing impression that it was a heartless beast."[17] Charles Lowenhaupt, a wealth manager from St. Louis, said in the same *New York Times* article that Gates's philanthropic outreach certainly helped "rebrand" his image.[18]

So has Gates truly changed from egomaniac to heartfelt man of the people? Or is it all a charade, aimed at advancing his own inner drives for domination and global control? He wasn't exactly a kid when his insufferable arrogance side showed. That puts a huge question mark beside his philanthropy. And it's a question that merits stiff thought, given the huge platform Gates was given to tout his coronavirus-related recommendations.

Gates, on COVID-19, was the go-to guy for advice with much of the media, with many on the left. Their rationale was that since Gates gave so many millions of his own dollars to race to the vaccine cure, and even more millions to the World Health Organization, that he must be a true-blue philanthropist bent only on curing humanity. But once again, the question of self-interest pops up. In a 2020 article from Paul Vallely in the *Guardian*, called, "How Philanthropy Benefits the Rich"—this excerpt:

Philanthropy, it is popularly supposed, transfers money from the rich to the poor. This is not the case. . . . A lot of elite philanthropy is about elite causes. Rather than making the world a better place, it largely reinforces the world as it is. Philanthropy very often favors the rich—and no one holds philanthropists to account for it."[19]

No one holds philanthropists to account because no one dares bite the hand that feeds. Gates, for example, is one of the top contributors to the World Health Organization, and has been for years. It's sparked some concerns. "'Big Concerns Over Gates Foundation's Potential to Become Largest WHO Contributor,' Devex.com wrote in mid-2020.[20] The story went on to report how the Gates Foundation provided roughly 45 percent of the WHO's annual funds, an extraordinary amount that positioned Gates himself as unelected leader of the global organization. Or as Lawrence Gostin, faculty director for the O'Neill Institute at Georgetown University, and the director of WHO's Collaborating Center on National and Global Health Law, was cited in the article as saying: "It would enable a single rich philanthropist to set the global health agenda."[21]

That's an astonishing amount of money. But it certainly would wield an astonishing amount of influence. The Left would like it believed everything Gates does is for the health of others, and since it's health—health!—then his donations, his recommendations, his advisements, and his policy suggestions are all automatically selfless, above reproach, above even suspicion. But that's not how the world of philanthropy works. Here's another interesting excerpt from that same *Guardian* piece by Vallely: "Philanthropy is always an expression of power. Giving often depends on the personal whims of super-rich individuals. Sometimes these coincide with the priorities of society, but at other times they contradict or undermine them."[22] Well said. And all that circles back and segues nicely to the whole reason for this chapter: how socialists, leftists, and collectivists are using the pandemic to advance long-held, long-desired, and utterly radical environmental causes.

And here we have Gates once again. Here we have Bill Gates, who's supposedly shed his egomaniac past to become the foremost philanthropic "expert" on coronavirus mitigation—whose very words were taken as near-commands to governments run amok with coronavirus shut down powers—and who now sees climate change as the even bigger challenge for the world.

Gates wants to do with climate change what he did with the coronavirus. He wants to move on from coronavirus clampdowns to climate change clampdowns. It's his post-coronavirus pet project. It's in his 2021 book, *How to Avoid a Climate Disaster: The Solutions We Have and the Breakthroughs We Need*, Penguin Random House, published February 2021—it's the Bill Gates playbook for fans and followers to put into effect all the crazy, nonsensible, nonsensical, redistribution-of-wealth, redistribution-of-resources, growth-stifling, anti-American policies the mad green scientists have been shoving down Americans' throats for years.

It's Alexandria Ocasio-Cortez's already steroided-out Green New Deal—on steroids. It's the next chain for elitists to enslave humanity. Do not take lightly the philanthropic approach to environmentalism—the line and logic that it's for the health of humanity. If Gates and his partners in pandemic fear mongering crime can shut down a country due to a virus, think what he can accomplish with climate change.

Think what he and all his money, all his partners, and all his like-minded left-leaning elitist friends can accomplish under the umbrella of the Great Reset, with all its woke corporatism and worldwide oligarchy, and with so many committed Democrats in public office, and the tech giants doing their social media censorship, and the media in general doing their anticonservative, anticapitalist, antifreedom coverage—and the coronavirus still hovering as the left's greatest tool of control. It's an easy pivot from the pandemic to climate change. Here we are, America. Ready, set, go. "Bill Gates says bioterrorism and climate change are the next biggest threats after pandemic," CNBC reported in February 2021.[23]

His goal is zero emissions. Zero. That's a complete overhaul of business, manufacturing, transportation, energy—everything. Gates said as much in his book, and in a February 2021 televised exchange with PBS host Judy Woodruff.

Woodruff: "What is so fascinating, among other things, about [your] book, is that you don't—it's not the usual prescriptions—use solar panels, recycle, think about electric vehicles. You're talking about a massive change in virtually the way we do everything, the way we make things, as you put it, the way we make electricity, how we make cement, steel."[24]

Gates: "Yes . . ."[25]

He said more. But what else, after "yes," is there that matters? Gates has the ears of the world; he commands the attention of governments and policymakers. And he's not alone. All of those on the left, the committed left, the elitist left, the globalist-minded left, have been pressing radical environmentalism for decades under the guise of protecting the planet from degradation. They've just never before had an opportunity like the pandemic, leading to the election of Joe Biden and his social justice crusading sidekick Kamala Harris into the White House, and Democrat majorities in both the House and Senate. It's go time for the socialists.

"The Pandemic Remade Every Corner of Society. Now It's the Climate's Turn," wrote Justin Worland, in an April 15, 2021 *Time* magazine headline that, despite its brevity, couldn't have spelled out the globalists' goals any clearer.[26] The opening lines expand on the Biden administration's strategies to do just that—use climate change to reshape all of society.

On her third day as the Secretary of Housing and Urban Development, Marcia Fudge phoned the White House. She had taken over an agency with a role to play addressing a range of crises as the lack of affordable housing in U.S. cities has left hundreds of thousands homeless and millions more in financial straits. She connected with Joe Biden's climate team. Fudge and Gina McCarthy, Biden's national climate adviser, talked about addressing climate change and the affordable housing shortage at the same time. Three weeks later, the Administration announced plans to provide for more than 1 million resilient and energy-efficient housing units.[27]

Suddenly, barely postpandemic, environmentalism was being rebranded as affordable housing. But it's worse than that. Postpandemic, environmentalism was being rebranded as a human right to affordable housing—which, in the hands of government, equates to taking from Peter to pay for Paul's affordable housing.

"Can an 'Activist HUD' Make Housing a Human Right?" Bloomberg asked in a January 2021 headline, about then nominee Fudge. Answer: Yes. Using the coronavirus and its halt to evictions as a starting point, Fudge and Biden moved quickly to exploit that perhaps understandable hiatus into a full-blown entitlement mindset. In fact, this was these Democrats' plan from the start—from even before Fudge's confirmation hearing was held, from even before Biden was elected. From Bloomberg:

> One of Biden's and Fudge's proposals could utterly transform the safety net [concept of subsidized housing] and is intended to make housing "a right, not a privilege," as the Biden campaign has described it. "The president has called for expanding . . . Section 8 to be a federal entitlement, meaning that anyone who qualifies for federal rental assistance under the program will receive it.[28]

Great. But who pays? Fudge said she favors a "universal voucher program." But again, who pays? Calling Peter. It's the home buyers who would suffer most by losing their mortgage interest tax deductions. That pays for only about $70 billion annually of the estimated $410 billion price tag for 10 years' worth of Section 8 vouchers for supposedly needy Americans—given the list doesn't grow longer, that is.[29] But after the homeowners, the middle class would suffer next. When rents rise due to the flood of government-paid vouchers, it's those squeezed between the wealthy and the poverty-stricken who would most feel the pinch to the pockets. That's environmentalism, postpandemic style.

The real goal with this housing plan is to reshape what it means to be an American. The real goal with environmentalism, going forward from the coronavirus, is to utterly reshape all of America. Nay, utterly reshape all of the world. Again, from *Time*:

From her perch in the West Wing, [Gina] McCarthy has been charged by Biden with overseeing a dramatic shift in the way the U.S. pursues action on climate change. Instead of turning to a select few environment-focused agencies to make climate policy, McCarthy and her office are working to infuse climate consider-ations into everything the Administrations does.[30]

Everything. McCarthy called for reports on how climate change affects national security, how it affects the financial sector, how it affects public health. Her dream, under Biden, was being realized. "Now, when I think of climate change, I see the face of my future grandson; he is the face of a changing climate for me," she wrote in 2018.[31]

It's everywhere. That's the left's strategy: expand green tentacles as far as possible, then use the expansion for political exploitation. "Now," *Time* wrote, "spurred by alarming science, growing public fury and a deadly pandemic, government officials, corporate bosses and civil-soci-ety leaders are finally waking up to a simple idea whose time has come: climate is everything."[32] It's everything.

The specifics of where this attitude will lead is frightening. Where once the worldview of Americans started with God and then moved to the Constitution—as in God-given rights, backed by a legal doc-ument called the Constitution—it will soon, under this socialist-communist-collectivist environmentalism, become climate change first, all else second. Green will be the new god. With all the partners in this endeavor, from Gates to the WEF to the Democratic Party to the media, and more—American citizens won't even know what hit them. They won't even see where much of the radical environmentalism comes from or whom to blame for this particular tax hike or that particular piece of regulation. They won't know whom to fight. They'll just feel the burden and suffer.

Klaus Schwab, World Economic Forum founder, wrote in mid-2020:

The second component of a Great Reset agenda would ensure that investments advance shared goals, such as equality and sustainability . . . This means, for example, [using funds for] building "green" urban infrastructure and creating incentives for industries to improve their track record on environmental, social and governance [ESG] metrics.[33]

It didn't take long for Biden to respond. To fall in line, really.

In April 2021, Biden released talking points of his climate change plan to the public. In a headline that speaks volumes of the crackdowns on freedoms that could come, the *Telegraph* reported, "How Biden's climate plan could limit you to eat just one burger a MONTH, cost $3.5K a year per person in taxes, force you to spend $55K on an electric car and 'crush' American jobs."[34]

The mainstream media jumped to Biden's defense, claiming Republicans were off their rockers for supposing Biden was going to ban hamburgers. But to achieve Biden's vision, cuts would have to come from somewhere. As the *Telegraph* wrote:

President Joe Biden's ambitious plan to slash greenhouse emissions by 50 to 52 percent over the next decade could prompt sweeping changes that could affect how Americans eat, drive and heat their homes. Biden announced the goal to cut emissions [in half] by 2030, compared with 2005 levels . . . He vowed the plan, which would set the US on a path of a zero emissions economy by no later than 2050, would create jobs and boost economies.[35]

Well, Biden can afford to promise that, can't he? After all, he won't be around in 2050 to see the economic devastation his no-growth climate policies would bring on the nation. Again, from the *Telegraph*:

Americans may have to cut their red meat consumption by a whopping 90 percent and cut their consumption of other animal based foods in half. Gradually making those changes by 2030 could see diet-related greenhouse gas emissions reduced by 50 percent, according to a study by Michigan University's Center for

Sustainable Systems. To do that, it would require Americans to only consume about four pounds of red meat per year, or 0.18 ounces per day. It equates to consuming roughly one average sized burger per month.[36]

Since when does the government get to tell free citizens what to eat and in what amounts?

But we knew this was coming. We knew a Joe Biden White House would bring back the kind of environmental regulations of Obama days, only more so. He started on practically Day One.

In January 2021, just days after taking over the White House, Biden signed an executive order "Tackling the Climate Crisis at Home and Abroad," and establishing the National Climate Task Force to do that tackling. Among the members? The secretaries of Treasury, Defense, Interior, Agriculture, Commerce, Labor, Health and Human Services, Housing and Urban Development, Transportation, Energy, Homeland Security—and more, including the attorney general of the United States. Talk about all-encompassing.[37]

In February 2021, at the first meeting of this National Climate Task Force, "Vice President Harris dropped by . . . [to] underscore her and President Biden's commitment to overseeing an unprecedented approach to tackling climate change . . . making sure that every agency plays a role . . . [She also] discussed the need to focus on those communities that are most vulnerable to climate change," according to a White House summary of the meeting.[38]

In March 2021, at the second meeting of this National Climate Task Force, discussions focused on realizing the "Biden-Harris Administration's whole-of-government approach to tackling the climate crisis, creating good-paying, union jobs, and prioritizing environmental justice," a White House summary of the meeting stated.[39] It continued,

Following th[is] task force meeting, the U.S. Department of Agriculture (USDA) Forest Service announced it will invest more than $218 million to leverage the Land and Water Conservation

Fund (LWCF) to fund projects that will help drive rural economic recovery and job creation, support the voluntary stewardship efforts of private landowners and better conserve America's public lands."[40]

So it begins. Pay to play. Carrot, meet climate change stick.

Just weeks into his administration, Biden's core policy pushes at the White House fell right in line with globalists' hope for their globalist futures—right in line with the Bill Gates message of what's up, what's hot, what's top-dog concern for worldwide policy, postpandemic.

The Barack Obama style of governing was back. Biden, like his Democratic predecessor, didn't bother to wait for Congress, but rather pulled out his pen, signed executive order after executive order, made czar-like appointments to issue czar-like rules, and looked to the global elites for marching orders. "Biden's climate duo of Kerry and McCarthy puts U.S. back in global warming fight," Reuters wrote in April 2021.[41] "Biden prepares sweeping order on climate-related risks," Politico wrote in April, 2021.[42] That story goes on to state: "In a draft executive order obtained by POLITICO, Biden reaches into all corners of the federal government with plans that would touch every sector of American industry, including banking and insurance, oil and gas, housing, agriculture, and federal contracting, purchasing and lending."[43] The order was issued in advance of the two-day climate summit Biden hosted in April.

Everywhere. Everything. The tentacles expand. So, too, the players in this massive move to restructure politics, economies, social and cultural activities, and human interactions and behaviors, all under the big umbrella of environmentalism.

In his order, which was titled "Climate-Related Financial Risk," and billed as a "predecisional draft," ostensibly the building block for the final climate solution, Biden called for:

- Treasury Secretary Janet Yellen, in her capacity as the head of the Financial Stability Oversight Council, a group that formed in 2008 due to the shaky Wall Street market, to determine climate-related risks in the financial sector—an assessment that could impact how banks do business, how loans are issued, how asset management companies choose to invest.[44]

- The Federal Insurance Office to work with state regulatory officials to determine climate-related risks that could lead to "major disruptions"—an assessment that could impact how developers are allowed to develop, how homeowners are allowed to build, at what price insurance is issued to consumers and businesses to cover these risks of climate-tied "major disruptions."[45]

- The Labor Department, the agency in charge of regulating retirement accounts, to rescind rules put in place by the Donald Trump administration, ordering pension fund managers to consider the financial interests of investors over the causes of social justice—an assessment that could lead to the reallocation of roughly $10 trillion of retirees' funds into companies that consider climate change more important than revenues to retirees.[46]

- The Federal Retirement Thrift Investment Board, the agency in charge of administering retirement savings for federal employees, including members of the military services, to look at pulling from all companies that do business in oil, natural gas, and coal, and to stop investing in fossil fuels—an assessment that could lead to a massive shift in the billions and billions of dollars the board oversees, meaning a massive shift in investments in particular companies.[47]

There was more. The Department of Housing and Urban Development was tasked to take climate change into consideration when it went about its loan underwriting business. The Department of Agriculture was tasked to do the same. The National Flood Insurance Program was tasked to do the same.[48]

That doesn't even touch on the contractors who do business with the federal government, the businesses that supply everything from food to military equipment. The impacts of putting climate concerns first, all else second, are massive. More than hirty-three million homeowners in America have loans that are backed by the government—insurance that is overseen by the government.[49] Even more do business with banks that are regulated by the government—with investment companies and financial services agencies and retirement funds that are overseen by the government. Where would be the work-around? Even consumers and citizens alert to the government's climate change agenda would find it difficult, under the Biden plan, under the Gates scenario, under the World Economic Forum vision, to opt out or sidestep. Tentacles.

"Look," Biden said in late January 2021, "this executive order I'm signing today also makes it official that climate change will be the center of [America's] national security and foreign policy." Referencing John Kerry, his special presidential envoy for climate, and an instrumental player in the negotiation of the Paris Climate Agreement, Biden then said, "With him, the world knows how serious I am."[50]

Kerry, just a few weeks later, was off and running. At a virtual Munich Security Conference in February 2021, Kerry cited climate change as "among the most complex security issues we've ever faced." He then said, "What these extreme weather events translate to on the ground should concern every single one of us." And he added: "When we talk about the impacts of climate change, we're talking about security, energy security, economic security, food security, even physical security. And the question now is, pregnantly, what will the world do about it?"[51]

At a meeting before the permanent representatives of the UN Security Council in March 2021, Biden, with Kerry by his side, committed America to joining the Group of Friends on Climate and Society, an organization started by the global body in 2018, to analyze national security policy for its impacts on climate change.[52] So much for America First. So much for America's defense.

It wasn't long before all the climate talk turned to actual walk. It wasn't long before Team Biden started throwing cash at what they had successfully labeled the climate crisis. From Press Trust of India, March 18:

> The United States Agency for International Development (USAID) and the US International Development Finance Corporation (DFC) have announced a USD 41 million-loan guarantee program to finance investment in renewable energy solutions by Indian SMEs [small and medium-sized enterprises] . . . including rooftop solar installations.[53]

Kerry, on the road to India and Bangladesh from April 5 to 9, highlighted several more specifics of this cash infusion. A little investigation shows just how tight and cozy the environmental partnerships go—using U.S. tax dollars from U.S. taxpayers, of course. From USAID's press office:

> USAID partners [since March 18] have already lined up projects worth $4 million for financing under the guarantee, including 50 solar-powered micro-cold chains in villages, and solar plus storage solutions to power 350 remote rural bank branches. USAID and the DFC are partnering with U.S.-based Encourage Capital and two Indian non-banking financial companies, cKers Finance and women-owned Electronica Finance Limited, on this this important initiative.[54]

USAID is funded by Congress—meaning, U.S. taxpayers. The DFC was established as a government agency in 2019, through the Better Utilization of Investments Leading to Development Act to partner with the private sector and help build up poorer nations. In an interesting shoulder shrug to the question "Are DFC services taxpayer funded?"—the DFC, on its website, states this: "DFC is committed to generating returns for the American taxpayer through its investments in development."[55] Well, isn't that nice. That's bureaucratic-speak for taking tax dollars from private citizens for seed money for overseas' development and hoping—that is, being committed to the hope—that they result in investments that yield return. And if the investment goes bust? Hmm. Oh well. The American taxpayer is probably none the wiser. So goes the bloat of government. The main point is this: Yes, USAID and the DFC are both funded by tax dollars.

The $41 million for solar rooftops and renewable energy development in India may have been billed as a loan, but (1) U.S. taxpayers didn't exactly agree to this loan—this was a Team Biden–announced deal and (2) U.S. taxpayers probably wouldn't have agreed to this loan if they knew all the particulars of the players involved in the loan.

Look at the $4 million in projects that were already in the works just a few weeks after the $41 million program was announced. Encourage Capital calls itself "a new kind of investment firm that seeks to change the way investment capital is used to solve critical environmental and social problems."[56] The Indian cKers Finance is a company that began in 2017 to grow clean energy resources, and that has since become a major player in the issuance of sustainable energy bonds—a means by which investors can fund risky environmental projects in their early stages of development, while avoiding double taxation issues inherent to India.[57] Electronica Finance Limited, meanwhile, is billed as "women-owned" by USAID, but the company's website, rather, lists the board of directors' as five males, S. R. Pophale, chairman emeritus; Milind Limaye and Mohan Tanksale, both independent directors; Sujit Natekar, additional director, nonexecutive; Ameya Bijoor, nominee director; and one female, Shilpa Pophale, managing director.[58] The ten-person leadership team is all male, save for the one female, Ashwini Shrivram, head of human resources and corporate social responsibility.[59] So why Electronica Finance Limited, if not "women-owned?"

In 2019, EFL began issuing green masala bonds in Indian NBFC space.[60] NBFC stands for nonbank financial companies, and they operate outside the normal regulatory boundaries.[61] They're not overseen by federal or state regulators, in other words. They're high risk, in other words. As the Corporate Finance Institute wrote of NBFCs:

> Many would argue that NBFCs are essential services that provide other services that are not met by traditional banks and are able to specialize in the services and perform better. Such institutions

help meet the demand for credit required by individuals and businesses that banks are not able to provide. *However, the fact that NBFCs are not regulated as heavily as banks poses an additional risk. Such a risk was highlighted during the 2008 Global Financial Crisis when the lending practices of the companies went unchecked and resulted in a disastrous outcome.*[62] (Italics added for emphasis.)

Also known as the housing bubble, this was the year all the heavy betting that banks did on real estate—and on unqualified buyers—came to a screaming halt. Financial institutions failed; mortgage lenders crashed; evictions, defaults, and bankruptcies soared; and then came the bailouts, stimulus, and rescues, also known as redistribution of tax dollars. This is where Biden sent U.S. dollars—into a quagmire where accountability, transparency, and security of investment are essentially nonexistent.

As for green masala bonds—read on, an explanation from ClearTax:

Masala bonds were introduced in India in 2014 by International Finance Corporation (IFC). The IFC issued the first masala bonds in India to fund infrastructure projects. Indian entities or companies issue masala bonds outside India to raise money. This issue of these bonds is in Indian currency [rupee] rather than local currency. Thus, if the rupee rate falls, the investor will bear the loss. . . . It benefits the borrower as there is no currency risk. It saves the borrower from currency fluctuations. Borrowers need not worry about rupee depreciation as the issuance of these bonds is in Indian currency rather than foreign currency.[63]

What a great deal for EFL. But what a risky deal for U.S. taxpayers funding any USAID and DFC loans to EFL, through the largely unregulated NBFC space.

But here's the icing on the cake shared by these environmental insiders: On its website, under the announcement of its entry into the green masala bonds market, EFL stated: "2019: Issuer of First Green Masala

Bonds in Indian NBFC Space; Equity Partnership with Encourage Capital."[64]

That's the same Encourage Capital that just benefited from a USAID and DFC promise of $4 million for cold chains and solar power. Are you beginning to see the tight circles of environmental partnerships? One hand washes the other, as they say. Just an interesting aside, cold chains are systems by which temperature-sensitive vaccines are transported to far parts of the world.[65] One coronavirus hand washes the other climate change other. Or is it more like killing two birds with one stone?

Either way, it all starts with U.S. tax dollars. It all starts, develops and finishes using Americans' hard-earned monies. That India-Bangladesh deal was just one in a long, long list of climate change projects the Biden administration pushed. It's just one small example of how convoluted the process of funding, the process of partnering becomes—and how difficult it is to check that tax dollars taken from hard-working Americans for the oft-dubious cause of climate change are being put to good and proper use.

Far too frequently, American citizens are paying for environmental developments in far corners of the world in ways they probably aren't even aware. The ones who truly benefit, though, aren't the taxpayers, so much as the nongovernmental organizations and private companies who play by the globalist visionaries' radical environmental rules—the same NGOs and private companies who, in turn, funnel money into their pet politicians' pockets, so as to guarantee these folks stay in political power, so as to guarantee the cycle of lucrative environmentalism continues, so as to guarantee their pots of taxpayer gold never go empty. The one clear question to ask in all this shifting of resources is this: Why does clean energy need so much taxpayer money to develop?

The answer the government will refuse to acknowledge is similarly clear: because it isn't cost-efficient, and frequently fails. If alternative energy worked in a manner that was reliable and affordable to consumers, the private sector would be all over it. That the sector needs so much taxpayer-infused assistance is the telling sign that all this money for clean energy, all this political talk for green energy, all this government grab at clean and green resource development is not genuinely about keeping the planet free of pollution, but about spreading wealth, redistributing wealth, concentrating wealth and resources into the hands of a few who can then control human actions and interactions and reshape society to their will.

From USAID's press office once again:

Special Presidential Envoy Kerry also highlighted [during this April trip to India and Bangledesh] that USAID will award up to $9.2 million to support the Coalition for Disaster Resilient Infrastructure (CDRI), hosted by the government of India. This initiative will help foster disaster and climate resilient infrastructure, pending the availability of funds. USAID will support the CDRI to develop and share innovations, policy recommendations, and best practices in developing disaster and climate resilient infrastructure worldwide in order to help countries incorporate best practices into their infrastructure planning and foster partnerships between governments and the private sector to expand disaster and climate resilient infrastructure.[66]

Infrastructure, infrastructure, infrastructure. Marcia, Marcia, Marcia.

CDRI, made up of national governments, UN agencies, banks and financiers, and private sector organizations, is yet another one of those groups that brings together partners in the global environmentalism agenda, and that serves as a conduit for funding and for future collaborations.[67] This one, CDRI, focuses on building "infrastructure" that's in line with the sustainable development goals of the United Nations.[68] There are seventeen SDGs, and they include everything from ending poverty and hunger, to providing work and economic opportunity, to ensuring peace and justice for all, all over the world, everywhere and including everyone.[69] They sound like worthy goals, but the devil's in the details. Whereas America might see these same goals advanced through capitalism and the Constitution, the United Nations, rather, wants to use tax dollars and then assume the position of power to redistribute those dollars at its bureaucratic whim. The socialists and communists in the United Nations want to control the money flow and pick who gets, who must give, and who, in the end, gets to flourish and grow. Where would America stand on that scale? Here's a hint: it's ain't in the line for getting.

The latest scheme is to align infrastructure with environmentalism and call it a global health and security crisis. Once again, Biden's right on board. "The idea of infrastructure has always evolved to meet the aspirations of the American people and their needs," Biden said in April 2021, pushing back against criticisms of his $2 trillion-plus American Jobs Plan, billed as an infrastructure package. "To automatically say that the only thing that's infrastructure is a highway, a bridge or whatever, that's just not rational. It really isn't."[70] Infrastructure, he argued, ought to instead be viewed "through its effect on the lives of working people in America."[71]

To come up with the $2 trillion, Biden wanted a 28 percent tax to corporations, a plan that was guaranteed to either hike prices on products so consumers would have to pay more, or send businesses fleeing to overseas' spots, as they did during the high-tax times of Obama's administration—resulting in higher costs on consumers for import fees. But the bigger issue was the conflating of environmentalism with road projects; the melding of bridge-building with climate change; the intermingling of jobs with the environment, with highway development as one seamless policy.

That's the way of leftists. They convolute, conflate, and confuse so as to ram through their agendas in hidden ways. "Biden believes . . . our environment and our economy are completely and totally connected," his presidential campaign pages put forth.[72] "This is essentially a jobs bill," White House press secretary Jen Psaki said, about the American Jobs Plan, which was nonetheless called Biden's infrastructure plan. "Yes, there is a lot in here that is infrastructure. Our workers, our workforce is part of the backbone and infrastructure of America's economy and communities."[73]

The White House, meanwhile, put out a statement about the Biden infrastructure plan that read like this:

Like great projects of the past, the president's plan will unify and mobilize the country to meet the great challenges of our time: the climate crisis and the ambitions of an autocratic China. It will invest in Americans and deliver the jobs and opportunities they deserve. But unlike past major investments, the plan prioritizes addressing long-standing and persistent racial injustice. This plan targets 40 percent of the benefits of climate and clean infrastructure investments to disadvantaged communities. And the plan invests in rural communities and communities impacted by the market-based transition to clean energy.[74]

What a total mish-mash of socialist redistribution opportunities. Expanding the classical understanding of infrastructure to incorporate environmentalism, the economy, and racial justice issues is massively advantageous for collectivists and globalists because it allows for the easy introduction of policies that, in a limited government and constitutional system, just wouldn't meet the smell test.

Among Biden's "infrastructure" plan for America, were these goals:[75]

- To fix highways, rebuild bridges, update public transit.
- To provide clean water to all Americans.
- To deliver high-speed Internet to all Americans.
- To build affordable housing that's updated with energy efficiency products.
- To "retrofit more than two million homes and commercial buildings" and fix up schools, child care centers, and federal facilities.
- To increase wages for homecare workers.
- To hire more caregivers to work in homes.
- To promote "Made in America" products—in part, by using tax codes to discourage corporations from moving offshore—and at the same time, to strengthen unions and address "systemic

discrimination" by opening doors to high-paying jobs for select segments of the population.

- To provide "better jobs and better transportation options to underserved communities," with roads, bridges, transit employment opportunities that "advance racial equity."
- To modernize roads in such a way to reduce crashes, "improve air quality, limit greenhouse gas emissions," "reduce congestion, "advance racial equity," and provide jobs and better transportation for "underserved communities," all for an infusion of about $115 billion.
- To "create good jobs electrifying vehicles."
- To "reconnect neighborhoods cut off by historic investments and ensure new projects increase opportunity, advance racial equity and environmental justice and promote affordable access," all for about $20 billion.
- To protect lands, forests, wetlands, watersheds, as well as "areas most vulnerable to flooding and other climate-change-related weather events," where "people of color and low-income people are more likely to live," all for about $50 billion.
- To replace water pipes, clean up abandoned mines, plug natural gas and oil wells, redevelop distressed properties—and use these properties to develop decarbonized hydrogen projects, i.e., green hydrogen.
- To establish a Civilian Climate Corps, and staff it with next-generation environmental stewards—for about $10 billion.
- To federalize zoning, which has always been the purview of local governments—but to do it in a way that doesn't call it that.
- To disburse tax dollars for business owners based on skin color—but to do it in a way that doesn't call attention to that.
- To force companies that rely on fossil fuels to pay, pay, pay—but to do it in a way that shows the government as the protector of humanity.

How so? According to Biden, according to Biden's American Jobs Plan, it's simple. It's called creative taxation. "The current tax code includes billions of dollars in subsidies, loopholes and special foreign tax credits for the fossil fuel industry," Biden's American Jobs Plan stated. "As part of the president's commitment to put the country on a path to net-zero emissions by 2050, his tax reform proposal will eliminate all these special preferences."[76] Zero emissions. There's that magic number once again.

But this is the world Democrats, socialists, globalists, collectivists envision for America:

- Live in an apartment, not a single-family home with land. From *USA Today*: "Eliminating exclusionary zoning as a way to build more climate-resilient multifamily housing can help address both the quality of life and the utility costs of low-income residents, said Richard Lamondin, CEO of Ecosystems, an energy conservation company. . . . 'It's a no-brainer to continue to push this.'"[77]
- Eat vegetables, not meat. From Bill Gates, on his blog: "[E]ating a meat substitute (or simply not eating meat) just once or twice a week will cut down on the emissions you're responsible for. The same goes for dairy products."[78]
- Eat insects. From *Time* magazine: "There is a sustainable alternative to going meat-free, the FAO [UN Food and Agriculture Organization] says: edible insects. Grasshoppers, crickets and mealworms are rich in protein, and contain significantly higher sources of minerals such as iron, zinc, copper and magnesium than beef. Yet pound for pound they require less land, water and feed than traditional livestock. Insect farming and processing produces significantly lower greenhouse gas emissions. Not only do insects produce less waste, their excrement, called frass, is an excellent fertilizer and soil amender."[19]

And it's all fast-forwarding furiously, thanks to the coronavirus.

- "The pandemic has created the opportunity for a 'great reset' of Africa's economies," the Brookings Institution wrote.[80]
- "Many of the root causes of climate change also increase the risk of pandemics," Harvard's School of Public Health wrote.[81]
- "The pandemic represents an unusual, short term opportunity to reflect, rethink and reboot our world," said Klaus Schwab, president of the World Economic Forum.[82]

It's coming. It's here. It's now. It's the coronavirus, climate change, social justice, infrastructure, affordable housing, job creation all rolled into one. It's whatever the Left deems is necessary to upset the natural order of capitalism, of limited government, of individualism, of liberties and freedoms, of the Constitution, of American exceptionalism, of sovereignty and self-rule. Moreover, it's not even necessarily a "short term opportunity" for Great Reset change, as Schwab said.

In Michigan, under Governor Gretchen Whitmer, it's this—from *Reason*:

> State bureaucrats are moving to impose permanent regulations that would mandate the following and more on all Michigan businesses: mask wearing whenever employees are within six feet of someone else, daily health screenings, extensive record keeping, and keeping a "COVID-19 safety coordinator" on-site. Retail stores, personal care services, and other businesses open to the public would have to become the mask police: They would be required to make all customers wear masks, vaccinated or not.[83]

Coronavirus is the gift to tyrants that keeps on giving. So long as they need it, they'll use it. But when the public gets tired, there's always climate change—or whatever the globalists and collectivists want to call it at that moment for political expediency's sake.

CHAPTER NINE

Lessons on Deception from George Orwell's *Animal Farm*

Do not be conformed to this world, but be transformed by the renewal of your mind, that by testing you may discern what is the will of God, what is good and acceptable and perfect.

Romans 12:2 (RSV)

Deception is a powerful political aphrodisiac.

It gives the deceiver a means of control while inflicting on the deceived a state of victimhood that can even become complicit over time—as when Democrats deceive Americans into believing they must rely on government to meet their every needs. Slowly, slowly, the lines of self-reliance move, the boundaries of limited governance shift, the expectations of what government should do versus what individuals should do morph, cloud, and convolute until one day, America finds herself at the steps of socialism, knocking at the door of communism, opening wide the gates to collectivism. This is what has happened in this country. This is where America now sits. This is what America must fight—or forever lose what it means to be an American.

Do you see what's happening? Do you see the battlefield? Face masking children is not scientific. Closing churches by government order, even for a pandemic, is not constitutional. Shutting down schools to keep students and teachers "safe" is not reasonable. Ordering businesses closed and forcing American citizens on the public dime is not freedom—particularly when government chooses which businesses can operate versus which must shut doors. A government of, by, and for the people, remember.

Doing all this more than a year after a pandemic is declared, more than a year after so-called scientists, so-called medical experts, and so-called health professionals said the goal was simply flattening a curve, is outrageous. It's ridiculous. It's offensive to individual intellect. It's an offense to liberty.

And it only underscores something else going on here. The pandemic is not about the pandemic. The pandemic is about shifting societies, changing the shape of government, and upsetting economies to usher in a single system that's been known by many names—the New World Order, the One World Order, the Great Reset—but which always leads down one road to one dead end: oppression of the masses to benefit the few. You're not supposed to notice. And that is the utter evil of it all.

In George Orwell's 1945 *Animal Farm,* a boar named Old Major tells his fellow barnyard friends of a dream he had in which they all rise up and rebel against their tyrannical human owners, then live forever after in freedom. Old Major dies, but his dream continues to live. Eventually, two other pigs, Snowball and Napoleon, seize an opportune moment—when the oft-drunken Mr. Jones and his farmhands fail to feed the animals—and lead an uprising. The animals successfully drive off Jones and his wife from the property and establish a new society where all animals are supposedly equal, united in spirit and flesh against a common enemy—the humans. They codify this egalitarianism with seven principles of "Animalism" painted for all to see on the side of the barn. The principles—like the Constitution of the United States, before politicians interpret it—are simple, straightforward, clear enough for even the least intelligent to understand:

- Whatever goes upon two legs is an enemy.
- Whatever goes upon four legs, or has wings, is a friend.
- No animal shall wear clothes.
- No animal shall sleep in a bed.
- No animal shall drink alcohol.
- No animal shall kill any other animal.
- All animals are equal.[1]

Easily understood, yes? About as easily understood as "We hold these truths to be self-evident, that all men are created equal, that they are endowed by their Creator with certain unalienable rights . . ." About as easily understood as "Congress shall make no law respecting the establishment of religion, or prohibiting the free exercise thereof; or abridging the freedom of speech, or of the press; or the right of the people peaceably to assembly, and to petition the government for a redress of grievances." Yet today's America must fight constantly for government to recognize that individual rights in this country are bestowed from above, from God, and not granted by government, at whim, at will. And today's Americans must fight constantly to remind bureaucrats the First Amendment, the Second Amendment, any of the Bill of Rights' amendments are not a starting points for debate and barter, but rather the ground rules for government's treatment of citizens. More to truth—the ground rules for government's deferential respect of citizens.

"No amendment, no amendment to the Constitution is absolute," said President Joe Biden in April 2021, as precursor to his rollout of executive orders on gun control.[2] "Nothing, nothing I am about to recommend in any way impinges on the Second Amendment," he said.[3] Does saying something twice make it so? The fact that Biden pretended expertise of the Constitution and Second Amendment while paving a path toward unilateral crackdown on citizen liberties via a power that's nowhere mentioned in the Constitution, and that has become a president's dictatorial step-around of congressional authority—that is, executive orders—is laugh-out-loud absurd.

Let the facts speak for themselves, though. It's not incumbent on American citizens to explain to government why we ought to keep our rights. It's incumbent on the government to explain to American citizens why we ought to cede certain aspects of our rights and for how long. Government needs the permission of the citizens to take their rights; citizens don't need the permission of government to have rights or to exercise rights.

Thomas Jefferson, in a June 1823 letter to William Johnson, one of three U.S. Supreme Court justices he seated while president, wrote, in part, "on every question of construction, carry ourselves back to the time when the [C]onstitution was adopted, recollect the spirit manifested in the debates, & instead of trying what meaning may be squeezed out of the text, or invented against it, conform to the probable one in which it was past [sic]."[4]

That's wisdom. That's the path toward discernment. That's a key that would easily show much of today's bills, pieces of legislation, policies, agendas, orders and laws as unconstitutional at root. But when the goal post is moved even a little, it becomes all the easier to move it more, even if just a little. Soon enough, inches turn to feet; feet turn to miles. What once was commonly accepted practice and belief becomes radical, right before our eyes.

After Old Major died, and the rebellion against Mr. Jones proved successful, a sort of power play between Snowball and Napoleon developed. Snowball wanted, as a priority, a windmill to be built and drew up plans for its construction. Napoleon, however, had different ideas. He joined forces with another pig, the smooth-talking Squealer, and stirred up strife while positioning the pigs, and himself, as the best able to lead. Napoleon also took away nine puppies born to the barnyard's Jesse and Bluebell, and stowed them far from all the other animals, explaining that he was going to educate them personally. Over time, all the other animals on the farm forgot about these puppies. They emerged as Napoleon's private police force and helped drive Snowball from the farm. Napoleon, aided by his dogs, was then left to lead, and he created a society where the pigs were held as a separate class, above reproach and intellectually superior.

It was not long before the principles of Animalism were reworded, in the middle of the night, under cloak of darkness, to reflect adherence to the pigs' changing behaviors. The pigs began sleeping in the house. The principle "No animal shall sleep in a bed" suddenly had two words added: "with sheets." When some of the animals expressed outrage over Snowball's banishment, Napoleon's security dogs slaughtered them publicly—and the principle "No animal shall kill any other animal" suddenly saw two more words: "without cause." When Squealer and the other pigs got drunk and the animals noticed their odd behavior, the principle "No animal shall drink alcohol" was suddenly seen as "No animal shall drink alcohol to excess." The pigs began wearing clothing. The pigs began doing business with other humans. The pigs began walking on their hind legs. The principles, on cue, changed.[5] From the notion that two legs were bad, four legs good, to: "Four legs good, two legs better."[6] From the notion that all animals were equal, to: "All animals are equal—but some are more equal than others."[7]

The story ends with the animals gazing through a farmhouse window at the pigs, who are seated and playing cards with humans. As Napoleon argues with a farmer, the animals look from one to the other, from the other back to one, and cannot tell the difference. The pigs are the humans are the pigs are the humans.

So, too, Democrats, progressives, socialists, communists, Marxists, and collectivists—and sadly, even some Republicans. Far too often in America, principles are pushed to the side for political purposes. The Constitution means what the Left wants it to mean. The idea of limited government gives way to the concept of general welfare, which is then stretched far beyond what the Founding Fathers ever intended to the point, where citizens become dominated and ruled, rather than respected and heeded.

And just like in *Animal Farm*, where the changes came secretively, today's pandemic-induced unconstitutional acts are not supposed to be noticed as moving into any state of permanence. Yet they are. The left's endgame of near-total clamping of civil liberties and constitutional rights is being steadily pursued.

"Virginia Adopts a Permanent COVID-19 Standard," *EHS Daily Advisor* wrote in February 2021.[8] The story went on to report:

> Virginia adopted the nation's first permanent standard for workplace exposures to the SARS-CoV-2 virus and COVID-19. The regulation includes requirements for written preparedness and response plans, as well as cleaning and sanitation, personal protective equipment (PPE), social distancing, training and record-keeping, and ventilation.[9]

Among the new rules forced onto businesses were ones requiring they "eliminate the need for employees to share work vehicles" and instead arrange transportation for them that allows for social distancing, and ones requiring they "provide employees with respiratory protection, such as an N95 filtering facepiece respirator" in instances where separate transportation is not possible. Employers were also tasked with providing the proper training to employees to make sure they knew how to wear the personal protective gear, and in certain cases, in certain businesses, with outfitting their facilities with new ventilation and filtration systems.[10] Guess who bears the costs for these regulations? The business owner, of course—and in turn, the customer.

Then it was Oregon's time. "Oregon Proposes Permanent COVID-19 Infectious Disease Standard," *EHS Daily Advisor* wrote, again in February 2021.[11] The sought-after regulations were essentially the same as what went forth in Virginia. So weren't the reasons. "The public health emergency triggered by COVID-19 remains a significant concern in Oregon—as we know, we have not yet defeated this disease and we clearly will not have done so by the time the temporary rule expires," said Michael Wood, Oregon's Occupational Safety and Health Administration (OSHA) administrator, in an early February 2021 statement. "As a result, it is critically important that we carry forward measures that we know are effective at combating the spread of this disease and reducing risks in the workplace."[12]

That sounds a little pie-in-the-sky—not to mention utterly unscientific. Last check, "defeated this disease" hadn't made it to the "Standards That Must Be Met to Return to Normalcy" list. And no wonder; it's a phrase that's essentially meaningless. It's a phrase aimed only at giving tyrannical politicians the dire sounding gongs they need to clang to keep clampdowns in place for a little while longer, just a little bit longer, just until the next fabricated dire sounding gong can be fashioned and formed and sent 'round the camp for tyrannical politician approval.

But this is the way of the deceivers. As Napoleon and his pigs changed the rules to accommodate their own evil ambitions, so the leftists do whenever they feel their grasp on power is slipping. They come up with a new warning, a new danger, a new crisis, complete with a new promise, a new hope, a new shiny object that dangles enticingly. From flattening the curve to defeating the virus—and lots of lies in between. "CDC 'looking' into whether masks are necessary outside," the *New York Post* wrote, April 22, 2021.[13] The justification? At the time, there were about 57,000 case counts of COVID-19 and about 700 deaths. Out of a nation of 330 million, mind you. With three vaccines available, mind you.

Has America gone crazy? From "wear one if you can't social distance" to "wear one while running track"—true story. From Michigan Governor Gretchen Whitmer in September 2020, this order, as described in the *Lansing State Journal*:

"Athletes participating in an organized sport, while on the field of play, are not subject to the social distancing requirements of this order found in sections 2(a) and 6(a)(1), but instead must maintain six feet of distance from one another to the extent compatible with that organized sport, and wear a facial covering except when swimming." Whitmer had thrown in a sizable caveat into executive order 2020-176: High school athletes, football players and cross country runners alike, would have to wear masks during competition. It stirred up a new side in the debate over masks, this time a more reasonable reaction: Is it safe for a teenager to compete in a football or soccer game or to run three miles while having their mouth and nose covered by a mask?[14]

That's a decent question. But it's not the main question. The main question is: Why? Asking if it's "safe" for high schoolers to wear masks while running track, batting tennis balls, or tackling with helmet on the football field presupposes the notion that it's sane and sensible for it to even be considered that kids wear masks during outdoor athletic competitions. It's not. Not by even the slightest of common sense considerations is it sane to think that in a world where viruses are as commonplace as the stars in the sky, that for some reason, that this particular virus, this particular strain of coronavirus requires humans to slap coverings over their faces while outdoors, while running around, while even running around outdoors in situations where they're distant from others—despite never having done this for viruses with similar or greater fatality counts, despite never having done this for viruses that affect youth to an even greater degree. Common sense alone shows the ridiculousness of this notion.

But this isn't about common sense. It isn't about safety and security of citizens, of youth. It's about control. It's about government's exertion of power.

A presupposition is just another way of moving the goalpost of norms—of leftists taking an issue and moving past all dissenting views by pretending they're already settled. It's a deception. It's the Left's way of shutting down talk before talk actually starts. The Left loves to do this with the "settled science" of climate change—which is actually far from settled.

They're doing the same with the coronavirus, with face masks, to keep free citizens in bondage, and to keep up the atmosphere of fear they need to bring about their ultimate globalist vision of total top-down governance.

The trick is to discern their trickery and force them back to the actual battlefield, to engage in the actual battle. The battle in America over the coronavirus is whether the crackdowns on liberty the Democrats are enforcing are (1) justified by science and (2) necessary for the health and safety of the citizens. Those are the standard considerations; those are the two questions, both in the here and now and going forward, that ought to be asked, and more important, answered.

In Animalism-speak, we've already gone from the rule of No Mask Is Fine, One Mask Is Good, to another rule: One Mask Is a Must, Two Masks Are Better. Now we're moving to an even newer rule about masks, kids, and outdoor sports? Whitmer, with her September 2020 executive order, was ahead of the tyranny game on that point. But the CDC, come April 2021, was catching that same crackdown fever. From the *New York Post*, in a story dated April 22, 2021:

> The Centers for Disease Control and Prevention is looking into whether people should continue to wear masks outdoors to prevent the spread of COVID-19, the agency's boss said . . . "This is a question that we're looking at," CDC director Dr. Rochelle Walensky said on the "Today" show when asked whether people still need to mask up outside when they're not close to others. Walensky noted that the US is still grappling with high numbers of new COVID-19 cases. "One of the things I think that's really important to understand is while there's wonderful news and we're getting more and more people vaccinated every single day, we still had 57,000 cases of COVID yesterday, we still had 733 deaths," she said. "And so now we are really trying to scale up vaccination, we have this complex message that we still have hot spots in this country. . . . "We will be looking at the outdoor masking question, but it's also in the context of the fact that we still have people who are dying of COVID," she said.[15]

Goalpost, meet crane.

Walensky's medical opinion only matters as much as the American people want it to matter. She's not an elected representative. She's not the gate guard of the Constitution. That role rests with the people—the people who pay her salary and who elect politicians, who are tasked with the job of keeping America a free country, based on a concept of individualism, and on a core principle of rights coming from God. What are 57,000 "cases of COVID" in a nation of 330 million? Remember, case counts aren't even really a thing, except that the oppressors of liberty want to make it a thing. After all, if 57,000 individuals come down with COVID, but zero die, zero go to the hospital, zero even feel sick, then what's the big deal about the virus, right? It's only the percentage of the whole who die, or percentage of the whole who are hospitalized, that matter. Only those who seek to destroy individual liberties and use the coronavirus for political agendas harp on case counts absent context. And seriously—733 deaths? For that, we would give up liberties?

No animal shall drink alcohol—to excess. No return to normalcy until death count curves are flattened—to zero. Change a mindset—and change a policy. Change the mindsets of an entire nation of people—and change the whole constructs and foundations of government. America is in twelfth-hour danger of losing all the nation stands for: all that makes us tick, all that keeps us exceptional. The deceptions are coming on strong.

Among the presuppositions the Democrats, the progressives and socialists, the globalists have been pushing:

- American citizens aren't equipped to make their own medical decisions.
- American citizens must be protected by the government.
- Americans who don't wear face masks are putting others in danger.
- Americans who refuse the COVID-19 vaccine are jeopardizing others' lives.
- Sometimes it's OK to exercise First Amendment speech and assembly rights in violent manners when the object of the protests uses rhetoric that's deemed by the protesters to be racist, hateful, or offensive.
- Scientists have no political biases and should never be questioned.
- Science is ever-changing, and citizens should recognize and accept that fluidity and simply obey scientific-based recommendations, even when guidance conflicts.

- Vaccines issued under emergency use authorization are 100 percent safe and effective, despite the definition of "emergency use authorization."
- Bill Gates and Anthony Fauci are experts, and they know best when it comes to dealing with pandemics.
- Teachers face higher-than-average coronavirus-catching risks than any other grouping of workers in the nation and must be accommodated at all costs.
- Face masks are the single most important protection against the coronavirus—better than social distancing, better than handwashing, better than vaccinations, better even than natural, God-given immunity.
- Some stores, restaurants, and businesses can stay open; some stores, restaurants, and businesses must stay closed; and only government officials can determine the safety of allowing some stores, restaurants, and businesses to stay open while others must close.
- Executive orders carry the weight of law.
- Contact tracing, especially when tied to technology, keeps you safe. Contact tracing, especially when tied to technology, keeps others safe.
- Private businesses have the right to control individuals' health decisions.
- Government has the right to control individuals' health decisions.
- A church is the same as a concert venue; as such, government can restrict attendance at churches in the same manner government can restrict attendance at concerts.

Those are the coronavirus-based deceptions. A few. They're the more prominent lingering ones; the mindset shifts that have taken this nation by storm, leading to government overreaches that are rapidly becoming permanent—and leading to even more government overreaches that threaten, similarly, to become permanent.

Hear that bell? Liberty is in peril.

If it's accepted that government has the right to close businesses based on fears of a pandemic, then it's all the more acceptable for government to keep these businesses closed, based on fears of a resurging pandemic, or a new pandemic—and it's then accepted that government must somehow provide financially for these out-of-work employees and employers.

"2021 Will Be the Year of Guaranteed Income Experiments," Bloomberg reported in January 2021.[16] The story went on to report that dozens of cities had already either announced intents or were considering intents to distribute direct-cash payments to citizens touched by the coronavirus. Bloomberg continued:

> Recent stimulus payments from the federal government have helped some Americans see the benefit of direct disbursements and may have chipped away at public resistance: A poll commissioned by the Economic Security Project found that 76% of respondents supported "regular payments that continue until the economic crisis is over," and a Gallup poll found widespread support for additional stimulus. Proponents hope these local efforts will normalize and popularize guaranteed income in the U.S. for potential future federal action.[17]

Redistribution of wealth. Free money; no work. Stay at home; the government will take care of you. What a recipe for societal disaster.

If it's accepted that only government can determine when it's safe to return to normalcy from the pandemic, then it's accepted that government can see all the threats that feed into the continuation, and even, expansion of the pandemic—and it's then all the more easily accepted that government can move to address other so-called health-based threats to society as part and parcel of addressing the pandemic, as part and parcel of emerging as a stronger society from the pandemic.

"Half of those surveyed are unaware of the link between climate change and diseases like COVID-19," the World Economic Forum wrote in January 2021.[18] The piece went on to argue that educating the public on this correlation could save lives. It then went on to state:

> WHO has stated there is no evidence of a direct link between climate change and the emergence or transmission of COVID-19. However, it adds that almost all recent pandemics originated in wildlife and points to evidence that disease emergence could be partly driven by human activity. What is more certain, WHO says, is that climate change can indirectly affect responses to the pandemic, by undermining the environmental determinants of health and [by] placing extra stress on health systems. Measures such as improved surveillance of infectious diseases in wildlife and humans, and greater protection of the natural environment, could help reduce the risk of future outbreaks.[19]

In layman's language: WHO acknowledges the link between pandemics and climate change issues is weak. Regardless, WHO also says that since some say that human activities are to blame for the emergence of some diseases, then it's best to control some human behaviors and implement environmental policies that might, perhaps, perchance, "reduce" the risk of another pandemic popping. How come bureaucrats always fall on the side of regulating and restricting?

Get the people used to government stepping in where government doesn't belong, so as to make it easier for government to step in more places government doesn't belong.

"Why Addressing Gun Violence as a Health Crisis Is Crucial for Change," Healthline wrote in January 2021.[20] The writer went on to opine:

Understandably, the COVID-19 pandemic captured most headlines for why the past year was particularly deadly—more than 300,000 deaths in the United States occurred as a result. While the pandemic took a disproportionate toll on American life, there was another devastating, enduring public health crisis that only got worse in 2020: gun violence.[21]

It's not as if the idea of gun violence as a public health threat hadn't been brought, by leftists, to the national stage in past years. The American Public Health Association, for instance, has called for a "public health approach" on Second Amendment issues for years.[22] But it's the timing that matters. What won't sell on peaceful Sunday could easily sell on bloody Monday. Hillary Clinton was mercilessly mocked for Hillarycare; Barack Obama was patted on the back for Obamacare. The difference? Timing.

Timing and the swaying of public opinion, in part, due to crafty messaging. "Gun violence in this country is an epidemic," President Joe Biden said, in White House Rose Garden remarks on April 8, 2021.[23] "This is an epidemic, for God's sake, and it has to stop," Biden said, during this same press event.[24]

First the pandemic. Then climate change. Then guns. Shut the people in their homes, clamp freedoms and redistribute resources based on broadly defined environmental policies, and then take away the guns. What a recipe for societal upheaval.

If it's accepted that only government can solve the problems of the world, and the bigger the problem, the bigger the government must be to solve that problem, then it's accepted that individuals must concede their individual freedoms for the greater good—and it's then all the more easily accepted that America must cede cherished liberties and stifle individualism, and ultimately, change foundational systems to flourish and thrive in modern times.

"Pandemics show us what government is for," wrote Susan Erikson, in the journal *Nature* in April 2020.[25] Her argument? As *Nature* summarized her commentary: "Too much dependence on the private sector weakened pandemic response, argues Susan Erikson."[26] Moreover, Erikson opined that governments that trim their workforce too much do so at the detriment of the taxpayer, who then pays a higher cost for the same services provided by the private sector. Postpandemic, Erikson said, it's time to start giving government its due respect—in the role of top priority, over that even of the private sector. Erikson continued:

> When the COVID-19 pandemic emergency ends, there needs to be a worldwide reckoning with what governments are for. Governments cut to the bone cannot respond easily or quickly. Pandemics are no longer unexpected events and those who claim otherwise are using old stochastic models and ignoring the world around us. It's not just that population pressures—for food, housing and income—will continue to push humans into wildlife habitat that will set off other unknown animal-human disease chains. Pandemics are also a result of economic growth-at-any-cost ideologies, those that call for ploughing down rainforests, systematically indenturing huge swathes of frontline healthcare workers and fighting the regulation of health sector profit-mongering. Governments cannot exist solely as payers-of-last-resort. They too need to be valued and nurtured back to health, so that they can sustain us when our needs hit pandemic proportions.[27]

The Great Reset? Capitalism that's more like communism in nature?

"Americans Want the Federal Government to Help People in Need," according to a March 2021 poll from the Center for American Progress.[28] Yes, the Center for American Progress is a far-left nonprofit headed by former Barack Obama Democratic pitbull attorney John Podesta, with a board that includes former Georgia Democrat gubernatorial candidate Stacey "Never

Concede" Abrams.[29] But since timing matters, it's worth paying attention to the rot they're pushing.

Among their findings:

- That most voters, regardless of political party, consider "access to clean water, a quality public education, adequate food, and housing as basic human rights that should be secured by the federal government."
- That more than 70 percent of voters, regardless of political party, support "major infrastructure investments, guaranteed sick days for employees, paid family and medical leave and increases to the Supplemental Nutrition Assistance Program," or food stamp program, for lower-income families.
- That more than 60 percent of voters, regardless of political party, support "increased housing assistance, a moratorium on evictions during the pandemic," and greater child tax credit allowances.
- That most voters want increases to the minimum wage and "new monthly payments to working families"—that is, a type of universal basic income, or guaranteed income award.[30]

No doubt, peer into the phrasing of the questions, pull back the curtain of the survey, and it will be revealed that the poll is about as unbiased as the socialist Center for American Progress outlet itself. But in these hotly charged partisan times, it's not about truth, but about what sells. It's all about the messaging, and the creating of a message that can swirl through the news cycles in short summary phrases so as to grab attention—enough attention that it keeps the message alive for the next news cycle.

The fact that the Center for American Progress conducted this poll and can now toss it into the ring of news fodder for similarly socialist-minded members of the media to pick and run with, is all that matters. Nobody will do the due diligence and look at the survey science. Nobody will look beyond the summaries presented by the leftists at the Center for American Progress, to the demographics, the phrasing and order of questions, the conflating of support for an issue with support for tax dollars being used to pay for the issue.

It's deception. But deception is a powerful political aphrodisiac in today's world. It's used, well-used, and it's used and well-used because it works. And it works in large part because most in the media have sunk to the level of propaganda. They'll pretend all individuals are equal, while sneering among themselves that some are more equal than others. Then they'll walk back into the news world's equivalent of a barnyard—in front of the television camera—and adopt the pretense once again that they're simply looking out for the downtrodden who don't have a voice.

Little Napoleon pigs.

And finally: if it's accepted that churches are no different from retail stores, then it's accepted that the Great Wall of America's Liberties has fallen. A nation that doesn't take its rights from a Creator, but rather gathers them from government, at the will of government, and in the face of changing government priorities, is a nation that is enslaved to government. You can't serve God and mammon; no one can serve two masters forever.

This is not just the battle. This is the entire war.

There's a reason communist countries are mostly secular and atheist; worshipping God gets in the way of the ruling tyrants' desire to be worshipped. Worshipping God gives the downtrodden a hope in something other than a human Dear Leader—and that makes the Dear Leader second best, at best. That puts the government in a role that's subservient to God.

That's the source of America's freedom—the fact that here in this country, individuals take their marching orders from above, rather than waiting for permission from politicians. At least, that's how it used to be. That's how it should be. That is the entire war.

If America loses the concept of rights coming from the Creator, then the government will have an open door to tread on individual rights as frequently as desired. If America loses the concept of rights coming from God, what is the difference between this country and any other? Without that distinction, without that difference, without that special asterisk of exceptionalism, America becomes just another plot of property, rather than a land of opportunity with a spirit of freedom—and that opens the door for globalists to treat this country the same—same as any other. That opens the doors for American citizens to believe this country is the same-same as any other. And like a self-perpetuating cycle, that opens the doors for America to actually become a country that's the same—same as any other. Be not deceived. Be not a tool of political exploiters.

The sanest people in America today are the gym owners in New Jersey who made national headlines by defying their governor's order to shut down and shut doors—who defied even to the point of pulling off wooden boards the government had nailed over their entrance—who defied even to the point of racking up tens of thousands of dollars in fines from local bureaucrats who had been handed enforcement powers to enforce bogus rules, all due to the pandemic.

The sanest people in America today are the moms and dads who stand before school boards in their communities and deliver impassioned pleas to open doors to students, to allow students to enter without masks, to return to a time when teachers actually taught on the things that mattered, and not on the things that mattered only to Black Lives Matter.

The sanest people in America today are those who dismiss Anthony Fauci and Bill Gates as either outright charlatans, or at best, as bureaucrats with overinflated senses of self-importance—and who instead decide for themselves, for their own families, for their own minor-age children, whether or not it makes sense to wear face masks, whether or not it's truly safe to take a coronavirus vaccine, whether or not they're going to gather with family, inside, at church and home, for Easter, the Fourth of July, Thanksgiving, Christmas, and whenever else they want.

The Left calls that selfish. The Democrats label these people as reckless—dangerous, even. The socialists, communists, and collectivists demand that these types of citizens must be controlled, regulated, stopped, and punished. Leftists see the sane as insane. Leftists are the insane.

Two legs bad, four legs good. Four legs good, two legs better. America needs only one basic commandment on the wall on the source of freedom for all citizens, and that's the phrase, "endowed by their Creator." No additions needed. No additions allowed. No changes or amendments or exemptions or clarifiers permitted. That is the war.

This is our war. "Children," 1 John 2:18 tells, "it is the last hour; and as you have heard that antichrist is coming, so now many antichrists have come; therefore we know that it is the last hour." Make it an hour that counts.

Epilogue . . . and an Exhortation

. . . and a little child shall lead them.

Isaiah 11:6 (RSV)

This is the part where the interested reader would ask: OK—now what do we do? And here's the sad and sorry answer: There is no shortcut solution to bring America back to the limited-government nation the founders envisioned. There are biblical reasons for this; there are Bible-based explanations for why we find ourselves, as a nation, crumbling the Constitution, fighting among selves, scrambling to retain our rights—before they're all stolen and usurped by government. Here's the biggest one: God will not be mocked.

Think of all the idolatrous behaviors we've engaged in and accepted as norm nowadays. We've rubber-stamped gay marriage. We've willingly given up privacies and individual liberties for the feeling of national security. We've chased money, wealth, and secular successes, giving little back in return—paying little heed to the warnings in Malachi about robbing God of the tithe. We've allowed the likes of adultery, promiscuity, and LGBTQ lifestyle choices to pass as entertainment and "rights." We've worshipped at the feet of celebrities and professional athletes, as if they're ordained to lead. We've elevated human education, that is, college degrees, to the point of godly wisdom—beyond the point of godly wisdom, pretending as if God does not matter, God does not know, God has no place in modern times. There's more, much more. But the simple matter of the fact is, God won't be mocked, and sooner or later, sins will catch up with the sinner.

So this is where we're at right now in America—paying the consequences for our idolatrous behavior. It's not that God's turned a blind eye and abandoned America. At least, not yet. But it is that too many Americans have abandoned God. Too many are secular and reveling in their secularism, demanding tolerance and acceptance for what should be contemptible and condemnable. Too many others are busily offering fake worship to God—the kind where the Bible is interpreted as a living breathing document, and the principles contained within subject to the whims of modern times.

This is why we now have an America that puts its hope in a face mask, in a medical degree, in a government bureaucrat. This is why we now see a nation of exceptionalism, like America, falling into a communist-like state of government control, run by socialist-like politicians who are plotting to seize even more control, aided and abetted by globalist-like tyrants whose every fiber of being is committed to the takedown of this country, to the lockdown of free citizenry.

We used to welcome the huddled masses. Now we've become the frightened huddled masses. It's our own fault. And yet God is not done with America. God is not done with his people. America can rebound. America is the king of the rebound. Our hope, at least when we're at our best, ultimately comes from God, and rests with godly individuals—and indeed, even this late in the hour, even as the hour of destruction comes, there are far too many individuals in this nation who aren't ready to call it quits.

Here's a story of one. My fourteen-year-old daughter, Chloe, won't wear a face mask because she sees the deceptions in the so-called science and doesn't want to take part in them. As she puts it: Wearing a face mask is about like a kid cowering under the blankets in the dark because of noises in the closet that sound like monsters. If the monster were real—and if the monster really wanted to get the kid—how's the blanket going to help? That's like the face mask, Chloe says. It's based on lies.

Her orthodontist office saw differently and threatened to refuse to see Chloe unless she wore a face mask—despite the fact the office was simultaneously making patients stay in their cars until their appointed times, so as to avoid any gatherings in the waiting room. The front office personnel—all wearing face masks—were still insistent; they confronted Chloe on two or three occasions, demanding she put on a face mask. Chloe refused, telling them that since they were taking responsibility for their own health decisions by choosing to wear face masks, she wanted to be allowed to take responsibility for her own health decisions by choosing not to wear a face mask—and as she pointed out, her refusal to wear a mask was not hampering their ability to still wear face masks. But it wasn't about safety and security. It was about control. At one point, an office worker even told Chloe to walk down the hallway to the orthodontist chair and just a hold a face mask in front of her face so as to appear to almost have a covering—to almost be obeying. Seriously.

Things came to a head when the orthodontist finally outright refused to treat Chloe unless she wore a mask. That—even as he was reminded that while face masks may be his office policy, the contract that was paid in full to finish Chloe's orthodontia was law, and a randomly enforced, randomly created policy, no matter how backed by bureaucracy or executive order, doesn't trump a legally binding contract. In the end, the orthodontist agreed to finish treating Chloe. He just treated her at a time when no other patients were scheduled. Fine. Fine and dandy.

But the takeaway is this: if a fourteen-year-old can stand her ground on principle, sound reasoning, and truth—well then, so can the rest of America.

If you're of the mind that face masks work and they make you feel better to wear one, by all means, go ahead and wear one. But don't insist others wear one just because you're frightened—just because you think your fright gives you the right to impose your will on others. Don't try to turn a land of individuals into a land of collectivists. Don't try to sell the collective good as sound, American, patriotic doctrine, and those who insist on freedom, choice, and individualism as problematic. It's un-American. It's anti-American. It's evil. And it's tearing down the constructs of our country.

Still think face masks "work"—as the Left likes to wail? Well, maybe so. But that's such a nebulous statement. Face masks certainly "work"— when they're donned by doctors who are operating in sterile rooms, and who are wearing gloves and don't touch their faces, their masks, or their eyes, ears, noses, and mouths until they've left the operating room. Face masks certainly "work" when they're used by doctors in sterile rooms who don't turn around and stuff them in their pockets for later reuse. Face masks certainly "work" when they're used by surgeons who don't leave the operating room, midsurgery, to grab a quick bite with their masks dangling about their necks—and then return an hour later, yank back up their masks, and finish the procedure. Face masks certainly "work" when they're used as intended—by medical professionals in medical surroundings, to perform medically necessary procedures.

But for regular Americans? Americans don't live in a sterile operating room, and Americans don't have nurses following them to tie their face masks behind their heads as a means of keeping fingers and masks clean. Americans don't, in general, pay attention to the same rules of sterility and cleanliness as hospital personnel.

This is where the whole "face masks work!" line of argument falls flat—at least, as far as the bureaucrats of the coronavirus crackdowns mean the word "work." At least, as far as the tyrants of the COVID-19 world mean it, as it pertains to stopping or slowing the spread of the virus.

Think about it. Think about it and look to the state statistics that have shown for some time now that face masks aren't leading to reduced coronavirus counts. If masks worked, why the need for closures, anyway? We don't live in operating rooms. We're not doctors in this experiment called life. This makes the wearing of face masks for most Americans, as preventive tools to stop or slow the spreading of the coronavirus, a farce. How many times have you seen Americans wearing these masks below their noses, with gaps on the side, beneath their chins, after pulling them from their pockets, their pocketbooks, or even the floors of their cars?

If you want to know one thing to do right now to save America from the tyrants who would cripple our freedoms, do this and do it forever after: take off the face mask. Quit wearing the face mask. It's not a scientifically sound remedy for stopping the spread of the virus. It's not a patriotic or Christian duty for neighbor and country. It's a sign of obedience more than anything. It reminds of the Mao Zedong badge of loyalty the communists used to advance the chairman's cult of personality during the Chinese Cultural Revolution. Those who wore the badge with Mao's image were easily identified as loyal to the chairman; those who didn't were easily identified as disloyal. Given the China connection to the pandemic, the widely reported Bill Gates and World Health Organization friendliness to China and the Chinese Communist Party's openly stated quest to dominate the world—with a cultural takeover being an authoritarian's best friend, don'tcha know—the analogy isn't that off base. Those who wear the face masks are easily identified as willing participants in the government's obedience training program called Pandemic Response; those who refuse to wear the face masks are just as easily identified as rebels. Why give the government that much information? Why take a chance?

Be a rebel. Just say no. When the sign in the window at the store says "Face Masks Required" or "No Face Mask, No Entry," walk in anyway, minus the face mask, and make the store employees approach you. Nine times out of ten, they won't. One time out of ten, they'll ask, "Do you need a face mask?" Say "No, thank you," smile and keep walking. It's your right as a free citizen to choose whether or not to wear a mask for health reasons. You're the customer. You're the citizens. More important, you're American. It's your right as an American to say no to health treatments you don't want. Or have you forgotten that?

The face mask is the beginning. The vaccinations are next. The proofs of vaccination as a condition of travel or entry are next. They're actually already here. This is the here; this is the now.

If you won't take a stand on face masks because it's too uncomfortable—because it's easier to go along to get along—then you probably won't take a stand on vaccinations the government says are for your good, or on vaccine papers the private business says are necessary to enter. Or on downloading the contact tracing app. Or on keeping your children away from parks, beaches, and open air spaces, because of threats of viruses. Or on keeping away from work and taking the stimulus check because of continued government business shutdowns. Or on any number of other government clamps on individual freedoms that are coming down the pike in the coming months, coming to a community near you. After all, rocking the boat is uncomfortable. Right?

From face masking to forced vaccination to vaccine passport to forced download and carry of contact tracing technology—these are rapid progressions of government controls that would be hard to reverse. These are rapid progressions that would soon become part and parcel of American culture. So long, culture of individualism. Hello, culture of collectivism. Goodbye, America.

So what's the answer? The answer to turning back the tyranny in America is two-fold: First, look to God. Next, look to self. Then, when the proper, moral, constitutional course of action comes to mind, stand strong. Stand strong and stand the ground, no matter how the mockers mock.

On April 28, 2020, as the pandemic was just sweeping into crackdown mode for Americans, I wrote this in *The Washington Times*: "Coronavirus hype biggest political hoax in history."[1] For that, I was vilified.

On May 1, 2020, as the crackdowns in America were growing harsher, despite the curious statistics, and even more curious science, I wrote this in *The Washington Times*: "Forced face masking is a civil rights offense."[2] For that, I was derided and scorned.

How'd I know so early when others in media, in politics, in the general public were busily buying into the bureaucrats' demands for clamps on freedoms and advocating for you to do the same? In a word: discernment.

Following God and knowing the Constitution, and being willing to fight for both, is the recipe that will save America, both in the here and now and the long term.

There is no other way to save America except turning back to God; turning back to godly ways; giving the boot to the many idols dotting the landscape; confessing, repenting, and praying to save the nation from socialists—and worse; getting back to church, getting your kids back to church—and then standing tall on whatever fight comes your way.

Standing tall on whatever bit of government overreach comes to your particular corner of the community. If it's an out-of-control school board—run for a school board seat. If it's an overzealous retail employee who disrespects your choice to not wear a face mask—call the manager, the manager's manager, the manager's manager of the manager, and complain. If it's a college campus, a public bus system, a private business, or an airline or train that advises proof of vaccine must be shown as a condition of entry—demand an exemption, sue if they refuse, and get a group of people to launch a class action suit if they still refuse. There are so many ways to fight. There are so many ways to make your voices heard. There are so many ways to defend individualism and individual liberties in America that those who don't, those who simply cower and shrug, those who profess powerlessness in the face of government power—well, maybe they don't deserve the liberties in the first place.

No excuses, America. No more going along to get along. If you want to know how to save America—fight to save America. That's it. Fight. It's on you. It's not easy. But it's simple. Simple enough that even a fourteen-year-old can do it. Now it's your turn. Because trust me on this: the socialists, the communists, the Marxists, the collectivists aren't quitting any time soon. And their common denominator? They're evil and won't be able to withstand the pushback from a God-centered, Constitution-knowing citizenry.

In this battle against principalities, it's always God's children who win.

Acknowledgments

I have many to thank. First and foremost, God, and my church family; second, the brave founders and their families, who gave so much without having benefit—in some cases, of ever experiencing first-hand the magnificence of their fruits; and third, the men and women of America's military, both past and present, who continue to sacrifice much so that even our nation's most ungrateful can enjoy personal liberties. I'd also like to thank Craig Shirley and Kevin McVicker of Shirley & McVicker Public Affairs, for their faith in my writings, for friendship and professionalism, for endless support and touching generosity; the esteemed staff of my publisher, Humanix—notably, Keith Pfeffer and Mary Glenn, for their excellent guidance and tireless efforts on my behalf; Chris Ruddy, Newsmax CEO, for providing a publishing and promotional experience that's both above and beyond the expected; for some key players at *The Washington Times* who've either directly or indirectly had a most beneficial impact on my media career: namely, Chris Dolan, Charlie Hurt, Joe Teipe, Kelly Sadler, Ann Wog, Martin Di Caro, Adam VerCammen, Nicole Kosar, Christine Reed, and Ian Bishop. I'd also like to thank the many, many pros in the broadcast media world who have granted me the gracious opportunities to appear on your respective shows and discuss issues of importance to liberty-loving Americans. Without your kind invitations, my passions for America and the Constitution and God-given freedoms wouldn't leave the printed page, and I'm grateful for your trust and your time. Similarly, I'm grateful for those in the public relations world who've reached out to me over the months to connect me with inspiring Americans who are in the trenches against the leftists, busily fighting for constitutional rights—some of whom I've showcased in my writings and in my *Bold and Blunt* podcast; many others who've served, mostly unwittingly, as guiding compasses and sparks of motivation for my own works. I'm especially honored and humbled by those who've consented to publicly endorse my work, and in some instances, works. Steve Bannon, Mike Huckabee, Rep. Jody Hice, Everett Piper, Marc Morano, Jack Kingston, Craig Shirley, Father Frank Pavone, Cal Thomas and Chris Salcedo—and on previous occasions, Michael Savage, Sam and Kevin Sorbo, Rep. Louie Gohmert, and more, many more: You are all tops in my book, titans of freedom, fierce defenders of truth and the American way, and it's energizing to be in this fight with you. And of course, it wouldn't be an acknowledgement list without naming my family: Savanna, Keith, Colvin, Chloe, and the newest, Sophie. You guys are the best. You make it all worthwhile. Thanks for being my light in the dark.

Notes

FOREWORD

1. Glenn Bracey, "Villanova Professor Openly Admits Critical Race Theory Is Marxist," YouTube, May 29, 2021, https://www.youtube.com/watch?v=giYlfIUfjS4.

CHAPTER 1

1. World Health Organization, "Archived: WHO Timeline—COVID-19," World Health Organization website, April 27, 2020, https://www.who.int/news/item/27-04-2020-who-timeline---covid-19.
2. Derrick Bryson Taylor, "A Timeline of the Coronavirus Pandemic," *The New York Times*, January 10, 2021, https://www.nytimes.com/article/coronavirus-timeline.html.
3. Will Stone, "1st U.S. Case of Coronavirus Confirmed in Washington State," NPR, January 22, 2020, https://www.npr.org/2020/01/22/798392221/1st-u-s-case-of-coronavirus-confirmed-in-washington-state.
4. Julie Steenhuysen, "Washington State Man Who Traveled to China Is First U.S. Victim of Coronavirus," Reuters, January 21, 2020, https://www.reuters.com/article/us-china-health-usa/washington-state-man-who-traveled-to-china-is-first-u-s-victim-of-coronavirus-idUSKBN1ZK2FF.
5. Connor Perrett and Aria Bendix, "The US Has Reported Its First Coronavirus Death: A Man in His 50s in Washington," *Business Insider*, February 29, 2020, https://www.businessinsider.com/coronavirus-death-us-washington-state-2020-2.
6. Ibid.
7. Sydney Brownstone, Paige Cornwell, Mike Lindblom and Elise Takahama, "Kind County Patient Is First in U.S. to Die of COVID-19 as Officials Scramble to Stem Spread of Novel Coronavirus," *Seattle Times*, February 29, 2020, updated March 1, 2020, https://www.seattletimes.com/seattle-news/health/one-king-county-patient-has-died-due-to-covid-19-infection/.

8. Stephanie Soucheray, "Coroner: First US COVID-19 Death Occurred in Early February," Center for Infectious Disease Research and Policy, April 22, 2020, https://www.cidrap.umn.edu/news-perspective/2020/04/coroner-first-us-covid-19-death-occurred-early-february.

9. Bill Chappell, "Coronavirus: Chaos Follows Trump's European Travel Ban; EU Says It Wasn't Warned," NPR, March 12, 2020, https://www.npr.org/sections/goatsandsoda/2020/03/12/814876173/coronavirus-trump-speech-creates-chaos-eu-says-it-wasnt-warned-of-travel-ban.

10. President Donald Trump, "Remarks by President Trump, Vice President Pence, and Members of the Coronavirus Task Force in Press Conference (February 26)," U.S. Embassy in Georgia, February 26, 2020, https://ge.usembassy.gov/remarks-by-president-trump-vice-president-pence-and-members-of-the-coronavirus-task-force-in-press-conference-february-26/.

11. John Fritze, "White House Requests $2.5 Billion for Coronavirus, Dems Say That's 'Woefully Insufficient,'" USA Today, February 24, 2020, updated February 25, 2020, https://www.usatoday.com/story/news/politics/2020/02/24/coronavirus-donald-trump-requests-2-5-billion-response/4822748002/.

12. President Donald Trump, "Remarks by President Trump, Vice President Pence, and Members of the Coronavirus Task Force in Press Conference (February 26)," U.S. Embassy in Georgia, February 26, 2020, https://ge.usembassy.gov/remarks-by-president-trump-vice-president-pence-and-members-of-the-coronavirus-task-force-in-press-conference-february-26/.

13. Bobby Allyn and Vanessa Romo, "Trump Suspends All Travel from Europe for 30 Days to Combat COVID-19," NPR, March 11, 2020, https://www.npr.org/2020/03/11/814597993/trump-set-to-deliver-address-as-coronavirus-deemed-a-pandemic.

14. Bill Chappell, "Coronavirus: Chaos Follows Trump's European Travel Ban; EU Says It Wasn't Warned," NPR, March 12, 2020, https://www.npr.org/sections/goatsandsoda/2020/03/12/814876173/coronavirus-trump-speech-creates-chaos-eu-says-it-wasnt-warned-of-travel-ban.

15. John Fritze, "White House Requests $2.5 Billion for Coronavirus, Dems Say That's 'Woefully Insufficient,'" USA Today, February 24, 2020, updated February 25, 2020, https://www.usatoday.com/story/news/politics/2020/02/24/coronavirus-donald-trump-requests-2-5-billion-response/4822748002/.

16. Nancy Pelosi, verified Twitter feed, February 25, 2020, https://twitter.com/SpeakerPelosi/status/1232171124169027584.

17. Nancy Pelosi, verified Twitter feed, February 25, 2020, https://twitter.com/SpeakerPelosi/status/1232171122474528768.

18. Nancy Pelosi, verified Twitter feed, February 25, 2020, https://twitter.com/SpeakerPelosi/status/1232171123321769990.

19. Nancy Pelosi, verified Twitter feed, February 25, 2020, https://twitter.com/SpeakerPelosi/status/1232171124169027584.

20. Nancy Pelosi, verified Twitter feed, February 25, 2020, https://twitter.com/SpeakerPelosi/status/1232171125070794754.

21. Lori Robertson, Jessica McDonald, and Robert Farley, "Democrats' Misleading Coronavirus Claims," FactCheck.org: A Project of The Annenberg Public Policy Center, March 3, 2020, https://www.factcheck.org/2020/03/democrats-misleading-coronavirus-claims/.

22. Joe Biden, verified Twitter account, February 1, 2020, https://twitter.com/JoeBiden/status/1223727977361338370.

23. Gregg Re, "After Attacking Trump's Coronavirus-related China Travel Ban as Xenophobic, Dems and Media Have Changed Tune," Fox News, April 1, 2020, https://www.foxnews.com/politics/dems-media-change-tune-trump-attacks-coronavirus-china-travel-ban.

24. Miriam Valverde, "Fact-checking Whether Biden Called Trump 'Xenophobic' for Restrictions on Travel from China," PolitiFact, March 27, 2020, https://www.politifact.com/factchecks/2020/mar/27/donald-trump/fact-checking-whether-biden-called-trump-xenophobi/.

25. Thomas J. Bollyky and Jennifer B. Nuzzo, "Trump's 'Early' Travel 'Bans' Weren't Early, Weren't Bans and Didn't Work," *The Washington Post*, October 1, 2020, https://www.washingtonpost.com/outlook/2020/10/01/debate-early-travel-bans-china/.

26. Ibid.

27. Charles Creitz, "Sanders Tells Fox News Town Hall He Wouldn't Close US Borders During Coronavirus-Type Contagion," Fox News, March 9, 2020, https://www.foxnews.com/media/bernie-sanders-wouldnt-close-us-borders-coronavirus.

28. Gregg Re, "After Attacking Trump's Coronavirus-Related China Travel Ban as Xenophobic, Dems and Media Have Changed Tune," Fox News, April 1, 2020, https://www.foxnews.com/politics/dems-media-change-tune-trump-attacks-coronavirus-china-travel-ban.

29. Chandelis Duster, "Pelosi on Trump's Coronavirus Response: 'As the President Fiddles, People Are Dying,'" CNN, March 29, 2020, https://www.cnn.com/2020/03/29/politics/nancy-pelosi-coronavirus-cnntv/index.html.

30. Bill de Blasio, verified Twitter account, March 2, 2020, https://twitter.com/BilldeBlasio/status/1234648718714036229.

31. Kristen Holmes, "Fauci: If Covid-19 Mitigation Efforts Started Earlier, 'You Could Have Saved Lives,'" CNN, April 12, 2020, https://www.cnn.com/world/live-news/coronavirus-pandemic-04-12-20/h_bd88a9d5d74575d502d005794d2d054d.

32. Lauren Egan, "Trump Calls Coronavirus Democrats' 'New Hoax,'" NBC News, February 28, 2020, https://www.nbcnews.com/politics/donald-trump/trump-calls-coronavirus-democrats-new-hoax-n1145721.

33. Daniel Funke, "Ad Watch: Biden Video Twists Trump's Words on Coronavirus," PolitiFact, March 15, 2020, https://www.politifact.com/factchecks/2020/mar/15/joe-biden/ad-watch-biden-video-twists-trumps-words-coronavir/.

34. Ben Chu, "Trump Has 'Blood on His Hands over Coronavirus,' Says Nobel Prize Winning Economist," *Independent*, April 15, 2020, https://www.independent.co.uk/news/world/americas/trump-joe-stiglitz-coronavirus-deaths-cases-us-nobel-prize-a9463666.html.

35. ASPPH, "Members in the News: South Carolina: Trump 'Has Blood on His Hands' for Downplaying Coronavirus Threat, Health Experts Say," Association of Schools and Programs of Public Health, September 18, 2020, https://www.aspph.org/south-carolina-trump-has-blood-on-his-hands-for-downplaying-coronavirus-threat-health-experts-say/.

36. Jorge L. Ortiz, "'Blood on His Hands': As US Surpasses 400,000 COVID-19 Deaths, Experts Blame Trump Administration for a 'Preventable' Loss of Life,"

USA Today, January 19, 2021, https://news.yahoo.com/blood-hands-us-nears -400-081115909.html.

37. Kristen Holmes and Kaitlan Collins, "White House Takes Aim at Fauci but Trump Has No Plans to Fire Him," CNN, July 13, 2020, https://www.cnn.com/ 2020/07/12/politics/fauci-trump-coronavirus/index.html.

38. John Sharman, "Donald Trump Admits 'I Have Germ Phobia' in Howard Stern Interview," *Independent*, September 26, 2017, https://www.independent.co.uk/ news/world/americas/us-politics/donald-trump-germ-phobia-howard-stern -melania-knauss-tapes-1993-interview-newsweek-factbase-a7967731.html.

39. Dan Mangan, "Donald Trump Says He Is a 'Germaphobe' as He Dismisses Salacious Activity," CNBC, January 11, 2017, https://www.cnbc.com/2017/01/ 11/donald-trump-says-hes-a-germaphobe-as-he-dismisses-salacious-allegations .html.

40. Daniel Lippman, "The Purell Presidency: Trump Aides Learn the President's Real Red Line," Politico, July 7, 2019, https://www.politico.com/story/2019/ 07/07/donald-trump-germaphobe-1399258.

41. Tim Haines, "Gov. Gavin Newsom: I'd Be Lying to Say Trump Hasn't Been Responsive to California's Coronavirus Needs," Real Clear Politics, April 2, 2020, https://www.realclearpolitics.com/video/2020/04/02/gov_gavin _newsom_id_be_lying_to_say_trump_has_not_been_responsive_to_californias _coronavirus_needs.html.

42. Laurel Rosenhall, "Why Is Newsom Suddenly Saying Such Nice Things About Trump?" Cal Matters, March 13, 2020, https://calmatters.org/politics/2020/03/ gavin-newsom-donald-trump-california-coronavirus/.

43. Aamer Mahdani, "Biden Declares 'America Is Back' in Welcome Words To Allies," Associated Press, February 19, 2021, https://apnews.com/article/biden- foreign-policy-g7-summit-munich-cc10859afd0f542fd268c0a7ddcd9bb6.

CHAPTER 2

1. Joe Biden, "Statement by Vice President Joe Biden and the Biden for President Public Health Advisory Committee on Testing," Medium.com, April 27, 2020, https://medium.com/@JoeBiden/statement-by-vice-president-joe-biden-and-the- biden-for-president-public-health-advisory-committee-6407f37c93da.

2. Representative Bobby Rush, "Rush Introduces Bipartisan Legislation to Fund $100 Billion Coronavirus Testing and Contact Tracing Effort," United States Congressman Bobby L. Rush media cen- ter, May 1, 2020, https://rush.house.gov/media-center/press-releases/ rush-introduces-bipartisan-legislation-to-fund-100-billion-coronavirus.

3. H.R. 6666 text, "H.R. 6666 – COVID-19 Testing, Reaching and Contacting Everyone (TRACE) Act," Congress.gov, May 1, 2020, https://www.congress.gov/ bill/116th-congress/house-bill/6666/text.

4. Bobby Rush, "Rush Introduces Bipartisan Legislation to Fund $100 Billion Coronavirus Testing and Contact Tracing Effort," United States Congressman Bobby L. Rush media center, May 1, 2020, https://rush.house.gov/media-center/press-releases/ rush-introduces-bipartisan-legislation-to-fund-100-billion-coronavirus.

5. Ibid.

6. ProPublica, "H.R.6666: COVID-19 Testing, Reaching and Contacting Everyone (TRACE) Act," May 1, 2020, https://projects.propublica.org/represent/bills/116/hr6666.
7. Elena Moore, "Matchup Set for New Jersey Rep. Van Drew, Who Switched Parties to GOP," NPR, July 7, 2020, https://www.npr.org/2020/07/07/888185916/matchup-set-for-new-jersey-rep-van-drew-who-switched-parties-to-gop.
8. H.R. 6666 text, "H.R. 6666 – COVID-19 Testing, Reaching and Contacting Everyone (TRACE) Act," Congress.gov, May 1, 2020, https://www.congress.gov/bill/116th-congress/house-bill/6666/text.
9. Ibid.
10. Ibid.
11. Ibid.
12. Rep. Bobby Rush, "Rush Introduces Bipartisan Legislation to Fund $100 Billion Coronavirus Testing and Contact Tracing Effort," United States Congressman Bobby L. Rush media center, May 1, 2020, https://rush.house.gov/media-center/press-releases/rush-introduces-bipartisan-legislation-to-fund-100-billion-coronavirus.
13. Ibid.
14. Ibid.
15. National Park Service, "What Is a National Heritage Area? Heritage Areas 101: What Is a NHA?" National Park Service website, undated, https://www.nps.gov/articles/what-is-a-national-heritage-area.htm#:~:text=National%20Heritage%20Areas%20(NHAs)%20are,a%20cohesive%2C%20nationally%20important%20landscape.&text=Consequently%2C%20NHA%20entities%20collaborate%20with,to%20local%20interests%20and%20needs.
16. Bobby L. Rush, "Rush Reintroduces the Bronzeville–Black Metropolis National Heritage Area," United States Congressman Bobby L. Rush, February 28, 2020, https://rush.house.gov/media-center/press-releases/rush-reintroduces-the-bronzeville-black-metropolis-national-heritage-act.
17. Congress.gov, "H.R. 670 – Bronzeville–Black Metropolis National Heritage Area Act," Congress.gov, introduced February 1, 2021, https://www.congress.gov/bill/117th-congress/house-bill/670/text?q=%7B%22search%22%3A%5B%22designating+national+heritage+area%22%5D%7D&r=2&s=3.
18. The Chicago Community Trust, "Black Metropolis National Heritage Area Commission," Chicago Community Trust webpage, undated, https://www.cct.org/what-we-offer/grants/black-metropolis-national-heritage-area-commission/.
19. Mark K. DeSantis, "Heritage Areas: Background, Proposals, and Current Issues," Congressional Research Service, updated August 20, 2020, https://fas.org/sgp/crs/misc/RL33462.pdf, pp. 8–9.
20. Centers for Disease Control and Prevention, "Contact Tracing for COVID-19," Centers for Disease Control and Prevention website, updated December 16, 2020, https://www.cdc.gov/coronavirus/2019-ncov/php/contact-tracing/contact-tracing-plan/contact-tracing.html#anchor_15900119.
21. Centers for Disease Control and Prevention, "Case Investigation and Contact Tracing: Part of a Multipronged Approach to Fight the COVID-19 Pandemic," CDC web page, updated December 3, 2020, https://www.cdc.gov/coronavirus/2019-ncov/php/principles-contact-tracing.html.

22. Johns Hopkins University, "COVID-19 Contact Tracing," course offered by Johns Hopkins University, https://www.coursera.org/learn/covid-19-contact -tracing?edocomorp=covid-19-contact-tracing.

23. Eagle Forum, "Contact Tracing = Government Surveillance, Not Health," Insights, an Eagle Forum e-publication, May 20, 2020, https://eagleforum.org/ publications/insights/contact-tracing-government-surveillance-not-health.html.

24. The History Makers, "The Honorable Bobby Rush," *The History Makers Archives*, May 15, 2015, https://www.thehistorymakers.org/biography/ honorable-bobby-rush.

25. Cheryl K. Chumley, "H.R. 6666 a Devil of a Government Surveillance Plot," *Washington Times*, May 12, 2020, https://www.washingtontimes.com/news/ 2020/may/12/hr-6666-a-devil-of-a-covid-19-government-surveilla/.

26. Jeremy M. Edwards, communications director, Congressman Bobby L. Rush, May 12, 2020, emails contained in author's records.

27. Radiant, "Social Distancing," Radiant RFID website, undated, https:// radiantrfid.com/social-distancing/?utm_campaign=10107239948&utm_ source=google&utm_medium=cpc&utm_content=436956598725&utm _term=automated%20contact%20tracing&adgroupid=101865395736 &gclid=EAIaIQobChMI4efQwqOI7wIVgbeGCh1vmgsbEAAYAiAAEgIKm PD_BwE&cn-reloaded=1.

28. Christine Lehmann, "Privacy Concerns Hindering Digital Tracing," WebMD, September 25,2020, https://www.webmd.com/lung/news/20200928/privacy -concerns-hindering-digital-contact-tracing.

29. Centers for Disease Control and Prevention, "Digital Contact Tracing Tools," CDC website, updated May 26, 2020, https://www.cdc.gov/coronavirus/2019 -ncov/php/contact-tracing/contact-tracing-plan/digital-contact-tracing-tools .html.

30. Josh Fruhlinger, "The OPM Hack Explained: Bad Security Practices Meet China's Captain America," CSO, February 12, 2020, https://www.csoonline .com/article/3318238/the-opm-hack-explained-bad-security-practices-meet -chinas-captain-america.html.

31. Martin Bosworth, "VA Loses Data on 26 Million Veterans," *Consumer Affairs*, May 22, 2006, https://www.consumeraffairs.com/news04/2006/05/va_laptop .html.

32. Andy Greenberg, "The Year of the Mega Data Breach," *Forbes*, November 24, 2009, https://www.forbes.com/2009/11/24/security-hackers-data-technology -cio-network-breaches.html?sh=798e321cd038.

33. Jim Finkle and Dustin Volz, "Database of 191 Million U.S. Voters Exposed on Internet: Researcher," Reuters, December 28, 2015, https://www.reuters.com/ article/us-usa-voters-breach/database-of-191-million-u-s-voters-exposed-on -internet-researcher-idUSKBN0UB1E020151229.

34. Nate Lord, "Top Ten Government Database Breaches of All Time in the U.S.," *Data Insider*, October 6, 2020, https://digitalguardian.com/blog/top-10-biggest -us-government-data-breaches-all-time.

35. Dan Swinhoe, "The 15 Biggest Data Breaches of the 21st Century," CSO, January 8, 2021, https://www.csoonline.com/article/2130877/the-biggest-data -breaches-of-the-21st-century.html.

36. Electronic Frontier Foundation, "COVID-19 and Digital Rights," EFF, undated, https://www.eff.org/issues/covid-19.

37. Tom Kertscher, "No Evidence Tying Bill Gates to a $100 Billion Covid-19 Deal Before the Outbreak," PolitiFact, June 22, 2020, https://www.politifact.com/factchecks/2020/jun/22/facebook-posts/no-evidence-tying-bill-gates-100-billion-covid-19-/.
38. Ibid.
39. The Aspen Institute, "Africa's Economic, Security, and Development Challenges and the U.S. Role, August 12-19. 2019," The Aspen Institute, https://www.aspeninstitute.org/wp-content/uploads/2020/02/Africa-2019-Report.pdf, pp. 37–38.
40. Tom Kertscher, "No Evidence Tying Bill Gates to a $100 Billion Covid-19 Deal Before the Outbreak," PolitiFact, June 22, 2020, https://www.politifact.com/factchecks/2020/jun/22/facebook-posts/no-evidence-tying-bill-gates-100-billion-covid-19-/.
41. World Health Organization Newsroom, "Tracking COVID-19: Contact Tracing in the Digital Age," World Health Organization, September 9, 2020, https://www.who.int/news-room/feature-stories/detail/tracking-covid-19-contact-tracing-in-the-digital-age.
42. Gopal Ratnam, "Biden Administration Likely to Leverage Tracing Apps Nationally," Government Technology, November 17, 2020, https://www.govtech.com/health/Biden-Administration-Likely-to-Leverage-National-Tracing-App.html.
43. Steven Findlay, "Contact Tracing Has Struggled During the Pandemic Surge; Biden Looks to Boost It," *U.S. News & World Report*, February 9, 2021, https://www.usnews.com/news/health-news/articles/2021-02-09/as-covid-surged-contact-tracing-struggled-biden-looks-to-boost-it.

CHAPTER 3

1. HRW.org, "Covid-19 Triggers Wave of Free Speech Abuse," *Human Rights Watch News*, February 11, 2021, https://www.hrw.org/news/2021/02/11/covid-19-triggers-wave-free-speech-abuse.
2. Ibid.
3. Ibid.
4. Jessica Jerreat, "Coronavirus the New Scapegoat for Media Censorship, Rights Groups Say," VOA, April 14, 2020. https://www.voanews.com/press-freedom/coronavirus-new-scapegoat-media-censorship-rights-groups-say.
5. Justin Sherman, "Russia Orders Tech Platforms to Remove Coronavirus 'Fake News,'" the Atlantic Council, March 27, 2020, https://www.atlanticcouncil.org/blogs/new-atlanticist/russia-orders-tech-platforms-remove-coronavirus-fake-news/.
6. Emelia Niemiec, "COVID-19 and Misinformation," EMBO Reports, October 26, 2020, https://www.embopress.org/doi/full/10.15252/embr.202051420.
7. Adrian Shahbaz, Allie Funk, "Information Isolation: Censoring the COVID-19 Outbreak," Freedom House, 2020, https://freedomhouse.org/report/report-sub-page/2020/information-isolation-censoring-covid-19-outbreak.
8. Rachel Lerman, Katie Shepherd and Taylor Telford, "Twitter Penalizes Trump Jr. for Posting Hydroxchloroquine Misinformation," *The Washington Post* via *Seattle Times*, July 28, 2020, https://www.seattletimes.com/nation-world/facebook

-deleted-a-viral-video-full-of-false-coronavirus-claims-then-trump-shared-it-on
-twitter/.

9. Sophia Ankel, "'Masks Work? NO': Twitter Removes Tweet by White House
Coronavirus Adviser That Says Face Coverings Are Not Effective Against COVID-
19," *Business Insider*, October 18, 2020, https://www.businessinsider.com/tweet
-removed-dr-scott-atlas-masks-dont-prevent-covid-19-2020-10.

10. Bill Chappell, "Instagram Bars Robert F. Kennedy Jr. for Spreading Vaccine
Misinformation," NPR, February 11, 2021, https://www.npr.org/sections/
coronavirus-live-updates/2021/02/11/966902737/instagram-bars-robert-f
-kennedy-jr-for-spreading-vaccine-misinformation.

11. Ibid.

12. Kamala Harris, via Twitter, CNN clip of interview with host Anderson Cooper,
October 1, 2019, https://twitter.com/KamalaHarris/status/1179066441372438533.

13. Donie O'Sullivan, "Twitter Tells Kamala Harris Why It Won't Suspend Trump's
Account," CNN, October 17, 2019, https://www.cnn.com/2019/10/16/
politics/twitter-kamala-harris-trump-account.

14. Ibid.

15. Brian Fung, "Twitter Bans President Trump Permanently," CNN Business,
January 9, 2021, https://www.cnn.com/2021/01/08/tech/trump-twitter-ban/
index.html.

16. Haley Messenger, "Twitter to Uphold Permanent Ban Against Trump, Even If
He Were to Run for Office Again," NBC News, February 10, 2021, https://
www.nbcnews.com/business/business-news/twitter-uphold-permanent-ban
-against-trump-even-if-he-were-n1257269.

17. Queenie Wong and Andrew Morse, "Parler Returns Online After Monthlong
Absence: Here's What You Need to Know," CNET, February 16, 2021, https://
www.cnet.com/news/parler-returns-online-after-month-long-absence-heres
-what-you-need-to-know/.

18. Lauren Fruen, "Now Dr. Seuss Is Canceled: Virginia School System Drops
Children's Favorite from Read Across America Day Because of 'Racial
Undertones' in His Writing," *Daily Mail*, updated March 1, 2021, https://
www.dailymail.co.uk/news/article-9309455/Now-Dr-Seuss-faces-cancel
-Virginia-school-says-books-strong-racial-undertones.html.

19. Renss Greene, "Count Complete: 2020 Election Turnout Neared 80% in
Loudoun," Loudoun Now, November 11, 2020, https://loudounnow.com/
2020/11/11/count-complete-2020-election-turnout-neared-80-in-loudoun/.
Katie Ishizuka and Ramon Stephens, "The Cat Is out of the Bag: Orientalism,
Anti-Blackness, and White Supremacy in Dr. Seuss's Children's Books," *Research
on Diversity in Youth Literature*, Volume 1, Issue 2, Article 4, https://
sophia.stkate.edu/rdyl/vol1/iss2/4/.

20. Lauren Fruen, "Now Dr. Seuss Is Canceled: Virginia School System Drops
Children's Favorite from Read Across America Day Because of 'Racial
Undertones' in His Writing," *Daily Mail*, updated March 1, 2021, https://
www.dailymail.co.uk/news/article-9309455/.Now-Dr-Seuss-faces-cancel
-Virginia-school-says-books-strong-racial-undertones.html.

21. Julia Barajas, "How Teachers in L.A. and Beyond Turned away from Dr. Seuss,"
Los Angeles Times, March 5, 2021, https://www.latimes.com/entertainment
-arts/books/story/2021-03-05/dr-seuss-read-across-america-los-angeles-county
-schools.

22. Ibid.
23. UCSanDiego, "Ramon Stephens," Department of Education Studies, undated, https://eds.ucsd.edu/explore/doctoral/phd/phd-students/PhD1-Profiles/Stephens_R.html.
24. This Picture Book Life, "Interview: The Conscious Kid Book Delivery Service," This Picture Book Life, September 26, 2017, http://thispicturebooklife.com/interview-the-conscious-kid-library-subscription-service/.
25. Today's Parent, "Katie Ishizuka and Ramon Stephens," *Today's Parent*, December 1, 2020, https://www.todaysparent.com/influential-parents-list/katie-ishizuka-and-ramon-stephens/.
26. This Picture Book Life, "Interview: The Conscious Kid Book Delivery Service," This Picture Book Life, September 26, 2017, http://thispicturebooklife.com/interview-the-conscious-kid-library-subscription-service/.
27. Valerie Strauss, "No, a Virginia School District Didn't Ban Dr. Seuss Books. Here's What Really Happened," *The Washington Post*, February 27, 2021, https://www.washingtonpost.com/education/2021/02/27/no-virginia-school-district-did-not-ban-drseuss-books/.
28. Julia Barajas, "How Teachers in L.A. and Beyond Turned away from Dr. Seuss," *Los Angeles Times*, March 5, 2021, https://www.latimes.com/entertainment-arts/books/story/2021-03-05/dr-seuss-read-across-america-los-angeles-county-schools.
29. Elizabeth Elizalde, "Disney Slaps 'The Muppet Show' with 'Offensive Content' Disclaimer," *New York Post*, February 21, 2021, https://nypost.com/2021/02/21/the-muppets-slapped-with-a-content-warning-by-disney/.
30. Allison Morrow, "Mr. Potato Head Tries to Be More Gender Neutral," CNN Business, February 26, 2021, https://www.cnn.com/2021/02/25/business/mr-potato-head-hasbro-gender-neutral/index.html.
31. John A. Burtka IV, "How Cancel Culture Came for ISI," Intercollegiate Studies Institute, Fox News posted Fox News interview, March 4, 2021, https://isi.org/intercollegiate-review/how-cancel-culture-came-for-isi/.
32. Johnny Burtka, "ISI President Johnny Burtka on Fox News's Tucker Carlson Tonight: How Cancel Culture Came to ISI," Fox News, via YouTube, March 4, 2021, https://www.youtube.com/watch?v=k12Ka0EeN80&feature=emb_logo.
33. Anna Eshoo and Jerry McNerney, Congress of the United States official letter to Mr. John T. Stankey, CEO, AT&T Inc., February 22, 2021, https://mcnerney.house.gov/sites/mcnerney.house.gov/files/McNerney-Eshoo%20TV%20Misinfo%20Letters%20-%202.22.21.pdf.
34. Ibid.
35. John Eggerton, "FCC's Carr: House Dems Are Trying to Censor Newsrooms," TV Tech, March 2021 edition, https://www.tvtechnology.com/news/fccs-carr-house-dems-are-trying-to-censor-newsrooms.
36. Andrew L. Whitehead (speaker) with Irina A. Faskianos (presenter), "Conference Call: The Rise of Christian Nationalism," Council on Foreign Relations text of webinar/conference call, February 9, 2021, https://www.cfr.org/conference-calls/rise-christian-nationalism.
37. Rachel S. Mikva, "Christian Nationalism Is a Threat, and Not Just from Capitol Attackers Invoking Jesus," *USA Today*, January 31, 2021, https://www.usatoday.com/story/opinion/2021/01/31/christian-nationalism-josh-hawley-ted-cruz-capitol-attack-column/4292193001/.

38. Tom Gjelten, "Militant Christian Nationalists Remain a Potent Force, Even After the Capitol Riot," NPR, January 19, 2021, https://www.npr.org/2021/01/19/958159202/militant-christian-nationalists-remain-a-potent-force.

CHAPTER 4

1. Kristen Carosa, "New COVID-19 Violation Reporting Policy at Colby-Sawyer College Causes Controversy on Campus," WMUR-9, updated March 2, 2021, https://www.wmur.com/article/new-covid-19-violation-reporting-policy-at-colby-sawyer-college-causes-controversy-on-campus/35703928.
2. IHE Staff, "Live Updates: Latest News on Coronavirus and Higher Education," Inside Higher Ed, March 21, 2021, https://www.insidehighered.com/news/2021/03/12/live-updates-latest-news-coronavirus-and-higher-education.
3. Ashley Humphreys, "Allowing Samantha Mohammed and Anna Allen Back into Their Colby-Sawyer Housing," Change.org, undated, https://www.change.org/p/colby-sawyer-college-allowing-samantha-mohammed-and-anna-allen-back-into-their-colby-sawyer-housing?redirect=false.
4. James Madison University, "About JMU," James Madison University website, undated, https://www.jmu.edu/about/.
5. James Madison University, "COVID-19 Stop the Spread Agreement," James Madison University, Spring 2021, https://www.jmu.edu/studentaffairs/files/sp2021-sts-agreement.pdf.
6. Ibid.
7. Ibid.
8. WebMD, "Coronavirus Recovery," WebMD, undated but noted as sourced from 2020 and 2019, https://www.webmd.com/lung/covid-recovery-overview#1.
9. James Madison University, "JMU Health Update-March 11," James Madison University News, March 11, 2021, https://www.jmu.edu/news/2021/03/11-jmu-health-update.shtml.
10. Nick Niedzwiadek and Andrew Atterbury, "Colleges Crack Down on Student Behavior as Virus Threatens More Closures," Politico, August 30, 2020, https://www.politico.com/news/2020/08/30/college-students-coronavirus-closures-404567.
11. Jeremy Bauer-Wolf, "Colleges Continue to Crack Down on Students Defying Coronavirus Safety Measures," Higher Ed Dive, November 6, 2020, https://www.highereddive.com/news/colleges-continue-to-crack-down-on-students-defying-coronavirus-safety-meas/588594/.
12. Bay Gammans, "Providence College Cracks Down Following Uptick in COVID-19 Cases," WPRI.com Channel 12, February 11, 2021, https://www.wpri.com/health/coronavirus/school-updates/providence-college-cracks-down-following-uptick-in-covid-cases/.
13. Ibid.
14. David Dowdy and Gypsyamber D'Souza, "COVID-19 Testing: Understanding the 'Percent Positive,'" Johns Hopkins Bloomberg School of Public Health, August 10, 2020, https://www.jhsph.edu/covid-19/articles/covid-19-testing-understanding-the-percent-positive.html.
15. Robin Lloyd, "The Problem with the Positivity Rate," *Intelligencer*, December 7, 2020, https://nymag.com/intelligencer/2020/12/the-problem-with-the-covid-19-positivity-rate.html.

16. Centers for Disease Control and Prevention, "Transitioning from CDC's Indicators for Dynamic School Decision-Making (released September 15, 2020) to CDC's Operational Strategy for K-12 Schools Through Phased Mitigation (released February 12, 2021) to Reduce COVID-19," CDC, February 18, 2021, https://www.cdc.gov/coronavirus/2019-ncov/community/schools -childcare/indicators.html.

17. EdW staff, "Map: Coronavirus and Schools Closures in 2019–2020," Education Week, updated September 6, 2020, https://www.edweek.org/ . leadership/map-coronavirus-and-school-closures-in-2019-2020/2020/03.

18. Betsy Foresman, "Here Are the U.S. Universities that Have Closed Due to Coronavirus," EdScoop, March 13, 2020, https://edscoop.com/universities -closed-due-coronavirus-2020/.

19. Davidson College staff, "Welcome to the C2i Dashboard!" The College Crisis Initiative at Davidson College, fall and spring 2020, https://collegecrisis .shinyapps.io/dashboard/.

20. Andrew Smalley, "Higher Education Response to Coronavirus (COVID-19)," National Conference of State Legislatures, March 15, 2021, https://www.ncsl .org/research/education/higher-education-responses-to-coronavirus-covid-19 .aspx.

21. Bay Gammans, "Providence College Cracks Down Following Uptick in COVID-19 Cases," WPRI.com Channel 12, February 11, 2021, https://www .wpri.com/health/coronavirus/school-updates/providence-college-cracks-down -following-uptick-in-covid-cases/.

22. Ibid.

23. Ibid.

24. Amanda Milkovits, "R.I. Governor Blames Students at Two Colleges for the States' Rise in Cases and Positivity Rates," Boston Globe, September 23, 2020, https://www.bostonglobe.com/2020/09/23/metro/rhode-island-sees-rises-cases -positivity-rate-week/.

25. Ibid.

26. Ibid.

27. U.S. News & World Report with various medical experts, "Webinar: Managing Children's Mental Health: A Pediatric Hospital Imperative," hosted by U.S. News & World Report, March 3, 2021, https://www.usnews.com/news/live -events/webinar-managing-childrens-mental-health-a-pediatric-hospital -imperative.

28. Elaine K. Howley, "Children's Mental Health Crisis Could Be a Next 'Wave' in the Pandemic," U.S. News & World Report, March 4, 2021, https://www.usnews .com/news/health-news/articles/2021-03-04/childrens-mental-health-crisis -could-be-a-next-wave-in-the-pandemic.

29. Ibid.

30. Ibid.

31. Ibid.

32. Ibid.

33. Hayley Roffey, "The Moment We're Living and Our Hope for the Future," Global Fund for Children, February 1, 2021, https://globalfundforchildren.org/ news/the-moment-were-living-and-our-hope-for-the-future/?gclid=EAIaIQ obChMI2fvr84W67wIVjLbICh1_7QVYEAAYASAAEgL9KPD_BwE.

34. Save the Children staff, "The Hidden Impact of Covid-19 on Children: A Global Research Series," Save the Children Resource Center, September 10, 2020, https://resourcecentre.savethechildren.net/library/hidden-impact-covid -19-children-global-research-series.

35. Hayley Roffey, "The Moment We're Living and our Hope for the Future," Global Fund for Children, February 1, 2021, https://globalfundforchildren.org/ news/the-moment-were-living-and-our-hope-for-the-future/?gclid=EAIaIQ obChMI2fvr84W67wIVjLbICh1_7QVYEAAYASAAEgL9KPD_BwE.

36. Elaine K. Howley, "Children's Mental Health Crisis Could Be a Next 'Wave' in the Pandemic," *U.S. News & World Report*, March 4, 2021, https://www.usnews .com/news/health-news/articles/2021-03-04/childrens-mental-health-crisis -could-be-a-next-wave-in-the-pandemic.

37. Ibid.

38. Ibid.

39. Emma Harville, "Twin Cities Teachers Unions Demand Schools Stay Closed this Fall," Pioneer Press/TwinCities.com, July 24, 2020, https://www.twincities .com/2020/07/24/twin-cities-teachers-unions-demand-schools-stay-closed -this-fall/.

40. Ibid.

41. Ibid.

42. Amelia Janaskie, "The Teachers Union Are Keeping the Schools Closed?" American Institute for Economic Research, December 20, 2020, https:// www.aier.org/article/the-teachers-unions-are-keeping-the-schools-closed/.

43. Ibid.

44. Ricardo Castagnoli, Martina Votto, Amelia Licari, et al., "Severe Acute Respiratory Syndrome Coronavirus 2 (SARS-CoV-2) Infection in Children and Adolescents," *JAMA Pediatrics*, April 22, 2020, https://jamanetwork.com/ journals/jamapediatrics/fullarticle/2765169.

45. American Academy of Pediatrics, "Pediatricians, Educators and Superintendents Urge a Safe Return to School This Fall," AAP News release, July 10, 2020, https://services.aap.org/en/news-room/news-releases/aap/2020/pediatricians -educators-and-superintendents-urge-a-safe-return-to-school-this-fall/.

46. Amelia Janaskie, "The Teachers Union are Keeping the Schools Closed?" American Institute for Economic Research, December 20, 2020, https://www .aier.org/article/the-teachers-unions-are-keeping-the-schools-closed/.

47. Madeline Will, "In Chicago and Other Big Cities, Teachers' Unions Are Delaying School Reopenings," EducationWeek, updated February 10, 2021, https://www.edweek.org/teaching-learning/in-chicago-and-other-big-cities -teachers-unions-are-delaying-school-reopenings/2021/02.

48. Ibid.

49. Ibid.

50. 50 Dana Goldstein, "The Union Leader Who Says She Can Get Teachers Back in Schools," *The New York Times*, updated February 10, 2021, https://www .nytimes.com/2021/02/08/us/schools-reopening-teachers-unions.html.

51. American Federation of Teachers, "Reopening Schools During a Time of Triple Crisis: Financial Implications," AFT, June 2020, https://www.aft.org/sites/ default/files/wysiwyg/reopen-schools-financial-implications.pdf.

52. Mike Kennedy, "Schools Need an Additional $116 Billion to Reopen Facilities Safely, the AFT Says," American School & University, June 11, 2020, https://

www.asumag.com/covid-19/article/21133830/schools-need-an-additional-116
-billion-to-reopen-its-facilities-safely-the-aft-says.

53. EdSource staff, "Quick Guide: California's plan for getting more kids back to school," EdSource, March 4, 2021, https://edsource.org/2021/quick-guide -how-does-gov-newsoms-safe-schools-for-all-plan-work/646111.

54. Amelia Janaskie, "The Teachers Union are Keeping the Schools Closed?" American Institute for Economic Research, December 20, 2020, https://www .aier.org/article/the-teachers-unions-are-keeping-the-schools-closed/.

55. Carolyn Thompson, "Schools Confront 'Off the Rails' Numbers of Failing Grades," NBC Channel 5, December 8, 2020, https://www.nbcdfw.com/news/ local/texas-news/schools-confront-off-the-rails-numbers-of-failing-grades -2/2499524/.

56. Ibid.

CHAPTER 5

1. Andrew Robbins, "President Biden: Getting COVID Shots a 'Patriotic Duty,'" WMUK/WKAR.org, February 19, 2021, https://www.wkar.org/post/ president-biden-getting-covid-shots-patriotic-duty#stream/0.

2. Arun Kristian Das, "President-elect Biden: Wearing a Mask Is Patriotic, Not Political," Fox5 New York, December 29, 2020, https://www.fox5ny.com/news/ president-elect-biden-wearing-a-mask-is-patriotic-not-political.

3. Dr. Michael Lederman, Maxwell J. Mehlman, and Dr. Stuart Youngner, "Defeat COVID-19 by Requiring Vaccination for All. It's Not un-American. It's Patriotic," USA Today, updated August 10, 2020, https://www.usatoday.com/ story/opinion/2020/08/06/stop-coronavirus-compulsory-universal-vaccination -column/3289948001/.

4. Rod Ledbetter, Rohin Gawdi, and Rachael Ledbetter, "The Winter of Our Discontent: The Patriotic Duty of Taking the COVID-19 Vaccine," Tennessean, December 3, 2020, https://www.tennessean.com/story/opinion/2020/12/03/ covid-19-vaccine-our-only-hope-gain/3800115001/.

5. Chelsea Simeon, "Ohio Sen. Sherrod Brown Receives COVID-19 Vaccine, Says It's Not Partisan—It's Patriotic," WKBN 27, December 19, 2020, https://www. wkbn.com/news/coronavirus/ohio-sen-sherrod-brown-receives-covid-19-vaccine -says-its-not-partisan-its-patriotic/.

6. Marsha Mercer, "Marsha Mercer Column: In 2021, Patriots Bare Their Arms," Richmond Times-Dispatch, March 18, 2021, https://richmond.com/opinion/ columnists/marsha-mercer-column-in-2021-patriots-bare-their-arms/article _0682f9d5-157e-5738-a32e-a6dbca7c8fb4.html.

7. Robert Williams, "Ford Appeals to Patriotic Duty With Campaign to Curb COVID-19," Marketing Dive, January 4, 2021, https://www.marketingdive.com/ news/ford-appeals-to-patriotic-duty-with-campaign-to-curb-covid-19/592738/.

8. Elizabeth Cohen, "FDA, CDC Advisers Say to Expect a Lot of Questions About AstraZeneca Covid-19 Vaccine," CNN, March 19, 2021, https://www.cnn.com/ 2021/03/19/health/astrazeneca-vaccine-us-questions/index.html.

9. The College of Physicians of Philadelphia, "The History of Vaccines: Vaccine Development, Testing and Regulation," HistoryOfVaccines.org, undated, https:// www.historyofvaccines.org/content/articles/vaccine-development-testing -and-regulation.

10. Ibid.
11. Ibid.
12. Ibid.
13. Ibid.
14. Ibid.
15. Ibid.
16. Ali Khan, F. Perry Wilson, Tasce Bongiovanni, and Joseph V. Sakron, "Op-Ed: Be a Patriot. Wear a Mask," MedPageToday, July 17, 2020, https://www .medpagetoday.com/infectiousdisease/covid19/87617.
17. Ibid.
18. Rachel Feltman, "Wearing a Face Mask Is Patriotic," *Popular Science*, July 22, 2020, https://www.popsci.com/story/health/covid-face-mask-patriotic-trump/.
19. CNN Wire, "President Trump Tweets Image of Himself Wearing a Mask and Calls It 'Patriotic,'" Fox 8 News, July 20, 2020, https://myfox8.com/news/ president-trump-tweets-image-of-himself-wearing-a-mask-and-calls-it-patriotic/.
20. Axios staff, "Trump Tweets Photo of Himself in a Face Mask and Calls It 'Patriotic,'" Axios, July 20, 2020, https://www.axios.com/trump-tweets-face -mask-patriotic-d1d8d442-dd94-4330-a483-971ae0be2a8a.html.
21. Sinead Baker, "Trump, Who Dismissed and Refused to Wear a Face Mask for Months, Now Says Wearing One Is 'Patriotic' Like Him," *Business Insider*, July 21, 2020, https://www.businessinsider.com/trump-says-wearing-face-mask -patriotic-months-of-refusal-2020-7.
22. Kevin Breuniger, "Trump Says Face Masks Are 'Patriotic' After Months of Largely Resisting Wearing One," CNBC, July 20, 2020, https://www.cnbc.com/ 2020/07/20/trump-says-coronavirus-masks-are-patriotic-after-months-of -largely-resisting-wearing-one.html.
23. Nicolas Reimann, "Trump Calls Mask Wearing 'Patriotic,' Tweets Photo Wearing One," *Forbes*, July 20, 2020. https://www.forbes.com/sites/ nicholasreimann/2020/07/20/trump-calls-mask-wearing-patriotic-tweets -photo-wearing-one/?sh=15dec9241cbe.
24. Andrew O'Reilly, "Trump Says He's a 'Believer in Masks,' But Stops Short of National Mandate in Coronavirus Fight," Fox News, July 19, 2020, https:// www.foxnews.com/politics/trump-says-he-a-believer-in-masks-but-stops-short -of-national-mandate-in-coronavirus-fight.
25. Ibid.
26. Ibid.
27. Rob Kuznia and Ashley Fantz, "They Swore to Protect America. Some Also Joined the Riot," CNN. January 15, 2021, https://www.cnn.com/2021/01/12/ us/military-extremism-capitol-riot-invs/index.html.
28. Statista, "Percentage of U.S. Population Who Are Veterans by 2019, by Age and Gender," Statista, September 2020, https://www.statista.com/statistics/250366/ percentage-of-us-population-who-are-veterans/.
29. Ibid.
30. Rob Kuznia and Ashley Fantz, "They Swore to Protect America. Some Also Joined the Riot," CNN. January 15, 2021, https://www.cnn.com/2021/01/12/ us/military-extremism-capitol-riot-invs/index.html.
31. American's Voice Online, "SPLC Annual Year in Hate Report: Center for Immigration Studies Is a Hate Group," America's Voice, February 15, 2017,

https://americasvoice.org/blog/splc-annual-year-hate-report-center-immigration
-studies-now-designated-hate-group/.

32. Merrill Perlman, "The Key Difference Between 'Nationalist' and 'Supremacist,'"
    Columbia Journalism Review, August 14, 2017, https://www.cjr.org/language
    _corner/nationalist-supremacist.php.

33. Ellen Mitchell, "Pentagon Watchdog to Launch Probe of White Supremacists
    in the Military," The Hill, January 14, 2021, https://thehill.com/policy/
    defense/534315-pentagon-watchdog-to-launch-probe-of-white-supremacists
    -in-the-military?rl=1.

34. Senator Richard Blumenthal et al, letter addressed to "The Honorable Sean
    O'Donnell, Acting Inspector General, Department of Defense," Blumenthal
    .Senate.Gov, January 14, 2021, https://www.blumenthal.senate.gov/imo/media/
    doc/2021.01.14%20Letter%20to%20DoD%20IG%20-%20Extremism%
    20in%20Military.pdf.

35. Mark Tapscott, "Marine Corps Officer Warns Congress Against Classifying
    Christians in Military as 'Religious Extremists,'" *Epoch Times*, March 24, 2021,
    https://www.theepochtimes.com/marine-officer-warns-congress-against
    -classifying-christians-in-military-as-religious-extremists_3748121.html?utm
    _source=morningbriefnoe&utm_medium=email&utm_campaign=mb-2021
    -03-25.

36. Ibid.

37. Morgan Lee, "Christian Nationalism Is Worse Than You Think," *Christianity
    Today*, January 13, 2021, https://www.christianitytoday.com/ct/podcasts/
    quick-to-listen/christian-nationalism-capitol-riots-trump-podcast.html.

38. Mark Galli, "Trump Should Be Removed from Office," *Christianity Today*,
    December 19, 2019, https://www.christianitytoday.com/ct/2019/december
    -web-only/trump-should-be-removed-from-office.html.

39. Morgan Lee, "Christian Nationalism Is Worse Than You Think," *Christianity
    Today*, January 13, 2021, https://www.christianitytoday.com/ct/podcasts/quick
    -to-listen/christian-nationalism-capitol-riots-trump-podcast.html.

40. Phillips Seminary/Center for Religion in Public Life, "Christian Nationalism
    May Be Different, and Closer, Than You Imagine," CRPL, February 17, 2021,
    https://www.ptstulsa.edu/rpli/christian-nationalism-may-be-closer/.

41. Christians Against Christian Nationalism, "Join More Than 22,000 Christians
    from Across the Country in Standing up to Christian Nationalism,"
    ChristiansAgainstChristianNationalism.org, undated, https://www
    .christiansagainstchristiannationalism.org/statement.

CHAPTER 6

1. Dan Mangan, "Trump Issues 'Coronavirus Guidelines' for Next 15 Days to
   Slow Pandemic," CNBC, March 16, 2020, https://www.cnbc.com/2020/03/16/
   trumps-coronavirus-guidelines-for-next-15-days-to-slow-pandemic.html.

2. Klaus Schwab, "Now Is the Time for a 'Great Reset,'" World Economic Forum,
   June 3, 2020, https://www.weforum.org/agenda/2020/06/now-is-the-time-for-a
   -great-reset/.

3. Hilary Sutcliffe, "COVID-19: The 4 Building Blocks of the Great Reset," World
   Economic Forum, August 11, 2020, https://www.weforum.org/agenda/2020/08/
   building-blocks-of-the-great-reset/.

4. Ibid.
5. Ibid.
6. Ibid.
7. Bob Zider, "How Venture Capital Works," *Harvard Business Review*, November–December 1998, https://hbr.org/1998/11/how-venture-capital-works.
8. Hilary Sutcliffe, "COVID-19: The 4 Building Blocks of the Great Reset," World Economic Forum, August 11, 2020, https://www.weforum.org/agenda/2020/08/building-blocks-of-the-great-reset/.
9. Ibid.
10. Ibid.
11. Ibid.
12. Jack Goodman and Flora Carmichael, "The Coronavirus Pandemic 'Great Reset' Theory and a False Vaccine Claim Debunked," BBC, November 22, 2020, https://www.bbc.com/news/55017002.
13. David Badash, "Libertarians Mocked for Freaking Out over 'Dystopian' Vaccine Passports: 'Have These People Never Attended School?'" The New Civil Rights Movement via Raw Story, March 30, 2021, https://www.rawstory.com/passport-vaccines-2651256332/.
14. ADL, "'The Great Reset,' Conspiracy Flourishes Amid Continued Pandemic," The Anti-Defamation League, December 29, 2020, https://www.adl.org/blog/the-great-reset-conspiracy-flourishes-amid-continued-pandemic.
15. Ibid.
16. Business Roundtable executives, "Business Roundtable Redefines the Purpose of a Corporation to Promote 'An Economy That Serves All Americans,'" Business Roundtable, August 19, 2019, https://www.businessroundtable.org/business-roundtable-redefines-the-purpose-of-a-corporation-to-promote-an-economy-that-serves-all-americans.
17. Klaus Schwab, "Why We Need the 'Davos Manifesto' for a Better Kind of Capitalism," World Economic Forum, December 1, 2019, https://www.weforum.org/agenda/2019/12/why-we-need-the-davos-manifesto-for-better-kind-of-capitalism/.
18. Ibid.
19. President Joe Biden, executive order, "Promoting COVID-19 Safety in Domestic and International Travel: Executive Order 13998," Federal Register, Signed by Biden January 21, 2021, Posted on Federal Register January 26, 2021, https://www.federalregister.gov/documents/2021/01/26/2021-01859/promoting-covid-19-safety-in-domestic-and-international-travel.
20. Kathryn Watson, "White House Leaves Vaccine 'Passports' to Private Sector," CBS News, March 30, 2021, https://www.cbsnews.com/news/biden-vaccine-passports-private-sector/.
21. Jen Psaki, "Press Briefing by Press Secretary Jen Psaki," White House Briefing Room, March 29, 2021, https://www.whitehouse.gov/briefing-room/press-briefings/2021/03/29/press-briefing-by-press-secretary-jen-psaki-march-29-2021/.
22. Klaus Schwab, "What Kind of Capitalism Do We Want?" Project Syndicate, December 2, 2019, https://www.project-syndicate.org/commentary/stakeholder-capitalism-new-metrics-by-klaus-schwab-2019-11?barrier=accesspaylog.

23. Business Roundtable, "Statement on the Purpose of a Corporation," BusinessRoundtable.org, Released August 19, 2019, Updated February 2021, https://system.businessroundtable.org/app/uploads/sites/5/2021/02/BRT -Statement-on-the-Purpose-of-a-Corporation-Feburary-2021-compressed.pdf.

24. Ibid.

25. Ibid.

26. PND, "PepsiCo Pledges $437.5 Million for Racial Equality Measures," *Philanthropy News Digest*, June 22, 2020, https://philanthropynewsdigest.org/news/pepsico-pledges-437.5-million-for-racial-equality-initiatives.

27. Ramon Laguarta, "PepsiCo's Racial Equality Journey/Black Initiative: A Message From Our CEO," PepsiCo.com, undated web site post, https://www.pepsico.com/about/diversity-and-engagement/racial-equality-journey-black -initiative.

28. James Quincey, "Where We Stand on Social Justice," prepared remarks for town hall with Coca-Cola employees, Coca-ColaCompany.com, June 3, 2020, https://www.coca-colacompany.com/news/where-we-stand-on-social-justice.

29. Rise, "PepsiCo Beverages Partners with RISE to Empower Sports Fans, Athletes and Leaders in the Industry to Fight Racism," RiseToWin.org, December 17, 2020, https://risetowin.org/stories/2020/12-17/pepsico-beverages-partners -with-rise/index.html.

30. Dominic-Madori Davis, "Ahead of Giving Tuesday, Coca-Cola Held a Virtual Dinner Series Event on Social Justice After Funding Millions in Grants This Year," *Business Insider*, December 1, 2020, https://www.businessinsider.com/coca-cola-co-sponsors-virtual-dinners-to-address-systemic-racism-2020-11.

31. Bradford Betz, "Coca-Cola Staff Told in Online Training Seminar 'Try to Be Less White,'" Fox Business, February 22, 2021, https://www.foxbusiness.com/lifestyle/coca-cola-staff-online-training-seminar-be-less-white.

32. Melisande Kingchatchaval Schifter, "How Companies Can Accelerate Racial Justice in Business," *Forbes*, January 25, 2021, https://www.forbes.com/sites/worldeconomicforum/2021/01/25/how-companies-can-accelerate-racial-justice -in-business/?sh=5a7dbb7239b2.

33. Craig Menear, "Message from Craig Menear—Racial Equality & Justice for All," Home Depot web page, June 1, 2020, https://corporate.homedepot.com/newsroom/message-craig-menear-%E2%80%93-racial-equality-justice-all.

34. Business & Human Rights Resource Centre, "Citi to Dedicate More Than $1 Billion to Initiative for Closing the Wealth Income Gap," Business-HumanRights.org, September 23, 2020, https://www.business-humanrights.org/en/latest-news/citi-to-dedicate-more-than-1-billion-to-initiative-for-closing -the-racial-wealth-gap/.

35. Business & Human Rights Resource Centre, "Ben & Jerry's Launches Podcast Examining the History of Racism & White Supremacy in the U.S.," Business-HumanRights.org, September 5, 2020, https://www.business -humanrights.org/en/latest-news/ben-jerrys-launches-podcast-examining-the -history-of-racism-white-supremacy-in-the-us/.

36. Business & Human Rights Resource Centre, "American Institute of Architects Expresses Commitment to Ending Racial Injustice & Violence," Business-HumanRights.org, December 15, 2020, https://www.business -humanrights.org/en/latest-news/usa-american-institute-of-architects-expresses -commitment-to-ending-racial-injustice-violence/.

37. Globe Newswire, "New Scorecards Compare 250 Largest S&P Companies on Racial Justice and Workplace Equity Disclosure," Intrado Globe Newswire, from As You Sow, November 18, 2020, http://www.globenewswire.com/news -release/2020/11/18/2129358/0/en/New-Scorecards-Compare-250-Largest-S -P-Companies-on-Racial-Justice-and-Workplace-Equity-Disclosure.html.
38. Vanessa Butterworth, "These Six Oil Companies Are Funding the Police (and Must Be Stopped!)," Greenpeace, October 14, 2020, https://www.greenpeace .org/usa/these-oil-companies-fund-the-police/.
39. Kari Paul, "How Target, Google, Bank of America and Microsoft Quietly Fund Police Through Private Donations," *Guardian*, June 18, 2020, https://www .theguardian.com/us-news/2020/jun/18/police-foundations-nonprofits-amazon -target-microsoft.
40. Jem Bendell, "Does Capitalism Need Some Marxism to Survive the Fourth Industrial Revolution?" World Economic Forum, June 22, 2016, https:// www.weforum.org/agenda/2016/06/could-capitalism-need-some-marxism-to -survive-the-4th-industrial-revolution/.

CHAPTER 7

1. Governor.NY.gov, "Governor Cuomo Announces Pilot Program Testing the Excelsior Pass at Madison Square Garden and Barclays Center," New York State Governor's Office, News, April 7, 2021, https://www.governor.ny.gov/news/ governor-cuomo-announces-pilot-program-testing-excelsior-pass-madison -square-garden-and.
2. Ibid.
3. Joanna Fantozzi, "Some States Are Moving to Restrict COVID 'Vaccination Passport' Mandates," Nation's Restaurant News, April 7, 2021, https://www.nrn .com/restaurants-ready/some-states-are-moving-restrict-covid-vaccination -passport-mandates.
4. Ibid.
5. Bailey Schulz, "Vaccine Passports Launched in Las Vegas But Privacy, Choice Still Concerns," *Las Vegas Review-Journal*, March 31, 2021, https://www.reviewjournal .com/business/casinos-gaming/vaccine-passports-launched-in-las-vegas-but -privacy-choice-still-concerns-2318935/.
6. Governor.NY.gov, "Governor Cuomo Announces Pilot Program Testing the Excelsior Pass at Madison Square Garden and Barclays Center," New York State Governor's Office, News, April 7, 2021, https://www.governor.ny.gov/news/ governor-cuomo-announces-pilot-program-testing-excelsior-pass-madison-square -garden-and.
7. American Queen Steamboat Company, Safecruise: Vaccinations, undated, https://www.americanqueensteamboatcompany.com/health-and-safety/.
8. Ibid.
9. Ryan Howard, "Could Vaccination Records Be Part of an Employment Background Check?" Verifirst, December 11, 2020, https://blog.verifirst.com/ could-vaccination-records-be-part-of-an-employment-background-check.
10. WebMD, "Coronavirus Recovery," WebMD, Reviewed by Hansa D. Bhargava, MD, August 7, 2020, https://www.webmd.com/lung/covid-recovery -overview#1.

11. Jordan E. Taylor, "The U.S. Has Had 'Vaccine Passports' Before–and They Worked," *Time* magazine, April 5, 2021, https://time.com/5952532/vaccine-passport-history/.
12. Ibid.
13. Ibid.
14. Ibid.
15. Mary Losure, "Smallpox Hit Lumber Camps Hard," Minnesota Public Radio, November 26, 2001, http://news.minnesota.publicradio.org/features/200111/26_losurem_smallpox/lumbercamp.shtml.
16. Jordan E. Taylor, "The U.S. Has Had 'Vaccine Passports' Before–and They Worked," *Time* magazine, April 5, 2021, https://time.com/5952532/vaccine-passport-history/.
17. Dave Roos, "The First 'Vaccine Passports' Were Scars from Smallpox Vaccinations," *History*, April 9, 2021, https://www.history.com/news/vaccine-passports-smallpox-scar.
18. Ibid.
19. Rebecca Coffey, "The Smallpox and Coronavirus Vaccines: 30 Facts from 'The Vaccine Vault,'" *Forbes*, November 20, 2020, https://www.forbes.com/sites/rebeccacoffey/2020/11/20/tales-from-the-vaccine-vault-30-facts-about-smallpox-and-the-coronavirus/?sh=3fd0677547a7.
20. American Museum of Natural History, "Smallpox: Lessons from the Past," AMNH, undated, https://www.amnh.org/explore/science-topics/disease-eradication/countdown-to-zero/smallpox#:~:text=Today%2C%20the%20virus%20only%20exists,million%20people%20since%201900%20alone.
21. World Health Organization, "COVID-19 Weekly Epidemiological Update," data from WHO national authorities, April 4, 2021, file:///C:/Users/cheryl/Downloads/20210406_Weekly_Epi_Update_34.pdf.
22. Roseanna Garza, "'Head-Spinning Discrepancy': Why Numbers for State and Local Covid-19 Deaths Don't Match," San Antonio Report, August 5, 2020, https://sanantonioreport.org/head-spinning-discrepancy-why-numbers-for-state-and-local-covid-19-deaths-dont-match/.
23. Louis Bolden, "Trust Index: News 6 Discovers Discrepancy in COVID-19 Deaths Reported in Florida," News 6, updated May 22, 2020, https://www.clickorlando.com/news/florida/2020/05/21/trust-index-news-6-discovers-discrepancy-in-covid-19-deaths-reported-in-florida/.
24. Sam Meredith, "Dr. Fauci Says 'Help Is on the Way' with Vaccines, But Doubts Covid Can Ever Be Eradicated," CNBC, November 12, 2020, https://www.cnbc.com/2020/11/12/coronavirus-dr-fauci-says-he-doubts-whether-covid-can-be-eradicated.html.
25. Ibid.
26. Rebecca Coffey, "The Smallpox and Coronavirus Vaccines: 30 Facts from 'The Vaccine Vault,'" Forbes, November 20, 2020, https://www.forbes.com/sites/rebeccacoffey/2020/11/20/tales-from-the-vaccine-vault-30-facts-about-smallpox-and-the-coronavirus/?sh=3fd0677547a7.
27. U.S. Food and Drug Administration, "Smallpox," FDA.gov, March 23, 2018, https://www.fda.gov/vaccines-blood-biologics/vaccines/smallpox#:~:text=During%20the%20smallpox%20era%2C%20the,insect%20reservoirs%20or%20vectors%20existed.

28. Max Roser, Sophie Ochmann, Hannah Behrens, Hannah Ritchie, and Bernadeta Dadonaite, "Eradication of Diseases," Our World in Data, published June 2014, revised October 2018, https://ourworldindata.org/eradication-of-diseases.

29. Agriculture and Consumer Protection Department, Animal Production and Health, "Questions & Answers: What Is Rinderpest?" Food and Agriculture Organization of the United Nations, updated November 18, 2015, http://www.fao.org/ag/againfo/programmes/en/rinderpest/qa_rinder.html#:~:text=Rinderpest%2C%20or%20cattle%20plague%2C%20is,include%20swine%2C%20giraffes%20and%20kudus.

30. Max Roser, Sophie Ochmann, Hannah Behrens, Hannah Ritchie, and Bernadeta Dadonaite, "Eradication of Diseases," Our World in Data, published June 2014, revised October 2018, https://ourworldindata.org/eradication-of-diseases.

31. Ibid.

32. Ibid.

33. Katherine J. Wu, "There Are More Viruses Than Stars in the Universe. Why Do Only Some Infect Us?" *National Geographic*, April 15, 2020, https://www.nationalgeographic.com/science/article/factors-allow-viruses-infect-humans-coronavirus.

34. Ibid.

35. Dirk Schulze-Makuch, "There Are More Viruses on Earth Than There Are Stars in the Universe," *Air & Space* magazine, March 17, 2020, https://www.airspacemag.com/daily-planet/there-are-more-viruses-earth-there-are-stars-universe-180974433/.

36. Katherine J. Wu, "There Are More Viruses Than Stars in the Universe. Why Do Only Some Infect Us?" *National Geographic*, April 15, 2020, https://www.nationalgeographic.com/science/article/factors-allow-viruses-infect-humans-coronavirus.

37. Dirk Schulze-Makuch, "There Are More Viruses on Earth Than There Are Stars in the Universe," *Air & Space* magazine, March 17, 2020, https://www.airspacemag.com/daily-planet/there-are-more-viruses-earth-there-are-stars-universe-180974433/.

38. Pfizer, "4 Things to Know About the Science of Coronavirus," Breakthroughs, 2020, https://www.breakthroughs.com/disease-decoded/4-things-know-about-science-coronavirus.

39. Medical News Today, "How Do SARS and MERS Compare with COVID-19?" *Medical News Today* newsletter, April 2020, https://www.medicalnewstoday.com/articles/how-do-sars-and-mers-compare-with-covid-19#MERS.

40. Dina Temple-Raston, "Officials Knew CDC Coronavirus Test Kit Was Prone to Failure," NPR, November 6, 2020, https://www.npr.org/2020/11/06/929078678/cdc-report-officials-knew-coronavirus-test-was-flawed-but-released-it-anyway.

41. Carolyn Crist, "Early CDC COVID-19 Test Kits 'Likely Contaminated,'" WebMD, June 23, 2020, https://www.webmd.com/lung/news/20200623/early-cdc-covid-19-test-kits-likely-contaminated.

42. Mike Stobbe, "Experts Say US Coronavirus Death Count Is Flawed, But Close," Associated Press, May 27, 2020, https://apnews.com/article/467387275ae5779c9bf031f3f2bcb2cf.

43. Michelle Rogers, "Fact Check: Hospitals Get Paid More If Patients Listed as Covid-19, on Ventilators," *USA Today*, April 24, 2020, updated April 27, 2020, https://www.usatoday.com/story/news/factcheck/2020/04/24/fact-check -medicare-hospitals-paid-more-covid-19-patients-coronavirus/3000638001/.

44. Cecelia Smith-Schoenwalder, "Fauci Sounds Alarm Over Coronavirus Variant First Found in U.K.," *U.S. News & World Report*, March 19, 2021, https:// www.usnews.com/news/health-news/articles/2021-03-19/fauci-sounds-alarm -over-coronavirus-variant-first-found-in-uk.

45. CNN Wire, "CDC Director Warns COVID Variants Could Spark Another Avoidable Surge as Travel Numbers Reach High," ABC 6 Action News, March 23, 2021, https://6abc.com/covid-surge-cdc-warning-air-travel-spring-break/ 10441253/.

46. Ibid.

47. National Center for Immunization and Respiratory Diseases (NCIRD), Division of Viral Diseases, "About Variants of the Virus That Causes COVID-19," Centers for Disease Control and Prevention, updated April 2, 2021, https://www.cdc.gov/coronavirus/2019-ncov/transmission/variant.html.

48. Chris Wilson, "The U.S. Has Flattened the Curve. Next Up Is 'Squashing It'– and That's Not Going Well," *Time* magazine, April 27, 2020, updated August 22, 2020, https://time.com/5827156/squashing-squash-curve-coronavirus -covid19/.

49. Julia Kollewe, "From Pfizer to Moderns: Who's Making Billions from Covid-19 Vaccines?" *Guardian*, March 6, 2021, https://www.theguardian.com/ business/2021/mar/06/from-pfizer-to-moderna-whos-making-billions-from -covid-vaccines.

50. Ibid.

51. Ibid.

52. Ibid.

53. Ibid.

54. Ibid.

55. Jeff Mason, "U.S. to Share 4 Million Doses of AstraZeneca COVID-19 Vaccine with Mexico, Canada," Reuters, March 18, 2021, https://www.reuters.com/ article/us-health-coronavirus-usa-mexico/u-s-to-share-4-million-doses-of -astrazeneca-covid-19-vaccine-with-mexico-canada-idUSKBN2BA22S.

56. Ibid.

57. David Bank and Rebecca Buckman, "Gates Foundation Buys Stakes in Drug Makers," *The Wall Street Journal*, May 17, 2002, https://www.wsj.com/articles/ SB1021577629748680000.

58. Keith Speights, "4 Coronavirus Vaccine Stocks the Bill & Melinda Gates Foundation Is Betting On," The Motley Fool, September 24, 2020, https:// www.fool.com/investing/2020/09/24/4-coronavirus-vaccine-stocks-the-bill -melinda-gate/.

59. Ibid.

60. Holly Ellyatt, "Covid Vaccine Maker Curevac Hopes Shot Will Get EU Approval in June," CNBC, April 8, 2021, https://www.cnbc.com/2021/04/08/ covid-vaccine-maker-curevac-hopes-shot-will-get-eu-approval-in-june.html.

61. Mohana Basu, "10-Year-Old US Firm with Harvard and MIT Brains Begins First COVID-19 Vaccine Trials," The Print, March 17, 2020, https://theprint

.in/health/10-year-old-us-firm-with-harvard-and-mit-brains-begins-first-covid
-19-vaccine-trials/382504/.

62. CEPI, "Creating a World in Which Epidemics Are No Longer a Threat to
    Humanity," CEPI.net, 2021, https://cepi.net/about/whyweexist/.

63. CEPI, "A Global Coalition for a Global Problem," CEPI.net, 2021, https://
    cepi.net/about/whoweare/.

64. International Finance Facility for Immunizations, "What Is Gavi?" IFFIM.org,
    2020, https://iffim.org/what-gavi.

65. Ibid.

66. Gavi.org, "Gavi's Partnership Model," Gavi.org, undated, https://www.gavi.org/
    our-alliance/operating-model/gavis-partnership-model.

67. Bill and Melinda Gates, "The Year Global Health Went Local," GatesNotes: The
    blog of Bill Gates, January 27, 2021, https://www.gatesnotes.com/2021
    -Annual-Letter.

68. Seth Berkley, "COVAX Explained," Gavi.org, September 2020, https://
    www.gavi.org/vaccineswork/covax-explained?gclid=EAIaIQobChMIgriE49
    D27wIVsQeICR35Ygo_EAAYASAAEgKGCfD_BwE.

69. Ibid.

70. Ibid.

71. Shivni Patel, "A COVID-19 Vaccine May Create New Problems," Johns
    Hopkins newsletter, April 11, 2021, https://www.jhunewsletter.com/article/
    2020/03/a-covid-19-vaccine-may-create-new-problems.

72. Julia Kollewe, "Moderna Forecasts $18bn in Sales of Covid Vaccine This Year,"
    Guardian, February 25, 2021, https://www.theguardian.com/business/2021/
    feb/25/moderna-forecasts-18bn-in-sales-of-covid-vaccine-this-year.

73. Kelly McSweeney, "The E Tattoo Is the Future of Healthcare Technology,"
    NOW.NorthrupGrumman.com, January 24, 2020, https://now
    .northropgrumman.com/e-tattoos-are-futuristic-healthcare-wearables/.

CHAPTER 8

1. Bill Gates, "What You Can Do to Fight Climate Change," GatesNotes.com,
   February 14, 2021, https://www.gatesnotes.com/Energy/What-you-can-do-to
   -fight-climate-change.

2. Dan Goodin, "Revisiting the Spectacular Failure That Was the Bill Gates
   Deposition," *Ars Technica*, September 10, 2020, https://arstechnica.com/tech
   -policy/2020/09/revisiting-the-spectacular-failure-that-was-the-bill-gates
   -deposition/.

3. John Naughton, "Let's Not Forget, Bill Gates Hasn't Always Been the Good Guy,"
   Guardian, August 29, 2020, https://www.theguardian.com/commentisfree/2020/
   aug/29/lets-not-forget-bill-gates-hasnt-always-been-the-good-guy.

4. Rob Larson, "Bill Gates' Philanthropic Giving Is a Racket," *Jacobin*, April 5,
   2020, https://www.jacobinmag.com/2020/04/bill-gates-foundation-philanthropy
   -microsoft.

5. John Naughton, "Let's Not Forget, Bill Gates Hasn't Always Been the Good Guy,"
   Guardian, August 29, 2020, https://www.theguardian.com/commentisfree/2020/
   aug/29/lets-not-forget-bill-gates-hasnt-always-been-the-good-guy.

6. Knowledge Ecology International, "Microsoft, Gates Foundation Timeline," KEIonling.org, November 29, 2010, revised January 4, 2011, https://www.keionline.org/microsoft-timeline.

7. Rose Berg and Victor Zonana, "Bill and Melinda Gates Make $25 Million Grant to International AIDS Vaccine Initiative," Bill & Melinda Gates Foundation, 1999, https://www.gatesfoundation.org/ideas/media-center/press-releases/1999/05/international-aids-vaccine-initiative.

8. David Bank, "Gates Steps Aside as Microsoft's CEO; Ballmer to Take Over Daily Operations," *Wall Street Journal*, January 14, 2000, https://www.wsj.com/articles/SB947799478575341462.

9. CNN staff, "Europe to Probe Microsoft," CNN London, February 9, 2000, https://money.cnn.com/2000/02/09/europe/monti_microsoft/.

10. Knowledge Ecology International, "Microsoft, Gates Foundation Timeline," KEIonling.org, November 29, 2010, revised January 4, 2011, https://www.keionline.org/microsoft-timeline.

11. Andrew Glass, "Judge Says Microsoft Violates Anti-trust Act, April 3, 2000," Politico, April 3, 2014, https://www.politico.com/story/2014/04/judge-says-microsoft-violates-antitrust-act-april-3-2000-105298#:~:text=U.S.%20District%20Judge%20Thomas%20Penfield,monopoly%20Sections%201%20and%202.

12. The New Humanitarian staff, "Funds Pledged to Fight AIDS," *New Humanitarian*, July 10, 2000, https://www.thenewhumanitarian.org/report/3876/botswana-funds-pledged-fight-aids.

13. Laurel Macklin and Trevor Neilson, "Bill & Melinda Gates Foundation Announces $1 Million Award for Global Health," Bill & Melinda Gates Foundation, October 12, 2000, https://www.gatesfoundation.org/ideas/media-center/press-releases/2000/12/gates-award-for-global-health.

14. Knowledge Ecology International, "Microsoft, Gates Foundation Timeline," KEIonling.org, November 29, 2010, revised January 4, 2011, https://www.keionline.org/microsoft-timeline.

15. Laurel Macklin and Trevor Neilson, "Bill & Melinda Gates Foundation Announces $1 Million Award for Global Health," Bill & Melinda Gates Foundation, October 12, 2000, https://www.gatesfoundation.org/ideas/media-center/press-releases/2000/12/gates-award-for-global-health.

16. Knowledge Ecology International, "Microsoft, Gates Foundation Timeline," KEIonling.org, November 29, 2010, revised January 4, 2011, https://www.keionline.org/microsoft-timeline.

17. Randall Smith, "As His Foundation Has Grown, Gates Has Slowed His Donations," *The New York Times*, May 26, 2014, https://dealbook.nytimes.com/2014/05/26/as-his-foundation-has-grown-gates-has-slowed-his-donations/.

18. Ibid.

19. Paul Vallely, "How Philanthropy Benefits the Rich," *Guardian*, September 8, 2020, https://www.theguardian.com/society/2020/sep/08/how-philanthropy-benefits-the-super-rich.

20. Catherine Cheney, "'Big Concerns' Over Gates Foundation's Potential to Become Largest WHO Contributor," Devex, June 5, 2020, https://www.devex.com/news/big-concerns-over-gates-foundation-s-potential-to-become-largest-who-donor-97377.

21. Ibid.
22. Paul Vallely, " How Philanthropy Benefits the Rich," *Guardian*, September 8, 2020, https://www.theguardian.com/society/2020/sep/08/how-philanthropy-benefits-the-super-rich.
23. Jessica Bursztynsky, "Bill Gates Says Bioterrorism and Climate Change Are the Next Biggest Threats After Pandemic," CNBC, February 11, 2020, https://www.cnbc.com/2021/02/11/bill-gates-says-bioterrorism-climate-change-are-the-next-big-threats.html.
24. Bill Gates and Judy Woodruff, "Bill Gates on Tackling Climate Change and the Ongoing Pandemic Response," PBS, February 22, 2021, https://www.pbs.org/newshour/show/bill-gates-on-tackling-climate-change-and-the-ongoing-pandemic-response.
25. Ibid.
26. Justin Worland, "The Pandemic Remade Every Corner of Society. Now It's the Climate's Turn," Time magazine, April 15, 2021, https://time.com/5953374/climate-is-everything/.
27. Ibid.
28. Kriston Capps, "Can an 'Activist HUD' Make Housing a Human Right?" Bloomberg, January 29, 2021, https://www.bloomberg.com/news/articles/2021-01-29/marcia-fudge-wants-to-transform-u-s-housing-rights.
29. Ibid.
30. Justin Worland, "The Pandemic Remade Every Corner of Society. Now It's the Climate's Turn," Time magazine, April 15, 2021, https://time.com/5953374/climate-is-everything/.
31. Gina McCarthy, "It's Time to Take Climate Change Personally," WBUR, May 31, 2018, https://www.wbur.org/cognoscenti/2018/05/31/global-warming-harvard-gina-mccarthy.
32. Justin Worland, "The Pandemic Remade Every Corner of Society. Now It's the Climate's Turn," Time magazine, April 15, 2021, https://time.com/5953374/climate-is-everything/.
33. Klaus Schwab, "Now Is the Time for a 'Great Reset,'" World Economic Forum, June 3, 2020, https://www.weforum.org/agenda/2020/06/now-is-the-time-for-a-great-reset/.
34. Emily Crane, "How Biden's Climate Plan Could Limit You to Eat Just One Burger a MONTH, Cost $3.5K a Year per Person in Taxes, Force You to Spend $55k on an Electric Car and 'Crush' American jobs," Telegraph, April 22, 2021, updated April 26, 2021, https://www.dailymail.co.uk/news/article-9501565/How-Bidens-climate-plan-affect-everyday-Americans.html.
35. Ibid.
36. Ibid.
37. Joseph Biden, "Executive Order on Tackling the Climate Crisis at Home and Abroad," The White House, January 27, 2021, https://www.whitehouse.gov/briefing-room/presidential-actions/2021/01/27/executive-order-on-tackling-the-climate-crisis-at-home-and-abroad/.
38. White House communications, "Readout of the First National Climate Task Force Meeting," The White House, February 11, 2021, https://www.whitehouse.gov/briefing-room/statements-releases/2021/02/11/readout-of-the-first-national-climate-task-force-meeting/.

39. White House communications, "Readout of the Second National Climate Task Force Meeting," The White House, March 18, 2021, https://www.whitehouse.gov/briefing-room/statements-releases/2021/03/18/readout-of-the-second-national-climate-task-force-meeting/.

40. Ibid.

41. Jeff Mason, "Biden's Climate Duo of Kerry and McCarthy Puts U.S. Back in Global Warming Fight," Reuters, April 16, 2021, https://www.reuters.com/business/environment/bidens-climate-duo-kerry-mccarthy-puts-us-back-global-warming-fight-2021-04-16/.

42. Lorraine Woellert, "Biden Prepares Sweeping Order on Climate-Related Risks," Politico, April 15, 2021, https://www.politico.com/news/2021/04/15/biden-climate-risks-executive-order-481962.

43. Ibid.

44. Jenny Leonard, "Biden Plans to Order Climate Risk Strategy for Financial Assets," Bloomberg, April 8, 2021, https://www.bloomberg.com/news/articles/2021-04-08/biden-plans-to-order-climate-risk-strategy-for-financial-assets.

45. Emily Aubert, "Biden Plans Exec Order on Climate-Related Financial Risk," Ballotpedia News, April 16, 2021, https://news.ballotpedia.org/2021/04/16/biden-plans-exec-order-on-climate-related-financial-risk/.

46. Jessica DiNapoli and Ross Kerber, "Labor Department Finalizes U.S. Rule Curbing Sustainable Investing by Pension Funds," Reuters, October 30, 2020, https://www.reuters.com/article/us-esg-rule/labor-department-finalizes-u-s-rule-curbing-sustainable-investing-by-pension-funds-idUSKBN27F35M.

47. The Action Network, "TSP Go Fossil Free! Protect the Retirement Assets of Federal Thrift Savings Plan Participants," petition from The Action Network, undated, https://actionnetwork.org/petitions/tsp-go-fossil-free/.

48. Lorraine Woellert, "Biden Prepares Sweeping Order on Climate-Related Risks," Politico, April 15, 2021, https://www.politico.com/news/2021/04/15/biden-climate-risks-executive-order-481962.

49. Jung Hyun Choi and Daniel Pang, "Six Facts You Should Know About Current Mortgage Forbearances," Urban Wire, the blog of the Urban Institute, April 18, 2020, https://www.urban.org/urban-wire/six-facts-you-should-know-about-current-mortgage-forbearances.

50. PTI, "Climate Change to Be Centre of National Security, Foreign Policy, Says Joe Biden," Financial Express, January 28, 2021, https://www.financialexpress.com/world-news/climate-change-to-be-centre-of-national-security-foreign-policy-says-joe-biden/2180352/.

51. Rebecca Beitsch, "Kerry: Climate Change Among 'Most Complex Security Issues We've Ever Faced,'" The Hill, February 19, 2021, https://thehill.com/policy/national-security/539619-kerry-climate-change-among-most-complex-security-issues-weve-ever.

52. AP, "Biden Meets with UN Security Council Members to Talk Climate," Associated Press, March 18, 2021, https://apnews.com/article/joe-biden-donald-trump-climate-climate-change-john-kerry-affbb64ad6f3df6b-4ca7a27295b2ed7c.

53. Press Trust of India, "USAID, DFC Announce $41 Million Financing for Renewable Energy in India," Press Trust of India via Business Standard, March 18, 2021, https://www.business-standard.com/article/current-affairs/usaid-dfc-announce-41-million-financing-for-renewable-energy-in-india

-121031800508_1.html#:~:text=USAID%2C%20DFC%20announce%20
%2441%20million%20financing%20for%20renewable%20energy%20in%20
India,-Press%20Trust%20of&text=The%20United%20States%20Agency%20
for,energy%20solutions%20by%20Indian%20SMEs.

54. Press, USAID, "U.S. Special Presidential Envoy for Climate John Kerry
Highlighted USAID Initiatives in India and Bangladesh to Combat Climate
Change," USAID, Office of Press Relations, April 9, 2021, https://www.usaid
.gov/news-information/press-releases/apr-9-2021-us-special-presidential-envoy
-climate-john-kerry-highlighted-usaid.

55. U.S. International Development Finance Corporation, "Overview," DFC,
undated, https://www.dfc.gov/who-we-are/overview.

56. Encourage Capital, "Who We Are," Encourage Capital website, undated,
http://encouragecapital.com/our-firm/who-we-are/.

57. PR Newswire, "New Energy Nexus and cKers Finance Grow Investment
Partnership to Build New Distributed Solar Segments in India," cKers Finance
Private Limited, March 11, 2020, https://www.prnewswire.com/in/news
-releases/new-energy-nexus-and-ckers-finance-grow-investment-partnership-to
-build-new-distributed-solar-segments-in-india-896529438.html.

58. EFL, "EFL, by Your Side: About Us," EFL.co.in, undated, https://www.efl.co
.in/about-us/.

59. Ibid.

60. Ibid.

61. CFI, "What Is a Non-Banking Financial Company (NBFC)?" Corporate
Finance Institute, undated, https://corporatefinanceinstitute.com/resources/
knowledge/finance/non-banking-financial-company-nbfc/.

62. Ibid.

63. ClearTax, "What Are Masala Bonds and Their Benefits?" ClearTax, updated
January 5, 2021, https://cleartax.in/s/masala-bonds.

64. EFL, "EFL, By Your Side: Milestones," EFL.co.in, undated, https://www.efl.co
.in/about-us/.

65. UNICEF, "Supply Division: What Is a Cold Chain?" UNICEF.org, undated,
https://www.unicef.org/supply/what-cold-chain.

66. Press, USAID, "U.S. Special Presidential Envoy for Climate John Kerry
Highlighted USAID Initiatives in India and Bangladesh to Combat Climate
Change," USAID, Office of Press Relations, April 9, 2021, https://www.usaid
.gov/news-information/press-releases/apr-9-2021-us-special-presidential-envoy
-climate-john-kerry-highlighted-usaid.

67. CDRI, "CDRI Overview," CDRI website, undated, https://cdri.world/cdri
-overview.

68. Ibid.

69. United Nations, "Department of Economic and Social Affairs: Sustainable
Development," SDGS.UN.org, undated, https://sdgs.un.org/goals.

70. Shannon Pettypiece and Lauren Egan, "Beyond Roads and Bridges, Biden Seeks
to Redefine 'Infrastructure' Amid GOP Criticism," NBC News, April 7, 2021,
https://www.nbcnews.com/politics/white-house/biden-push-back-criticism
-infrastructure-bill-goes-too-far-n1263293.

71. Ibid.

72. Biden-Harris campaign, "The Biden Plan for a Clean Energy Revolution and Environmental Justice," Biden-Harris Climate Campaign Plan, 2020, https://joebiden.com/climate-plan/.

73. Shannon Pettypiece and Lauren Egan, "Beyond Roads and Bridges, Biden Seeks to Redefine 'Infrastructure' Amid GOP Criticism," NBC News, April 7, 2021, https://www.nbcnews.com/politics/white-house/biden-push-back-criticism-infrastructure-bill-goes-too-far-n1263293.

74. The White House, "Fact Sheet: The American Jobs Plan," the White House briefing room, March 31, 2021, https://www.whitehouse.gov/briefing-room/statements-releases/2021/03/31/fact-sheet-the-american-jobs-plan/.

75. Ibid.

76. Ibid.

77. Romina Ruiz-Goiriena, "Biden's Infrastructure Plan Calls for Cities to Limit Single-Family Zoning and Instead Build Affordable Housing," *USA Today*, April 14, 2021, https://www.usatoday.com/in-depth/news/nation/2021/04/14/zoning-biden-infrastructure-bill-would-curb-single-family-housing/7097434002/.

78. Bill Gates, "What You Can Do to Fight Climate Change," GatesNotes, February 14, 2021, https://www.gatesnotes.com/Energy/What-you-can-do-to-fight-climate-change.

79. Aryn Baker, "They're Healthy. They're Sustainable. So Why Don't Humans Eat More Bugs?" *Time* magazine, February 26, 2021, https://time.com/5942290/eat-insects-save-planet/.

80. Ede Ijjasz and Aloysius Uche Ordu, "Climate Adaptation and the Great Reset for Africa," Brookings Institution, April 7, 2021, https://www.brookings.edu/blog/africa-in-focus/2021/04/07/climate-adaptation-and-the-great-reset-for-africa/.

81. Harvard staff, "Coronavirus and Climate Change," Harvard T.H. Chan School of Public Health, 2021, updated regularly, https://www.hsph.harvard.edu/c-change/subtopics/coronavirus-and-climate-change/.

82. Klaus Schwab, "Great Reset: For a Healthier, More Equitable and Prosperous Post COVID-19 World," Iberdrola, undated, https://www.iberdrola.com/innovation/great-reset.

83. Jarrett Skorup, "Michigan Moving to Make 'Emergency' COVID-19 Mandates Permanent," *Reason*, April 16, 2021, https://reason.com/2021/04/16/michigan-moving-to-make-emergency-covid-19-mandates-permanent/.

CHAPTER 9

1. Orwell, George, *Animal Farm*, London, Seeker and Warburg, 1945.

2. Joe Biden, The White House, "Remarks by President Biden on Gun Violence Prevention," The White House Briefing Room, April 8, 2021, https://www.whitehouse.gov/briefing-room/speeches-remarks/2021/04/08/remarks-by-president-biden-on-gun-violence-prevention/#:~:text=But%20no%20amendment%20%E2%80%94%20no%20amendment,weapon%20you%20wanted%20to%20own.

3. Ibid.

4. Thomas Jefferson, "Extract from Thomas Jefferson to William Johnson," Library of Congress repository via Monticello.org, June 12, 1823, https://tjrs.monticello.org/letter/417#X3184736.
5. Orwell, George, *Animal Farm*, London, Seeker and Warburg, 1945.
6. Ibid.
7. Ibid.
8. Guy Burdick, "Virginia Adopts a Permanent COVID-19 Standard," *EHS Daily Advisor*, February 1, 2021, https://ehsdailyadvisor.blr.com/2021/02/virginia-adopts-a-permanent-covid-19-standard/.
9. Ibid.
10. Ibid.
11. Guy Burdick, "Oregon Proposes Permanent COVID-19 Infectious Disease Standard," *EHS Daily Advisor*, February 12, 2021, https://ehsdailyadvisor.blr.com/2021/02/oregon-proposes-permanent-covid-19-infectious-disease-standard/.
12. Aaron Corvin, public information officer, "Oregon OSHA proposes permanent rule addressing COVID-19 in all workplaces," State of Oregon Newsroom, February 1, 2021, https://www.oregon.gov/newsroom/Pages/NewsDetail.aspx?newsid=54135.
13. Jackie Salo, "CDC 'Looking' into Whether Masks Are Necessary Outside," *New York Post*, April 22, 2021, https://nypost.com/2021/04/22/cdc-looking-into-whether-masks-are-necessary-outside/.
14. Graham Couch, "Couch: Masks for High School Athletes? It's Safe, Health Experts Insist," *Lansing State Journal*, published September 8, 2020, updated September 9, 2020, https://www.lansingstatejournal.com/story/sports/columnists/graham-couch/2020/09/08/high-school-athletes-football-players-runners-wearing-masks-while-competing-is-safe/5746725002/.
15. Jackie Salo, "CDC 'Looking' into Whether Masks Are Necessary Outside," *New York Post*, April 22, 2021, https://nypost.com/2021/04/22/cdc-looking-into-whether-masks-are-necessary-outside/.
16. Sara Holder, "2021 Will Be the Year of Guaranteed Income Experiments," Bloomberg, January 4, 2021, https://www.bloomberg.com/news/articles/2021-01-04/guaranteed-income-gains-popularity-after-covid-19.
17. Ibid.
18. Natalie Marchant, "Half of Those Surveyed Are Unaware of the Link Between Climate Change and Diseases Like COVID-19," World Economic Forum, January 20, 2021, https://www.weforum.org/agenda/2021/01/climate-change-link-infectious-diseases-covid-19-study/.
19. Ibid.
20. Brian Mastroianni, "Why Addressing Gun Violence as a Health Crisis Is Crucial for Change," Healthline, Janaury 14, 2021, https://www.healthline.com/health-news/why-addressing-gun-violence-as-a-health-crisis-is-crucial-for-change.
21. Ibid.
22. APHA, "Gun Violence," American Public Health Association, undated, https://www.apha.org/Topics-and-Issues/Gun-Violence.
23. David Smith, "Gun Violence in This Country Is an Epidemic," *Guardian*, April 8, 2021, https://www.theguardian.com/us-news/2021/apr/08/joe-biden-gun-violence-executive-actions-epidemic.

24. Ibid.
25. Susan Erikson, "Pandemics Show Us What Government Is For," *Nature*, April 3, 2020, https://www.nature.com/articles/s41562-020-0871-4.
26. Ibid.
27. Ibid.
28. John Halpin, "Americans Want the Federal Government To Help People in Need," Center for American Progress, March 10, 2021, https://www.americanprogress.org/issues/politics-and-elections/reports/2021/03/10/496744/americans-want-federal-government-help-people-need/.
29. Center for American Progress, "Board of Directors," AmericanProgress.org, 2021, https://www.americanprogress.org/about/c3-board/.
30. John Halpin, "Americans Want the Federal Government to Help People in Need," Center for American Progress, March 10, 2021, https://www.americanprogress.org/issues/politics-and-elections/reports/2021/03/10/496744/americans-want-federal-government-help-people-need/.

EPILOGUE

1. Cheryl K. Chumley, "Coronavirus hype biggest political hoax in history," *The Washington Times*, April 28, 2020, https://www.washingtontimes.com/news/2020/apr/28/coronavirus-hype-biggest-political-hoax-in-history/.
2. Cheryl K. Chumley, "Forced face masking is a civil rights offense," *The Washington Times*, May 1, 2020, https://www.washingtontimes.com/news/2020/may/1/forced-face-masking-civil-rights-offense/.

Index

About the Author

Cheryl Chumley is an author, commentary writer, and the online opinion editor for *The Washington Times*, where she also hosts a podcast, *Bold and Blunt*, about politics and culture from a Christian, conservative perspective. Her first book, *Police State USA: How Orwell's Nightmare Is Becoming Our Reality*, hit the bookshelves at a time of great societal unrest, when police faced criticisms for their handling of a black Ferguson, Missouri, eighteen-year-old named Michael Brown, and rioters took to the streets of St. Louis—much in the vein of the Black Lives Matter and Antifa uprisings of 2020, stemming from outrage over the death of George Floyd at the hands of officers. Her second book, *Devil in DC: Winning Back the Country from the Beast in Washington*, was a solution-oriented look at the political and cultural ills of America, as described in Police State USA. Her third book, *Socialists Don't Sleep: Christians Must Rise or America Will Fall*, was an Amazon bestseller in several categories and for several months, and provided a dire warning of the societal, cultural, and political ills that were befalling America, and then explained why Christians were particularly well-positioned to fight and win.

Cheryl is a Robert Novak Journalism Fellow, and spent a year researching and writing about National Heritage Areas and the state of private property rights in the country. She's an award-winning journalist with recognition in state contests for her use of the Freedom of Information Act to root out government corruption and track money in politics. And she's a frequent media guest on national television and radio, and an experienced public speaker, passionate about topics related to Christianity and conservativism and the Constitution, and how to keep God-given rights intact in America.

Cheryl is also a certified private investigator and principal of Chumley Investigations, LLC in Virginia. Previously, Cheryl was a Court Appointed Special Advocate (CASA) volunteer, helping judges make the difficult placement decision for abused and neglected children. She served in the active Army as a 63H (tank-track and wheeled vehicle repairer), and as a diesel mechanic in the civilian sector. She lives in Northern Virginia with two of her four children—named Savanna, Keith, Colvin, and Chloe—and enjoys running and reading in her spare time.